Best Bike Rides
Cape Cod and the Islands

The Greatest Recreational Rides
in the Area

DR. GREGORY WRIGHT

FALCONGUIDES

GUILFORD, CONNECTICUT
HELENA, MONTANA

For Rachel and our children
Hayley, Emma, Lukas, Myles, and Sophie

An imprint of Rowman & Littlefield
Falcon, FalconGuides, Outfit Your Mind, and Best Bike Rides are registered trademarks of
Rowman & Littlefield.

Distributed by NATIONAL BOOK NETWORK
Copyright © 2015 Rowman & Littlefield

Photos on pages 145, 160, 215, 268, 275, and 289 courtesy of Hayley C. Wright; photo on
page 121 courtesy of Rachel S. Lajoie. All other photos are by the author.

British Library Cataloguing in Publication Information Available
Library of Congress Cataloging-in-Publication Data is available on file.

ISBN 978-1-4930-0755-4
ISBN 978-1-4930-1427-9 (ebook)

∞™ The paper used in this publication meets the minimum requirements of American
National Standard for Information Sciences—Permanence of Paper for Printed Library
Materials, ANSI/NISO Z39.48-1992.

**The author and FalconGuides assume no liability for accidents happening
to, or injuries sustained by, readers who engage in the activities described
in this book.**

Contents

Map Overview

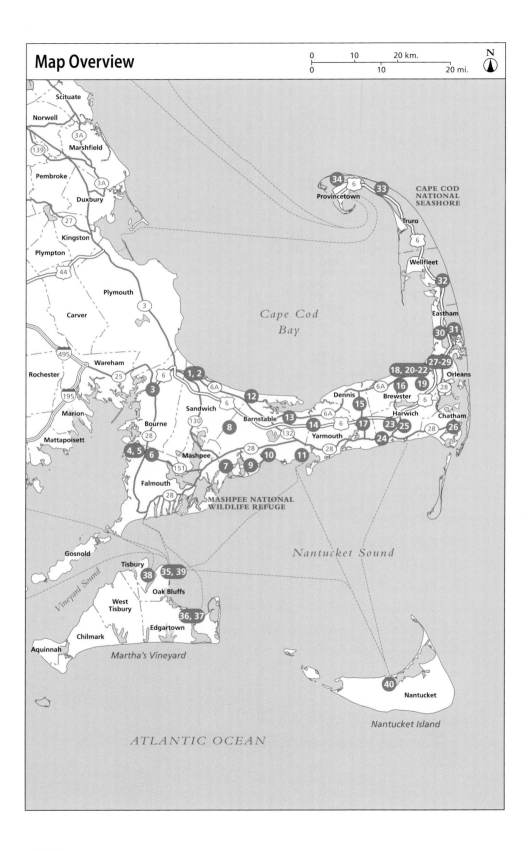

The Islands

Martha's Vineyard

Nantucket

Key to icons used in this edition:

 Road Bike   **Mountain Bike**   **Hybrid**

Preface

One of my best memories is of summer vacation and my family's many trips to Nickerson State Park and Coast Guard Beach. The first bike path I ever rode was the one at Salt Pond Visitor Center at Cape Cod National Seashore in Eastham. I couldn't have been more than 10 years old, and it was a roller coaster of a ride that opened up to a beach with big surf. That ride is etched in my memory, one of the greatest joys of my life. The annual trip to the Cape almost always included swimming at Coast Guard Beach, a kettle pond in Brewster, or a hike along massive cliff beaches or through forest. I can still smell the scent of pine needles baking in the sun on those hot, summer days. Our daytime activities were often followed by a dinner of fresh lobster, steamers, or fried clams, and ice cream with my brothers and sisters. Always the ice cream. My father was a connoisseur of chocolate ice cream and clam shacks. One summer we finished with a bonfire and traditional clambake on the beach, with singing, laughter, and roasting marshmallows under the stars. I was hooked. I'll always remember the laughter.

My parents were eager to explore the vast outer region of Cape Cod made famous by so many writers and artists and preserved as a 43,500-acre national park in 1961 by President John F. Kennedy. The Cape Cod National Seashore was an easy trip from Greater Boston. I remember seeing the Sagamore Bridge for the first time, which soon became synonymous with the real beginning of vacation. When I was a little boy, I actually believed our car tires would travel on top of the curved steel arches of the Sagamore Bridge. They looked like tracks to me, and it was an exciting possibility. Crossing the Cape Cod Canal was entering into another world, the symbolic separation from school, work, and the stresses of life on the other side. I can still remember feeling the sudden change in temperature upon crossing "the bridge"—cooler in summer, warmer in winter. I remember my young nose and face filling with salty air, car windows always open in summer. I loved it here as a kid. It's why I moved here over twenty years ago, married here, and am raising a family here. I still love it. It's a great place to live and a great place to ride a bike. It is a place that is best seen riding a bike. I hope to see you out riding on the roads, trails, and beaches when you visit us and our large, friendly cycling community.

Introduction

When given the opportunity to map, write, and photograph the forty "best bike rides" on Cape Cod and the islands, my first thoughts were, "How much has already been written on the topic?" and, "What new could be written?" After all, Cape Cod is only 65 miles long from Sandwich to Provincetown along its inner coastline, 20 miles wide at its widest, and only 1 mile at its narrowest near the end of the hook. While Cape Cod is a breathtakingly beautiful place, that's not a lot of room for bicycle routes. The roadways on Cape Cod and the Islands have changed very little in the past several decades, even centuries. Indeed, some road rides here are so scenic and beautiful no one would ever want to change them. I decided not to try. Striking a balance between old and new became important in deciding which rides could not be left out, even if we've all seen them before. Fortunately, there are more back roads and rides on Cape Cod and the islands than meet the eye, and the combinations of rides one can put together are surprisingly varied. I also chose to highlight in new and different ways some of the sights and attractions that have not changed. So much of the history and beauty of this place deserves a fresh look.

And while there are some things about this region that are timeless and never seem to change—elegant historic houses, gorgeous sunsets, and seemingly endless miles of barrier beaches—there also have been several changes in the cycling landscape over the past ten years, as well as the landscape of Cape Cod and the islands themselves. Cape Cod has become a much busier place, with heavy traffic in summer, especially during the peak vacation months of July and August. Many of the previously well-established routes cannot be recommended anymore due to the heavier traffic on those roads in summer, with some of those "old back roads" now resembling main roads year-round—repaved and widened, the vehicular traffic increasing in speed and number. But positive changes in the area's cycling landscape have occurred, too.

For one, Massachusetts is consistently ranked as one of the most bicycle-friendly states in the country. Bicycling is getting friendlier on Cape Cod and the islands, too. The Cape Cod chapter of the Massachusetts Bicycle Coalition (MassBike) has played a very important role, educating children and local organizations on the Cape and islands, providing advocacy for cyclists and safe cycling. The Massachusetts Department of Transportation's GreenDOT initiative promotes bicycling as one of its central goals. And Cape Cod National Seashore and the Cape Cod Commission are currently working on making Cape Cod—particularly the stretch from Wellfleet to Provincetown—a more

Wing Pond, along the Shining Sea Bikeway, North Falmouth

enjoyable and safer experience, with input from the community and plans for a safer route between those towns. Cape Cod recently held its first-ever Bike Summit, which was organized by the Barnstable County Department of Human Services, the Town of Barnstable, the office of State Senator Dan Wolf, and the Cape Cod Chapter of MassBike to promote better and safer bicycling on Cape Cod. The Cape Cod Regional Transit Authority recently published its "Getting To and Through Cape Cod" map to promote multimodal transportation, including bicycles. The political landscape for cycling on Cape Cod looks very bright indeed.

Another good change in the cycling landscape is an ever-growing number of bikeways, both on Cape Cod and the islands. I have included all the best ones in this book. The Shining Sea Bikeway in Falmouth has been extended and the newer Old Colony Rail Trail extending from the Harwich Bike Rotary to Chatham provides access to those two towns without vehicular traffic. The long-awaited westward extension of the Cape Cod Rail Trail looks like it is finally going forward, with bids having gone out in 2014 for the first phase of building from South Dennis to Yarmouth. The Province Lands Bike Trail in Provincetown has also recently undergone a great number of improvements since its original design in the 1960s. And the Nauset Trail in Eastham has been repaved and widened, with a new bridge over Nauset Marsh to replace one that was blown away in a recent storm. On Nantucket, there have been several miles of bike trails added since 2004, including the Hummock Pond Bike Path, the South Shore Bike Path, and an airport bike path that links to every other path on the island. Nantucket now has more than 30 miles of paved bike paths and Martha's Vineyard more than 40, with more scheduled to be built in the near future. Between Cape Cod and the islands there are more than 155 miles of paved bike (multi-use) paths, most of them family-friendly.

But this guidebook isn't just for road cyclists and paved trail riders. It also includes mapped mountain bike trails, cyclocross trails, and something relatively new to Cape Cod: fat tire bike rides. It is a very sandy place, and Cape Cod has hundreds of miles of gorgeous trails suitable for both mountain bikes and fat tire bikes, the trails listed in this book being the most popular and well-maintained ones. Every ride in the book was mapped with GPS, and the maps provide more detail than any cycling guidebook for the Cape and islands to date, to get you where you want to go without getting lost.

Choosing and then mapping the forty rides for this book was the fun part, as these rides are some of my personal favorites. They are beautifully scenic at almost every turn. Cape Cod and the islands have much to offer despite their limited area. I avoided many of the routes that are more dangerous, and did my best to completely avoid Routes 6, 6A, and 28, as much as that was possible. I also included shorter and more child-friendly rides, making a distinction between rides for older and younger children. I included every family-friendly paved bikeway on Cape Cod, and chose rides on Martha's Vineyard and Nantucket that either travel along paved bike paths or provide easy access to them. Cycling is for everybody, of all ages, so parents with children visiting Cape Cod and the islands need safe routes for their families. As a father of five, I spend extra time discussing safety issues in this book. Good planning for safety will make bike riding on Cape Cod, Martha's Vineyard, or Nantucket a much more pleasurable experience for all.

The longer rides in the book are for road riders looking for rides of about 30 miles or longer, the longest being Ride 29, Grand Tour of the Outer Cape, at 53.7 miles. For mountain bikers looking for something more challenging, there are several other routes to be explored within the ride areas mapped. The mountain bike rides are challenging rides from 5.5 to 8.6 miles, highlighting the most popular mountain biking areas on Cape Cod. In short, there are rides for all kinds: seasoned cyclists, fat tire enthusiasts, novice riders, lighthouse admirers, beach bums looking for sandy getaways, hill climbers, and flatlanders.

Although I know not every ride will appeal to everybody, I sincerely hope the variety of routes, terrain, scenery, and locations will provide a very enjoyable experience for anyone visiting to ride a bicycle on Cape Cod, Martha's Vineyard, and Nantucket. This is one of the most pristine and beautiful places in the country to ride a bike. If by chance this book can inspire you to get back on a bicycle and explore a new place, or try a new kind of bike riding, then it will have succeeded. So, go have an adventure and enjoy!

Ride Finder

RIDES WITH VIEWS OF SURF BEACH

2. Sandwich Historical Tour
3. Villages of Bourne
4. Shining Sea Bikeway
5. Tour of Falmouth
9. Osterville-Centerville Loop
10. Centerville to Hyannis
11. Hyannis to the Cape Cod Rail Trail
24. West Harwich and West Dennis Beaches
25. Harwich Port and South Chatham Tour
26. Chatham Harbors Tour
27. Orleans Center to Nauset Beach Loop
29. Grand Tour of the Outer Cape
30. Nauset Trail at Salt Pond Visitor Center
31. Nauset Light and the Three Sisters
32. Wellfleet Ocean-to-Bay Tour
33. Head of the Meadow Trail
34. Province Lands Trail
35. Oak Bluffs to Edgartown Beach Road
36. Chappaquiddick
37. Edgartown to South Beach Loop
38. Vineyard Up Island Tour
39. Oak Bluffs–East Chop–Vineyard Haven
40. Nantucket-Siasconset-Wauwinet Tour

RIDES WITH VIEWS OF KETTLE PONDS

3. Villages of Bourne
11. Hyannis to the Cape Cod Rail Trail
15. Dennis Bayside Beaches
16. Oh No, It's Signal Hill!
17. Cape Cod Rail Trail, South Dennis to Nickerson State Park
18. Cape Cod Rail Trail, Nickerson State Park to Wellfleet
19. Cliff Pond Killer Loop
20. Flax Pond–Owl Pond Loop
22. Nickerson State Park Kids' Ride
23. Old Colony Rail Trail, Harwich to Chatham
24. West Harwich and West Dennis Beaches
28. Orleans and Eastham Bayside Beaches
29. Grand Tour of the Outer Cape
32. Wellfleet Ocean-to-Bay Tour

RIDES WITH VIEWS OF BAY BEACH

7. Cotuit and Mashpee
9. Osterville-Centerville Loop
11. Hyannis to the Cape Cod Rail Trail
12. Sandy Neck Fat Tire Dune Ride

RIDES FOR OLDER CHILDREN

1. Cape Cod Canal
4. Shining Sea Bikeway
17. Cape Cod Rail Trail, South Dennis to Nickerson State Park
18. Cape Cod Rail Trail, Nickerson State Park to Wellfleet
22. Nickerson State Park Kids' Ride
23. Old Colony Rail Trail, Harwich to Chatham
30. Nauset Trail at Salt Pond Visitor Center
33. Head of the Meadow Trail
34. Province Lands Trail
35. Oak Bluffs to Edgartown Beach Road

RIDES ALONG THE NATIONAL SEASHORE

27. Orleans Center to Nauset Beach Loop
29. Grand Tour of the Outer Cape
30. Nauset Trail at Salt Pond Visitor Center
31. Nauset Light and the Three Sisters
32. Wellfleet Ocean-to-Bay Tour
33. Head of the Meadow Trail
34. Province Lands Trail

RIDES WITH HILLS

3. Villages of Bourne
5. Tour of Falmouth
6. Otis
7. Cotuit and Mashpee
8. Trail of Tears
9. Osterville-Centerville Loop
10. Centerville to Hyannis
14. Willow Street
15. Dennis Bayside Beaches
16. Oh No, It's Signal Hill!
19. Cliff Pond Killer Loop
20. Flax Pond and Owl Pond Loop
22. Nickerson State Park Kids' Ride
23. Old Colony Rail Trail, Harwich to Chatham
25. Harwich Port and South Chatham Tour
26. Chatham Harbors Tour
29. Grand Tour of the Outer Cape
30. Nauset Trail at Salt Pond Visitor Center
31. Nauset Light and the Three Sisters
32. Wellfleet Ocean-to-Bay Tour
34. Province Lands Trail

Map Legend

195	Interstate Highway	†	Church
6	US Highway		Dining
6	State Highway		Lighthouse
6	Featured State/Local Road		Lodging
	Local Road		Marina
	Featured Bike Route	17.1	Mileage Marker
	Bike Route		Museum
	Trail	P	Parking
	Railroad		Picnic Area
	Ferry		Ranger Station
	Airfield/Runway		Restroom
	State Line		Scenic View/Viewpoint
	Small River or Creek		School/College/University
	Marsh/Swamp		Small Park
	Body of Water		Spring
	State Park/Forest/Wilderness/ Preserve/Recreational Area		Swimming
	Airport		Tower
	Boat Launch	1	Trailhead
	Bridge		Visitor/Information Center
■	Building/Point of Interest		Water

Cape Cod Canal

A flat, often windy, scenic, and smooth paved path that hugs the curves of the Cape Cod Canal, gateway to the Cape Cod peninsula. A favorite spot for fishermen where you can watch ships from around the world pass through, and see travelers overhead on the Sagamore and Bourne Bridges.

Cape Cod

Start: Sandwich Recreation Area, at the end of Freezer Road adjacent to the Sandwich Marina, off Tupper Road, which is accessible from Route 6A in Sandwich, east of the Sagamore Bridge

Distance: 13.2 miles out-and-back

Approximate riding time: 1 to 2 hours depending on stops

Best bike: Road, hybrid

Terrain and surface type: Smooth, flat, paved bike (multi-use) path along the canal, with one railroad track crossing (Cape Cod Canal Railroad Bridge)

Traffic and hazards: Pedestrians, in-line skaters, fishermen (with fishing rods and lines), dogs, and other riders on a two-way bike path that has no barrier between the path and the canal other than a grass strip and sharp rocks descending quickly into the water. It's often very windy and dangerous for smaller children (and lighter riders), who could literally get blown off the trail into the rocks or canal.

Things to see: Cape Cod Canal Visitor's Center, Sagamore Bridge, Bourne Bridge, Aptucxet Trading Post and Museum, Cape Cod Canal Railroad Bridge, big sky and the 480-foot-wide Cape Cod Canal known internationally for its sports fishing and strong currents

Map: *Arrow Street Atlas: Cape Cod including Martha's Vineyard & Nantucket,* p. 76

Getting there: By car: From Boston, take Route 93 South to Route 3 South to the Sagamore Bridge. Take exit 1C (the first exit after the bridge

1

on right), take a right onto Sandwich Road, go under the Sagamore Bridge, and merge with Route 6A. Take a left onto Tupper Road, then left on Freezer Road, bearing left (Sandwich Marina on right). Parking lot straight ahead. **From Route 495/25 and Bourne Bridge:** Cross over Bourne Bridge, go around rotary and proceed onto Sandwich Road. **From points east on Cape Cod:** Take exit 2 off Route 6 and proceed north on Route 130 toward Sandwich. Take a right on Tupper Road at the Sandwich Glass Museum, cross Route 6A, then right onto Freezer Road and follow to Sandwich Recreation Area parking lot.

GPS coordinates: N41 46.32' / W70 30.33'

THE RIDE

This easy, very flat ride at sea level along the Cape Cod Canal covers 13.2 miles out-and-back from the Sandwich Recreation Area. As you ride out of the far left corner of the parking lot toward the canal, the Cape Cod Canal Service Road entrance is marked by a sign that first reads "Authorized Motor Vehicles Only" and you might think you're in the wrong place. The US Army Corps of Engineers maintains the 100-year-old Cape Cod Canal, but vehicles are almost never seen on this multi-use paved path, where you are far less likely to see a motor vehicle than someone riding, running, in-line skating, walking, or fishing. As you start out toward the canal, enjoy the big sky and vastness of the canal, 30-plus feet deep and up to 700 feet wide in some spots, with a view of the Sagamore Bridge off in the distance. No permit or license is required to line fish from the shores of the canal, so fishermen armed with jigs and pogies, some on bicycles, are a common sight. There are plentiful bluefish, cod, stripers, and even the occasional tuna or mackerel caught off the rocky banks of the canal, or as local anglers like to call it, the Ditch or Big Ditch. Ride past them all and see the catch of the day.

Large ships and smaller boats from around the world pass to the right, navigating the strong currents of the canal that change direction every six hours and can reach speeds of 5 mph with the change of the tides. The bike path soon veers a little left and then a little right just after the Canal Power Plant to the left.

The path soon passes under the Sagamore Bridge, so enjoy the view of sea and sky and get a new perspective on what probably got you here: the car traffic overhead. That traffic backs up for miles on Fridays headed onto Cape Cod, and Sundays headed off Cape Cod especially in summer. The steel-arched, four-lane bridge, built in 1933, looms large above, recently stripped of its old lead paint and repainted in 2014 for $12.3 million. You've just passed into the town of Bourne and the village of Sagamore, very close to the border of the Massachusetts Military Reservation, now known as Otis Air National Guard Base. Otis makes up most of the area of the town of Bourne, which lies on both sides of the canal. But there is little visible sign of anything military on this ride—just a sense of openness and freedom.

Continuing past the Sagamore Bridge, the path goes up slightly and then down again. And that's it for climbs on this path, with a maximum elevation of 25 feet. However, what this ride lacks in elevation it more than makes up for with frequent windy conditions, true of Cape Cod bicycling conditions in general. Serious Cape Cod racing cyclists say, "The wind is our hill training." Winds of 70 mph or higher have threatened to close the bridges over the Cape Cod Canal in the past, and are sometimes strong enough to blow cyclists off course or even off their bicycles. Use caution on windy days.

Continue onward where the canal takes a big bend left and then right with your first view of the Bourne Bridge. The Bourne Bridge is the Sagamore Bridge's twin, built in the same year to almost the same specifications in 1933, although the approach to the Bourne Bridge is much longer at both ends. The Bourne Bridge connects Route 495 and traffic coming from the west to the Cape Cod peninsula. Travel under its shadow and ride past the Aptucxet Trading Post and Museum on your left. Aptucxet is the site of the first Pilgrim trading post and where Pilgrims adopted the New World's currency, *wampum*.

Just past Aptucxet is the Cape Cod Canal Railroad Bridge, also built and maintained by the US Army Corps of Engineers in 1933. The Railroad Bridge is the third-longest vertical railroad bridge in the world, and is usually found in the "up" position. Marine traffic has statutory right-of-way over rail traffic, and it takes 2.5 minutes to lower the railroad bridge from its elevation of 135 feet to mean high water (average water level). If you arrive at this spot around

Bike Shops

Sailworld Bikes & Boards, 139 Main St., Buzzards Bay, Bourne, (508) 759-6559, sailworld.com
Eastern Mountain Sports, 2 Bridge Approach St., Bourne, (508) 759-7620, ems.com

9:30 a.m. or 5 p.m., you might see it descend to track level, which is a pretty impressive sight. The rail line over the bridge is owned by the Massachusetts Department of Transportation (DOT), and is mostly used to haul trash from Yarmouth and Otis Air National Guard Base off Cape Cod. But recently, it has also become the railway of the *Cape Flyer*, a new train service started in 2013 that carries passengers from South Station in Boston to Hyannis in just two hours. It also carries bicycles at no charge. The *Cape Flyer* and DOT have made bicycling tourism a top priority by dedicating an entire train car to bicycle

View from the Cape Cod Canal Service Road, Sandwich

transport so that cyclists who wish to avoid driving and traffic can still ride Cape Cod and the islands. The 78-mile journey makes stops in Braintree, Middleboro, Wareham, and Buzzards Bay on the way to Hyannis. In Hyannis, there is a special bus that carries both cyclists and their bicycles to the Outer Cape and Cape Cod National Seashore. DOT's investment plan through 2018 includes a $31 million budget "to complete track and signal projects necessary to restore permanent, seasonal *Cape Flyer* passenger service to Cape

Cod." That's great news for cycling the Cape! In 2013, during the July 4 holiday weekend, 672 people traveled back from Hyannis to Boston on the last train of the weekend, on the same Sunday a traffic jam and gridlock at the Sagamore Bridge had traffic backed up 25 miles on Route 6 on Cape Cod. So take the train on weekends (Memorial Day to Labor Day). The bridge backup traffic has become so bad that regional transportation planners are talking about building a third motor vehicle bridge over the canal. But the Cape Cod Canal Railroad Bridge never has any traffic! It does have lots of happy travelers with bicycles, though.

Ride over the tracks and arrive at the turnaround point of this ride, at the Tidal Flats Recreation Area parking lot. Stop here and connect to Ride 3 (Villages of Bourne) or ride over the tracks and return to the start along the canal, now to the left. In 2014, the Cape Cod Canal celebrated its 100-year anniversary with fireworks, maritime events, historical exhibits, a tugboat parade, and tall ships on display, including the *Charles W. Morgan*, the last surviving wooden whaling ship.

Approach the Sandwich Recreation Area now, where you can have a picnic (picnic tables and restrooms are here) or opt to ride to the historical town of Sandwich in a matter of minutes (see Ride 2, Tour of Sandwich). Also located here is the Cape Cod Canal Visitor's Center, where you can board a retired 40-foot patrol boat, be the captain on a virtual boat ride through the canal, explore flora and fauna living in and around the canal, or view films about the history of the Cape Cod Canal. The Visitor Center is owned and operated by the US Army Corps of Engineers and is located at 60 Ed Moffitt Dr., across the marina from the ride finish parking lot. There is also a deck with rocking chairs where you can just sit, relax, and enjoy the view. It's all free.

MILES AND DIRECTIONS

0.0 The bike path starts at the Sandwich Recreation Area parking lot, at the back left of the oval.

2.0 Ride under the Sagamore Bridge.

5.3 Ride under the Bourne Bridge.

6.2 Pass the Aptucxet Trading Post and Museum on your left.

6.5 Pass the Cape Cod Canal Railroad Bridge on your right and go over the tracks cautiously.

6.6 Turn around at the Tidal Flats Recreation Area parking lot and return the way you came.

13.2 Arrive back at the start/finish in Sandwich along the canal.

Cape Cod Canal

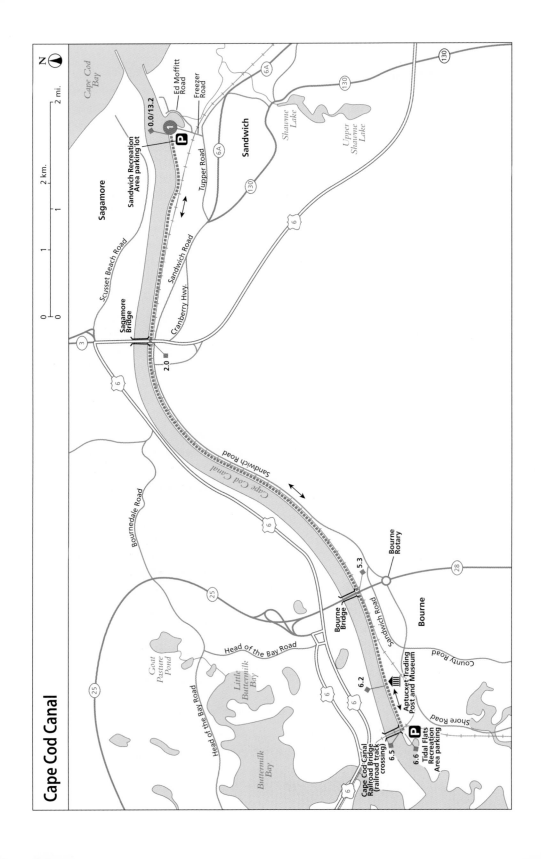

Local Events/Attractions

Aptucxet Trading Post and Museum: 24 Aptucxet Rd., Bourne; (508) 759-9487; bournehistoricalsociety.org/aptucxet-museum. A replica of the first privately owned business in the New World. Also home to president Grover Cleveland's personal train station and a replica of an early Cape Cod saltworks. Gift shop housed in a restored windmill. A slice of early Plymouth colony and Wampanoag culture. Bring your wampum.

Cape Cod Canal Visitor's Center: 60 Ed Moffitt Dr., Sandwich; (508) 833-9678; nae.usace.army.mil/Missions/Recreation/CapeCodCanal.aspx. Small, kid-friendly, with smart interactive exhibits for kids and nearby playground at the Sandwich Marina. Short films about the canal history, wildlife. Sit on the deck in rocking chairs overlooking the Cape Cod Canal. Children can "steer" the 45-foot canal patrol boat in the wheelhouse, watch live radar of vessels in the canal, then eat hot dogs and ice cream at nearby Shipwreck Ice Cream. Free.

Restaurants

Shipwreck Ice Cream: 2 Freezer Rd., Sandwich; (508) 888-3444. A huge variety of flavors, with bunnies, a fish pond, and turtles.

Sagamore Inn: 131 MA 6A, Sagamore; (508) 888-9707. A stone's throw from the Sagamore Bridge, owners Michael and Suzanne Bilodeau serve northern Italian fare with an old-Cape Cod feel, with veal parmesan, clams casino, fish cakes, and baked beans among the favorites. Two outside decks, one reserved for patrons with dogs.

Sunset Grille at the Brookside Club: 11 Brigadoone Rd., Buzzards Bay; (508) 743-0705; thebrooksideclub.com/index.php/sunsetgrille. Chef Adam Borowski has a unique and diverse menu. You can watch golf or spectacular sunsets from the outdoor terrace overlooking miles of rolling hills, or just sit at the gorgeous new bar, have a cocktail, and enjoy the stone fireplace and good company.

Restrooms

Sandwich Recreation Area (Start), Bourne Recreation Area (mile 5.3), Aptucxet Trading Post and Museum (mile 6.2), and Tidal Flats Recreation Area parking lot (mile 6.6)

Sandwich Historical Tour

An easy cruise from the Cape Cod Canal to historic Sandwich, Cape Cod's first town (1637). Can be combined with Ride 1 or done separately. Don't miss the Sandwich Boardwalk or the Sandwich Glass Museum. Fill your bike bottles with fresh spring water from the town's public faucets.

Start: Sandwich Recreation Area, at the end of Freezer Road adjacent to the Sandwich Marina, off Tupper Road, which is accessible from Route 6A in Sandwich, east of the Sagamore Bridge

Distance: 5.2 miles, modified double-lollipop

Approximate riding time: 1 hour or more depending on stops

Best bike: Road, hybrid

Terrain and surface type: Smooth, flat pavement on main roads and quiet residential roads throughout historical Sandwich; one railroad track crossing ridden two times

Traffic and hazards: Traffic can be very congested, especially in summer on Route 6A and Route 130. Sandwich is the oldest Cape Cod town, with many historical sites where drivers, cyclists, and pedestrians stop to take pictures. Route 6A, the "Old King's Highway," is sometimes backed up through town with traffic waiting to leave Cape Cod by one of two bridges over the Cape Cod Canal.

Things to see: Sandwich Boardwalk and Beach (continue on Harbor Street to Boardwalk Road, not to be missed), Sandwich Glass Museum, Dexter Grist Mill, Shawme Lake, Hoxie House, Daniel Webster Inn & Spa, Heritage Museum and Gardens, Cape Cod Canal, Cape Cod Canal Visitor Center

Map: *Arrow Street Atlas: Cape Cod including Martha's Vineyard & Nantucket*, p. 76

Getting there: **By car:** From Boston, take Route 93 South to Route 3 South to the Sagamore Bridge. Take exit 1C (the first exit after the bridge on right), take a right onto Sandwich Road, go under the Sagamore Bridge, and merge with Route 6A. Take a left onto Tupper Road, then left on Freezer Road, bearing left (Sandwich Marina on right). Parking lot straight ahead. **From Route 495/25 and Bourne Bridge:** Cross over Bourne Bridge, go around rotary, and proceed onto Sandwich Road. **From points east on Cape Cod:** Take exit 2 off Route 6 and proceed north on Route 130 toward Sandwich. Take a right on Tupper Road at the Sandwich Glass Museum, cross Route 6A, then right on Freezer Road and follow to Sandwich Recreation Area parking lot.

GPS coordinates: N41 46.32' / W70 30.33'

THE RIDE

This short, flat ride on main roads and some back roads starts at the Sandwich Recreation Area and heads south out of the parking lot around the Sandwich Marina, away from the Cape Cod Canal. Just a mile away, after crossing Route 6A, is the tiny town of Sandwich Village, the first incorporated town on Cape Cod and the first settlement in the "East Ham" of Plymouth Colony. The town was founded in 1637 by Edmund Freeman, a more open-minded Pilgrim than his Puritan counterparts in Boston, and Sandwich is the site of the oldest continuous monthly Quaker meetings in America.

This is a ride through early American history, and riders may want to park their bikes and walk around town on foot. Also, there are three optional side routes on this ride: the first to the Heritage Museum and Gardens with its auto museum and landscaped gardens; the second, to Cape Cod's oldest house, the Hoxie House built in 1675; and the third to the Sandwich Boardwalk, where you can walk or just relax on Boardwalk Beach, truly the first Cape Cod Bay beach of the Cape Cod peninsula.

After crossing Route 6A, ride past the marsh on Tupper Road, approach the village, and turn left onto Main Street at the intersection of Route 130 (Water Street), bending around to the left past the Sandwich Glass Museum. As an option, take Grove Street to the right of Sandwich Town Hall (with the big Greek columns), and ride the out-and-back to the Heritage Museum and Gardens. This is a long, beautiful, and shaded uphill ride that turns around at the museum for an easy cruise downhill and back to town. Just to the left of the front steps of Town Hall, on the sidewalk, there are public faucets that pump fresh artesian well water, a great place to fill your water bottles. Just

The Sandwich Boardwalk to Cape Cod Bay

behind the faucets to the left is Shawme Lake and the entrance to Dexter Grist Mill, where herring run in spring. As another side-trip option, ride up Water Street (Route 130) a little farther to the saltbox Hoxie House, Cape Cod's oldest house. There are many places for coffee, lunch, or snacks along the route through Sandwich Village Center on Main Street.

Turn left onto Jarves Street, named after founder of the Boston & Sandwich Glass Company, Deming Jarves. Cross Route 6A, continue on Jarves Street, take a left on Factory Street past the old train station, and imagine the once-bustling glass factory that doubled the population of Sandwich from 1825 to 1850. Jarves brought in the best glassblowers and glassmakers from England and Ireland, and turned Sandwich into the major glass-producing center of the United States. The factory was open twenty-four hours a day, employed 550 workers, and produced an incredible 5.2 million pieces of glassware each year until its closure after the Civil War. This neighborhood still has many of the homes and factory buildings from that time in history, with half-cape, three-quarter cape, and full cape houses that were the common architecture of the day.

Factory Street ends on Harbor Street, and as an option, follow Harbor Street to its end to the Sandwich Boardwalk. This "option" really is not to be missed. The boardwalk connects you to Cape Cod Bay with views of marshes, dunes, and Mill Creek flowing from Dexter Grist Mill all the way to the estuary, and it is one of the most beautiful sites on Cape Cod. In 1991 Hurricane Bob destroyed the 1,350-foot boardwalk, but it was rebuilt with planks purchased individually by locals who donated to the rebuilding, with inscriptions of their

Best Bike Rides Cape Cod and the Islands

names and personal messages on each plank. National Geographic listed the Sandwich Boardwalk in their top ten rankings of boardwalks of the United States, but without the Coney Island or Atlantic City neon and amusements. It is simply raw, untouched Cape Cod here, and the boardwalk seems to go on forever, with miles of beach, marsh, and dunes past Sandwich Harbor. Double back from the boardwalk on Harbor Street, where there are thousands of pieces of sea glass to be found in the marsh at the end of this street where it bends toward the boardwalk. Take a few twists and turns in the old glass-factory neighborhood, and try to find the original factory location on Factory Street. Cross Route 6A back onto Main Street via Dewey Avenue. It really doesn't matter how lost you get in the old factory village, you're only going to escape it one of two ways—on Jarves Street or Dewey Avenue. To continue, ride to Dewey Avenue from Liberty Street.

> ### Bike Shop
> **Ecotourz LLC,** 20 Jarves St., Sandwich, (508) 888-1627, ecotourz.net

Return back to the center of town on Main Street and pass by several historic homes on this end of Main Street belonging to nineteenth-century Sandwich settlers, like Fessenden, Fish, Hamblin, Holway, and many others. Continue past Jarves Street on Main Street and take note of the Daniel Webster Inn on the right at mile 3.7, where US Senator and Secretary of State Daniel Webster took time to relax during the tense years building up to the Civil War. Stop for coffee and an apple toffee scone at the Coffee Roost, lunch and a wine tasting at the Belfry Inn & Bistro, or gourmet food, wine, or lunch on the quiet back patio of the Brown Jug on the corner of Jarves Street and Main Street. There is a lot to explore in this tiny village. Take the shortcut and turn right on River Street back to Tupper Road and retrace your way back to the Sandwich Recreation Area. Stop by the Cape Cod Canal Visitor Center where you can relax on the deck in a rocking chair, board a 40-foot patrol boat, take a virtual boat ride through the canal, or learn its history.

MILES AND DIRECTIONS

0.0 Ride starts at the Sandwich Recreation Area parking lot.

0.1 Exit parking lot onto Freezer Road.

0.2 Turn left onto Ed Moffitt Drive and hug the Sandwich Marina to your left.

0.5 Turn right onto Gallo Road.

0.7 Turn right onto Town Neck Road.

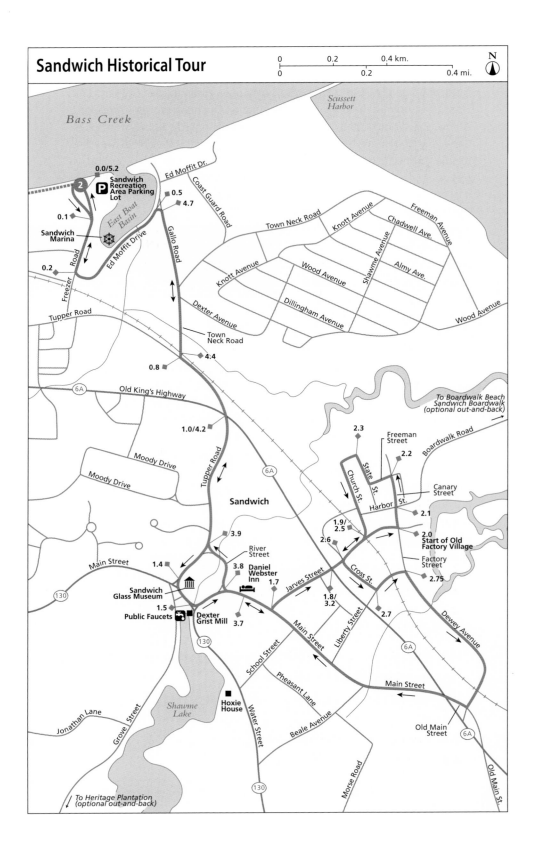

Sandwich Historical Tour

N

0   0.2   0.4 km.
0   0.2   0.4 mi.

Bass Creek

Scussett Harbor

Ed Moffit Dr.

0.0/5.2

2

P **Sandwich Recreation Area Parking Lot**

0.5
4.7

Coast Guard Road

0.1

East Boat Basin

Sandwich Marina

0.2

Freezer Road

Ed Moffit Drive

Gallo Road

Town Neck Road

Knott Avenue

Chadwell Ave.

Freeman Avenue

Knott Avenue

Wood Avenue

Shawme Avenue

Almy Ave.

Wood Avenue

Dexter Avenue

Dillingham Avenue

Tupper Road

Town Neck Road

0.8   4.4

6A   Old King's Highway

1.0/4.2

To Boardwalk Beach Sandwich Boardwalk (optional out-and-back)

2.3

Freeman Street

2.2

Boardwalk Road

Moody Drive

Moody Drive

Tupper Road

6A

Sandwich

Church St.

State St.

Harbor St.

Canary Street

2.1

1.9/2.5

2.0 **Start of Old Factory Village**

2.6

Factory Street

3.9

River Street

1.4

3.8 **Daniel Webster Inn**

1.7

Jarves Street

Cross St.

2.75

2.7

Dewey Avenue

Main Street

130

Sandwich Glass Museum

1.5

Public Faucets

Dexter Grist Mill

3.7

1.8/3.2

Liberty Street

6A

130

School Street

Main Street

6A

Pheasant Lane

Main Street

Old Main Street

6A

Shawme Lake

Hoxie House

Water Street

Beale Avenue

Morse Road

Old Main St.

Jonathan Lane

Grove Street

130

To Heritage Plantation (optional out-and-back)

0.8 Cross the railroad tracks and turn left on Tupper Road.

1.0 Cross Route 6A and continue on Tupper Road. Heavy traffic (with traffic lights).

1.4 Turn left onto Main Street, around the Sandwich Glass Museum on your left. (Option: Take Grove Street, to the right of Sandwich Town Hall's big Greek columns, and ride the out-and-back to the Heritage Museum and Gardens. This is a long, beautiful, and shaded uphill ride that turns around at the museum for an easy cruise downhill and back to town.)

1.5 Turn left and continue on Main Street. (Option: Ride straight ahead, up Water Street on Route 130 a little farther to the saltbox Hoxie House, Cape Cod's oldest house.)

1.7 Turn left onto Jarves Street.

1.8 Cross Route 6A and continue on Jarves Street.

1.9 Cross the railroad tracks.

2.0 Turn left on Factory Street.

2.1 Turn right on Harbor Street and take a quick left on Canary Street. (Option: Continue on Harbor Street to the Sandwich Boardwalk via Boardwalk Road. Add about a mile to your distance for this out-and-back ride to the Boardwalk. Turn around and turn right on Canary Street.)

2.1 Continue ride on Canary Street.

2.2 Turn left on Freeman Street.

2.25 Turn right on State Street.

2.3 Turn left on Church Street, which bends 90 degrees left.

2.5 Turn right on Jarves Street and cross the railroad tracks.

2.6 Turn left on Cross Street.

2.7 Turn left on Liberty Street.

2.75 Turn right on Dewey Avenue and follow it to its end.

3.15 Turn right on Old Main Street.

3.2 Cross Route 6A and continue on Main Street back into town.

3.7 Pass the Daniel Webster Inn on the right.

3.8 Turn right on River Street.

3.9 Turn right on Tupper Road.

4.2 Cross Route 6A.

4.4 Turn right onto Town Neck Road and cross the railroad tracks.

4.5 Turn left onto Gallo Road.

4.7 Turn left onto Ed Moffitt Drive.

5.0 Turn right onto Freezer Road.

5.2 The ride ends at the Sandwich Recreation Area parking lot where it started.

RIDE INFORMATION

Local Events and Attractions

Heritage Museum and Gardens: 67 Grove St., Sandwich; (508) 888-3300. Hike the beautiful gardens (look for the bug sculptures) in spring or summer (not fall), check out the antique car collection of the Lily family (the pharmaceutical company family) year-round, and ride the carousel. Try the new zip line.

Sandwich Boardwalk: Boardwalk Road (at the end of Harbor Street), Sandwich. Very long boardwalk, with incredible views of the marsh and Cape Cod Bay. Not to be missed. I dare you to jump!

Sandwich Glass Museum: 129 Main St. (on the corner of Route 130, Main Street, and Tupper Road), Sandwich; (508) 888-0251. The entrance is on Tupper Road. See beautiful works of glass and master glassblowers in this historic museum and former factory.

Cape Cod Canal Visitor's Center: 60 Ed Moffitt Dr., Sandwich; (508) 833-9678; nae.usace.army.mil/Missions/Recreation/CapeCodCanal.aspx. See the listing under Ride 1.

Restaurants

The Brown Jug: 155 Main St., Sandwich; (508) 888-4669. Enjoy a great sandwich in Sandwich, along with coffee, a great selection of wines and cheeses, with a quiet patio in back.

The Coffee Roost: 132 Route 6A, Suite 2, Sandwich; (508) 888-7000. Coffee, tea, scones, pastries, on the way to the Boardwalk. Did I mention the apple toffee scone?

Daniel Webster Inn: 149 Main St., Sandwich; (508) 833-3217. Eat in the tavern or main restaurant with great atmosphere and try to figure out what Daniel Webster liked so much about this spot.

Ice Cream Sandwich: 66 Route 6A, Sandwich; (508) 888-7237. Homemade ice cream and nicely decorated little shop. Great lobster roll.

Sagamore Inn: 131 Route 6A, Sagamore; (508) 888-9707. See the listing under Ride 1.

Restrooms

Sandwich Recreation Area (Start), Cape Cod Canal Visitors Center (60 Ed Moffitt Dr.), Daniel Webster Inn (3.7 miles), and Sandwich Boardwalk and Beach (option)

Villages of Bourne

A tour through the villages of Bourne, from the Cape Cod Canal and Bourne Village through Mashnee Neck, Monument Beach, Wing's Neck, Pocasset, and Cataumet. Ride the coast for the first half of the ride, with spectacular views of the ocean and bays, then return inland through countryside along rolling hills back to the start under the Bourne Bridge.

Start: Bourne Recreation Area parking lot, off Sandwich Road, under the Bourne Bridge in Bourne

Distance: 27.7-mile out-and-back and loop

Approximate riding time: 2 to 3 hours, depending on stops

Best bike: Road

Terrain and surface type: Smooth, flat pavement on main roads and quiet residential roads through the villages of Bourne (on the south side of the Cape Cod Canal)

Traffic and hazards: Traffic is quieter in Bourne, with most tourists passing it by to other Cape Cod locations. Route 28A has heavier traffic, especially in summer.

Things to see: Cape Cod Canal, Bourne Bridge, Cape Cod Railroad Bridge, Aptucxet Trading Post and Museum, Gray Gables site, Mashnee Neck and Island, Monument Beach, Wing's Neck and Lighthouse, Four Ponds Conservation Area, Pocasset Town Forest, Pocasset River

Map: *Arrow Street Atlas: Cape Cod including Martha's Vineyard & Nantucket,* p. 22

Getting there: By car: From Boston, take Route 93 South to Route 3 South to the Sagamore Bridge. Take exit 1C (the first exit after the bridge on right), take a left onto Sandwich Road toward the Bourne Bridge. Sandwich Road splits in two just before the Bourne Rotary as the road starts to go uphill toward the rotary. Go right just before the road goes uphill to the Bourne Recreation Area. Parking lot by the canal under the bridge. **From Route 495/25 and Bourne Bridge:** Cross over Bourne Bridge, go around the rotary, and proceed onto Sandwich Road. Take your first left onto Sandwich Road (I know that sounds wrong, but it isn't). **From points east on Cape Cod:** Take exit 1C off Route 6 and turn left onto Adams Street (the first left), then left onto Sandwich Road, and turn right onto Sandwich Road just before the Bourne Bridge (as above).

GPS coordinates: N41 44.80' / W70 35.30'

THE RIDE

This is a challenging road ride for more seasoned road cyclists at a distance of almost 30 miles, but it can easily be cut shorter or made longer depending on your level of energy. This ride overlaps Ride 1, Cape Cod Canal, and Ride 5, Tour of Falmouth. It has several challenging short climbs and rolling hills for several long stretches, especially in the middle of the ride and at the end of the ride along County Road in Bourne. On some main roads but mostly back roads, it starts at the parking lot under the Bourne Bridge by the Cape Cod Canal and takes a little side trip to the Aptucxet Trading Post and Museum. Check out the 100-year-old Victorian personal train station of President Grover Cleveland as you ride by, moved here in 1976 from its original location farther along this ride at mile 2.7. The Aptucxet Trading Post is the site of the first Pilgrim trading post with the Wampanoag Native Americans (see Ride 1, Cape Cod Canal). Turn left under the railroad tracks (tunnel with mural) and make a right onto Shore Road. Make a right onto Bell Road and head to the Tidal Flats Recreation Area parking lot. This is an alternate parking lot in case the Bourne Recreation Area lot is full, but it's also another great way to see the Cape Cod Canal and the Railroad Bridge.

Return to Shore Road and take a right onto Monument Neck Road. At mile 2.7, the corner of Monument Neck Road and President's Road, the original site of President Cleveland's personal train station is marked by an engraved stone (1892) partially covered over with flowers. Take a right on President's Road into the village of Gray Gables, where President Cleveland spent his summers fishing at nearby ponds, searching for trout. At the end of President's Road off Shore Road is the site of Cleveland's summer home from 1888 to 1896, the first presidential "summer White House." He referred to the house as Gray Gables since the weathered cedar shingles turned gray and the three-story house had numerous gables. The president's home was later turned into an

Gone for a swim at Mashnee Neck, Bourne

inn after being sold by Cleveland's son in 1920, becoming the Gray Gables Ocean House Inn, which stood until 1973, when a fire completely destroyed it.

From the Gray Gables neighborhood of Bourne, the ride takes you to a long neck of sandy beach and dune called Mashnee Neck, which can be very crowded in summer with cars, but presents no problem for touring cyclists who want to park their bikes and go to the beach for a swim. It is an area of Cape Cod that most Cape Codders have never heard of, even confusing the name of "Mashnee" with "Mashpee," a town on the other side of Otis Air National Guard Base. Mashnee Neck is a beautiful strip of land with ocean views everywhere.

Leaving Mashnee and Gray Gables, turn right onto Shore Road and continue past the Lobster Trap restaurant over the Back River Bridge. The water views are spectacular along Shore Road, and here the ocean to your right flows under you into the Back River estuary and Eel Pond to your left. Enter the village of Monument Beach, passing through town with a quick right and left past Whistle Stop Ice Cream to continue on Shore Road to the beach. Monument Beach is large and rarely crowded. Enjoy watching the boats navigating in and out of adjacent Monument Beach Marina, admire the frequent windsurfers, or comb the beach for shells, beach glass, and rocks that are abundant here. Just after Monument Beach is the start of a short but steeper climb past conservation area, into a shaded forest summit. The road descends quickly over the Pocasset River Bridge into the village of Pocasset, with excellent views of sea and marsh.

Turn right onto Barlow's Landing Road and then quickly onto Wing's Neck Road and ride about a mile to Wing's Neck Island, where you ascend Wing's Neck Road through oak, pine, and cedar forest. Descend the other side and turn around at Lighthouse Lane, a private road. You can see the Wing's Neck Lighthouse from this cul-de-sac and there are only a little more than a dozen houses in this private, gated neighborhood. The Wing's Neck Lighthouse was formerly a US Coast Guard lighthouse that was sold in 1947, and the light tower is still attached to a three-bedroom keeper's house that can be rented (sleeps up to 8) weekly for $4,500. Turn around here and return over the hill via South Road to the neck and take a right back to Shore Road through Pocasset.

Bike Shops

Sailworld Bikes & Boards, 139 Main St., Buzzards Bay, Bourne, (508) 759-6559, sailworld.com
Eastern Mountain Sports, 2 Bridge Approach St., Bourne, (508) 759-7620, ems.com

The next village of Bourne is Cataumet, and at mile 17.0 you'll descend Shore Road and pass over the Red Brook Bridge with a scenic view of Red Brook Harbor on the right. At mile 17.5, turn right on Red Brook Harbor Road and enjoy the views. Cross over Scraggy Neck Road and enjoy the views of Squeteague Harbor on your right. On Megansett Road, cross over into Falmouth for a short stretch on Garnet Avenue. At mile 19.5, turn left onto County Road (or turn right to add another 31 miles to this ride, and follow directions for Ride 5, Tour of Falmouth).

Turn left on Old Main Street and head back to Bourne just a few minutes from here. Turn left on Route 28A (Bourne town line), left again onto County Road (Bourne) at mile 20.6, and ride a long stretch of rural road over rolling hills all the way back to Bourne Village and the start. This longer stretch on County Road will challenge your legs, but makes for a nice finish to this ride. Cross Shore Road onto Sandwich Road and turn left into the Bourne Recreation Area parking lot under the Bourne Bridge.

MILES AND DIRECTIONS

0.0 Start the ride at the Bourne Recreation Area under the Bourne Bridge.

0.1 Turn right onto Sandwich Road.

0.7 Turn right on Perry Avenue.

0.9 Turn left on Aptucxet Road.

1.0 Pass Aptucxet Trading Post and Museum.

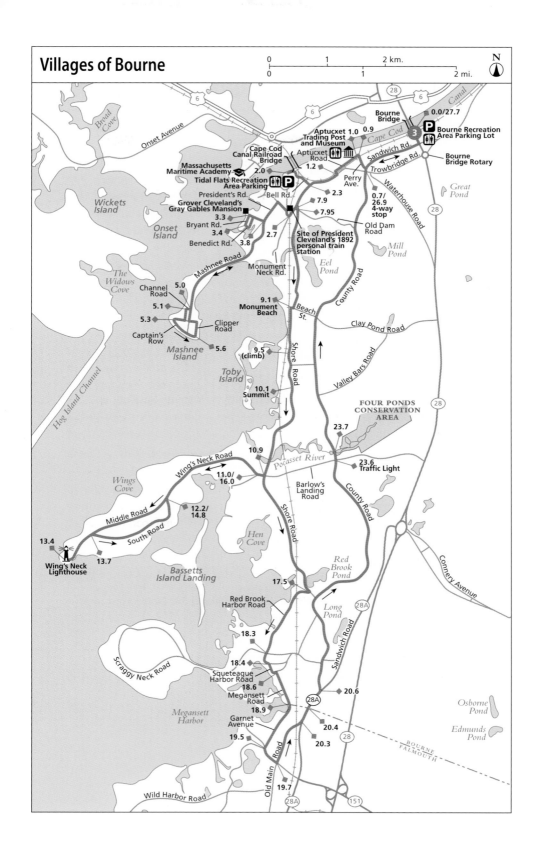

Villages of Bourne

0 1 2 km.
0 1 2 mi.

N

Bread
Cove

Onset Avenue

Wickets
Island

Onset
Island

The
Widow's
Cove

Hog Island Channel

Mashnee Road

Channel
Road 5.0

5.1

5.3

Captain's
Row

Clipper
Road

5.6

Mashnee
Island

Toby
Island

Wings
Cove

Wing's Neck Road

Middle Road

South Road

13.4

13.7

Wing's Neck
Lighthouse

Bassetts
Island Landing

Scraggy Neck Road

Megansett
Harbor

Bourne
Bridge

0.0/27.7

Bourne Recreation
Area Parking Lot

Cape Cod
Canal

Aptucxet 1.0 0.9
Trading Post
and Museum

Aptucxet
Road 1.2

3

Bourne
Bridge Rotary

Sandwich Rd.

Trowbridge Rd.

Cape Cod
Canal Railroad
Bridge 2.0

Massachusetts
Maritime Academy

Tidal Flats Recreation
Area Parking

President's Rd.

Grover Cleveland's
Gray Gables Mansion

3.3

Bryant Rd.

3.4

Benedict Rd. 3.8

Bell Rd.

2.3

7.9

7.95

2.7

Monument
Neck Rd.

Perry
Ave.

0.7/
26.9
4-way
stop

Waterhouse Road

Great
Pond

Old Dam
Road

Mill
Pond

Eel
Pond

County Road

Great
Pond

28

Site of President
Cleveland's 1892
personal train
station

Monument
Beach 9.1

9.5
(climb)

10.1
Summit

Beach St.

Shore Road

Clay Pond Road

Valley Bars Road

FOUR PONDS
CONSERVATION
AREA

23.7

28

10.9

Pocasset River

11.0/
16.0

12.2/
14.8

Hen
Cove

23.6
Traffic Light

Barlow's
Landing
Road

County Road

Shore Road

Red
Brook
Pond

Connery Avenue

17.5

Red Brook
Harbor Road

Long
Pond

Sandwich Road

28A

18.3

18.4

Squeteague
Harbor Road

18.6

Megansett
Road

18.9

Garnet
Avenue

19.5

28A

20.6

20.4

20.3

28

Osborne
Pond

Edmunds
Pond

BOURNE
FALMOUTH

Old Main Road

19.7

28A

151

Wild Harbor Road

1.2 Turn left under the small railroad bridge tunnel with kids' mural painting and make an immediate right turn on Shore Road.

1.5 Turn right on Bell Road.

1.7 Turn right on Canal Service Road into the Tidal Flats Recreation Area parking lot. This is an alternate parking lot and ride start if the Bourne Recreation Area parking lot is full.

2.0 Turn around at the end of the Tidal Flats Recreation Area parking lot.

2.3 Turn right on Shore Road.

2.6 Bear right onto Monument Neck Road.

2.7 Turn right on President's Road, original site of Cleveland's train station.

2.8 Bear left and continue on President's Road.

3.1 Bear right and continue on President's Road.

3.3 Turn left on Bryant Road, passing the Gray Gables site.

3.4 Turn left on Benedict Road and loop around back to President's Road.

3.6 Turn right back onto President's Road.

3.8 Turn right on Mashnee Road. Continue on Mashnee Neck about 2 miles. Stop and park your bike for a swim and magnificent views of the bay on both sides of the neck.

5.0 Turn right on Channel Road, entering Mashnee Island.

5.1 Turn left on Rope Walk Road.

5.2 Turn right on Mooring Road.

5.3 Bear left and continue on Captain's Row. Commanding views on all sides.

5.6 Turn left on Clipper Road.

5.8 Turn left on Mooring Road.

5.9 Turn right on Mashnee Road and return along the 2-mile Mashnee Neck causeway to the end.

7.4 Continue straight on President's Road.

7.6 Bear right.

7.8 Turn left on Monument Neck Road.

7.9 Turn right on Old Dam Road.

7.95 Turn right on Shore Road.

9.0 Bear right (Beach Street).

9.1   Bear left and continue on Shore Road past Monument Beach on the right.

9.5   Start of climb on Shore Road (at Emmons Road).

10.1   Summit of Shore Road climb.

10.9   Turn right on Barlow's Landing Road.

11.0   Turn right on Wing's Neck Road.

12.2   Continue straight up the climb on Wing's Neck Road (Middle Road).

13.4   Turn around at the end of Wing's Neck Road (Middle Road) at the cul-de-sac and view the Wing's Neck Lighthouse.

13.7   Turn right onto South Road.

14.8   Turn right, back onto Wing's Neck Road.

16.0   Turn left onto Barlow's Landing Road.

16.1   Make a quick right onto Village Road and turn right on Shore Road through Pocasset.

17.5   Turn right on Red Brook Harbor Road through Cataumet.

18.3   Cross Scraggy Neck Road and continue on Squeteague Harbor Road.

18.4   Bear right.

18.6   Turn right on Megansett Road.

18.9   Continue on Garnet Avenue (Falmouth town line).

19.5   Turn left on County Road (Falmouth).

19.7   Turn left on Old Main Road (Falmouth).

20.3   Turn left on Route 28A/North Falmouth Highway.

20.4   Continue on 28A/Sandwich Road (Bourne town line).

20.6   Turn left on County Road (Bourne).

23.6   Cross Barlow's Landing Road (traffic light).

23.7   Pass Pocasset River and Four Ponds Conservation Area.

26.9   Cross Shore Road/Trowbridge Road at stop sign; continue on Sandwich Road.

27.6   Turn left into Bourne Recreation Area and return to parking lot.

27.7   Ride ends in the Bourne Recreation Area parking lot under the Bourne Bridge where it started.

3

RIDE INFORMATION

Local Events and Attractions
National Marine Life Center: 120 Main St., Buzzards Bay (Bourne); (508) 743-9888; nmlc.org. NMLC is on the north side of the Cape Cod Canal, adjacent to Massachusetts Maritime Academy. NMLC is a nonprofit rehabilitation and release hospital for the treatment of stranded sea turtles and seals, with future plans to expand to treat dolphins, porpoises, and small whales. Every year, up to 56 live seals, 98 live dolphins, and 144 live sea turtles get stranded on Cape Cod beaches in need of medical care. Programs for kids and adults include the popular annual Mermaid Ball in August and the Cape Cod Wildlife Festival in September.

Bourne Scallop Festival (September): Recently moved to the Cape Cod Fairgrounds (Barnstable County Fairgrounds) in East Falmouth (which many in Bourne are not happy about), this popular festival attracts more than 50,000 people each year. Professional, juried arts and crafts, rides, games, entertainment, and famous fried scallop and herb-roasted chicken dinners. Free hamburgers, hot dogs, and ice cream for kids. Kids under 5, free admission.

Restaurants
Sunset Grille at the Brookside Club: 11 Brigadoone Rd., Buzzards Bay; (508) 743-0705; thebrooksideclub.com/index.php/sunsetgrille. See the listing under Ride 1.

The Lobster Trap: 290 Shore Rd., Bourne; (508) 759-7600. A kid-friendly, fried seafood place with a great view and a fresh-fish market. Sit outside on the deck on a nice day and enjoy the view.

The Chart Room: 1 Shipyard Ln., Bourne (off Shore Road at the Cataumet Marina, mile 17.2, on Red Brook Harbor); (508) 563-5350. Get a reservation or get there early, dine with the locals, and get a table in the outer dining room, where there are sunset views. No fried seafood on the menu here, and it's expensive. Great "chowdah."

Courtyard Restaurant & Pub: 1337 County Rd., Bourne; (508) 563-1818. Former Boston Bruins NHL enforcer Jay Miller owns this sports bar and restaurant, with its own penalty box (where Jay spent a lot of time) and spacious outdoor dining area with fire pit and big-screen TV for sports. Live music. Ask Jay about his "wicked good" classmates at Natick High School.

Whistle Stop Ice Cream: 435 Shore Rd., Monument Beach, Bourne; (508) 759-8958. I've never seen cranberry chip ice cream anywhere else.

Restrooms
Bourne Recreation Area (start), Tidal Flats Recreation Area (1.7), and Monument Beach (9.1)

Shining Sea Bikeway

A flat, smoothly paved path from North Falmouth through West Falmouth, Falmouth Center, and along Surf Drive to Woods Hole and back. Panoramic views of Great Sippewissett Marsh, Little Sippewissett Marsh, Salt Pond, Oyster Pond, Surf Beach, and Vineyard Sound. Lots to do and see in Falmouth Center and Woods Hole, great for kids and families.

Start: North Falmouth, off County Road in the dirt parking lot across from Pine Street

Distance: 21.2 miles out-and-back

Approximate riding time: 2 to 3 hours

Best bike: Road, hybrid

Terrain and surface type: Smooth, flat, paved bike and multi-use path. Some gentle hills.

Traffic and hazards: Pedestrians, dogs, and other riders on a two-way bike path that is great for kids and families, several crosswalks, car traffic in Steamship Authority parking lot with drivers sometimes in a hurry to catch the ferry to Martha's Vineyard and posing a real danger to cyclists along the Woods Hole end of the Bikeway

Things to see: Cranberry bogs, wildlife, Bourne Farm (1775), Great Sippewissett Marsh, Little Sippewissett Marsh, Wampanoag history, West Falmouth Village (Old Dock Road), Falmouth Center (Depot Avenue), Corner Cycle, Maison Villatte Bakery, Surf Drive Beach, Woods Hole

Map: *Arrow Street Atlas: Cape Cod including Martha's Vineyard & Nantucket*, p. 50

Getting there: From Route 495/25 and the Bourne Bridge: Go around Bourne Rotary and proceed onto Route 28 South. Take the exit for Route 151 and head west. Cross Route 28A, and continue on County

Road to the dirt parking lot opposite Pine Street on the right. **From Route 6 (and Route 3, points north):** Cross over the Sagamore Bridge and take exit 1C to the Sandwich Road. Turn left (west) at the end of the exit ramp and follow the Cape Cod Canal (should be on the right), heading west to the Bourne Rotary. Exit the rotary onto Route 28 South and exit at Route 151, following the directions to County Road and the dirt parking lot opposite Pine Street (above).

GPS coordinates: N41 38.85' / W70 36.85'

THE RIDE

The official start of the Shining Sea Bikeway is in Woods Hole at the Steamship Authority (the turnaround point of this ride), but this ride starts in North Falmouth in a dirt parking lot across from Pine Street on County Road. Although the parking lot is unglamorous here, with a porta-potty next to the chain-link fence, parking is free, and you won't have to deal with the heavy traffic in Woods Hole in summer, or the long line of slow-moving traffic on the Woods Hole Road to get there. The Shining Sea Bikeway, named for the anthem "America the Beautiful" by Falmouth native Katherine Lee Bates, is one of the best anywhere in New England. This is a great ride for children and families, as the pavement is very smooth and wide, and the views and activities along the route are perfect for a day's outing with the little ones. Make sure the kids watch out for turtle crossings along the Bikeway, especially the endangered diamondback terrapin turtle. It's best to ride around them.

Turn left out of the sandy parking lot on County Road and then right onto the bikeway, heavily marked with railroad crossing lights and signs. For the first 2 miles there isn't much to see other than trees and crosswalks, signs for turtles, and Bikeway Rules (riders should read them), but the path soon opens up for a view of active cranberry bogs, where you might see cranberries harvested in September or October. Just past the bogs is Bourne Farm, a forty-nine-acre farm that dates back to 1775 and overlooks Crocker Pond.

At Old Dock Road, you can opt to turn left off the bikeway for some much-needed organic coffee or ice cream at the Village Cafe (restrooms, but not open on Sunday) or Eulinda's Ice Cream (open Sunday) in West Falmouth. Or you can opt to turn right off the bikeway to see the boats in Snug Harbor. Continue on and arrive at a vast open space, Great Sippewissett Marsh, with a diverse ecology of salt marsh, coastal beach, and marine tidal habitats for birds and other coastal fauna. Salt hay and tall sea grasses line the route here, opening up to allow panoramic views across the 140-acre marsh, with osprey, herons,

Riders on the Shining Sea Bikeway, Woods Hole, Falmouth

all kinds of terns, gulls, and shorebirds. Buzzards Bay is visible from Great Sip-pewissett Marsh on the bikeway, and there are a few rest stops where you can park your bike and inhale the fresh salt air. One mile farther on the bikeway is Little Sippewissett Marsh, with a rest stop and placards describing Wampa-noag history. Opposite the marsh, the Sippewissett Campground has teepees visible through the trees. It turns out that the bikeway, and the Penn Central Railroad before it, follow old Wampanoag routes along the way to Woods Hole.

The history of the route is as old as the Wampanoag Native Americans who lived here before European arrival. In 1872, the first railroad tracks were laid from Monument Village in Bourne to Falmouth and Woods Hole by the Penn Central Railroad along the old Wampanoag paths. The railroad ran from that year until 1957, eighty-five years of service, and in 1973, the Town of Falmouth procured the title to the abandoned railroad bed. In 1974, the town raised $4,000, matched with another $4,000 by Woods Hole Oceanographic Institute and Marine Biological Labs of Woods Hole, to clear the old railroad bed. By 1976, the 3.3-mile Shining Sea Bikeway was completed with a path from Woods Hole to Locust Street. Over the years the path has been extended several times and now measures 10.7 miles, avoiding most of the traffic in summer by staying closer to the coast for the first 7 miles.

After Little Sippewissett Marsh, the bikeway enters downtown Falmouth, and reaching Depot Avenue, there is the option to turn left and explore the busy town center. Corner Cycle is on the corner of Route 28 and Palmer Avenue, and you can park and rent bicycles there. Say hello to owner and all-around good guy George Sykes, one of the best bicycle mechanics in the United States. And he ought to be, having wrenched for US National Champion Mark McCormack, the first American cyclist to win national championships in both road cycling and cyclocross. You're likely to run into any one of a number of national champions or professional cyclists here. Yet the place is unassuming, not very big, good-humored, and resembles a museum devoted to the history of New England cycling. Corner Cycle also hosts the only USA Cycling-sanctioned race on Cape Cod, the Coonamessett Farm Eco-Cross cyclocross race in North Falmouth, usually held in November during the week of Veteran's Day. It doesn't happen every year, but check with the bike shop for more information and go out and watch the fastest growing sport in the United States. Cyclocross is a great spectator sport that kids and families will love, with cowbells, mud, and beer tents à la Belgium, where the sport is as popular as baseball.

Bike Shops

Art's Bike Shop, 91 County Road, North Falmouth, (508) 563-7379, artsbikeshop.com
Bike Zone, 13 County Road #3, North Falmouth, (508) 563-2333, bikezone capecod.com
Corner Cycle, 115 Palmer Ave., Falmouth, (508) 540-4195, cornercycle.com

Continue past downtown and cross the Woods Hole Road, where the flavor of the bikeway changes again, and approach the Atlantic Ocean past Salt Pond on the way to Surf Drive. At mile 8.3, cross Elm Road and go past Oyster Pond to your right, where the path opens up for a view of Vineyard Sound and Martha's Vineyard along Surf Drive Beach. This is the place to watch fireworks on the Fourth of July if you're in the neighborhood, or watch sailboats cruise Vineyard Sound. The seal population has been growing over the past few years on Cape Cod, and they're sometimes seen swimming and lying around on the beach here. After about a mile of unobstructed ocean view to the left, the path heads into a forested area, over the 7-mile Falmouth Road Race course on a wooden bridge, through a long parking lot and into Woods Hole by the Steamship Authority ferry docks. In Woods Hole, you can see the start of an international running race in August, a film festival in July, the oldest aquarium in the country, and the place where Rachel Carson lived and worked, or board a ferry to Martha's Vineyard, go to lectures and an excellent science exhibit at the world-renowned Woods Hole Oceanographic Institute (WHOI), visit the world-famous Marine Biological Labs (MBL), whale watch, deep-sea fish, eat at any number of ocean-view restaurants, or just hang out and people-watch.

The village of Woods Hole is an international center for natural science. In addition to MBL and WHOI, the Woods Hole scientific community includes the National Marine Fisheries Service, the United States Geological Survey, the National Academy of Sciences, Sea Education Association, and the Woods Hole Research Center. There are lots of Nobel Prize–winning scientists walking around. Take a right at the end of the bikeway, walk up the hill a little bit, and head into the Pie in the Sky Bakery and Internet Cafe on the left for sandwiches, pies, coffee, and cold drinks. Refuel for the ride back to North Falmouth, or just book a room in Woods Hole and stay right here.

MILES AND DIRECTIONS

0.0 Begin in the dirt parking lot on County Road across from Pine Street. (The official start of the Shining Sea Bikeway is in the Steamship Authority parking lot in Woods Hole, but traffic in Woods Hole is often very congested and parking is metered, so this ride starts in North Falmouth.)

0.6 Cross Winslow Road.

1.0 Cross Curley Boulevard.

1.4 Cross Wing Road and view Wing Pond on the right.

2.0 View cranberry bogs on the right.

2.2 Pass Bourne Farm and Crocker Pond on the left.

2.7 Cross Chase Road.

3.3 Cross Old Dock Road. (Option: Turn left for the Village Cafe.)

3.6 Cross Chapoquoit Road.

3.9 Cross Little Neck Bars Road.

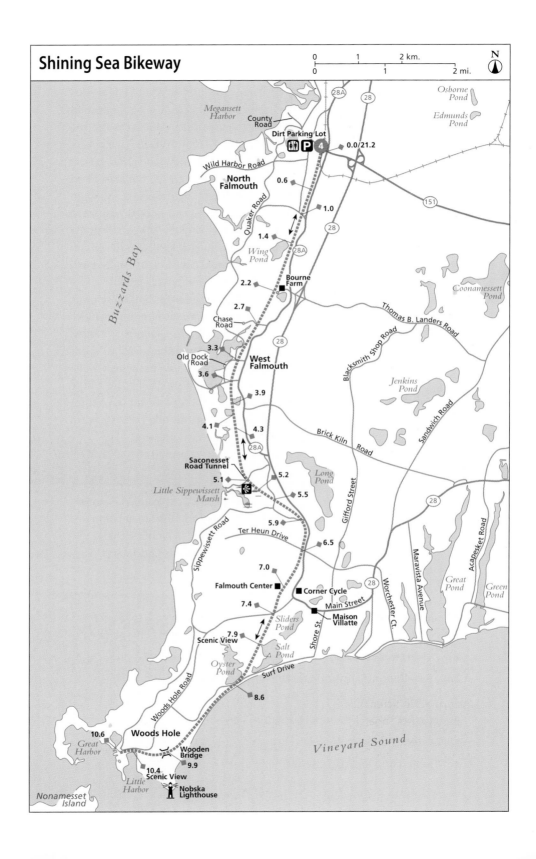

Shining Sea Bikeway

0 1 2 km.

0 1 2 mi.

N

Osborne Pond

Edmunds Pond

Megansett Harbor

County Road

28A

28

Dirt Parking Lot

🅿 4 0.0/21.2

Wild Harbor Road

North Falmouth

0.6

151

1.0

Quaker Road

28

1.4

Wing Pond

28A

Coonamessett Pond

2.2

Bourne Farm

Thomas B. Landers Road

2.7

Chase Road

28

3.3

Old Dock Road

West Falmouth

Buzzards Bay

Jenkins Pond

3.6

Blacksmith Shop Road

Sandwich Road

3.9

4.1

4.3

Brick Kiln Road

28A

Saconesset Road Tunnel

5.1

5.2

Long Pond

Little Sippewissett Marsh

5.5

Gifford Street

28

5.9

Ter Heun Drive

6.5

Sippewissett Road

7.0

Maravista Avenue

Acapesket Road

Falmouth Center

■ **Corner Cycle**

Great Pond

Green Pond

7.4

Main Street

28

Shore St.

Worchester Ct.

■ **Maison Villatte**

7.9

Scenic View

Sliders Pond

Salt Pond

Oyster Pond

Surf Drive

8.6

Woods Hole Road

Woods Hole

10.6

Great Harbor

Wooden Bridge

9.9

10.4 **Scenic View**

Little Harbor

🔦 **Nobska Lighthouse**

Nonamesset Island

Vineyard Sound

4.1 Cross Quahog Pond Road.

4.3 View Great Sippewissett Marsh on your right.

5.1 Pass under Saconesset Road (tunnel).

5.2 View Little Sippewissett Marsh and get a little Wampanoag history.

5.5 Cross Palmer Avenue.

5.9 Cross Palmer Avenue again.

6.5 Cross Ter Heun Drive (Falmouth Hospital). Watch out for ambulances.

7.0 Cross Depot Avenue. (Option: Take a quick side trip to visit Corner Cycle, and bring the employees a snack from Coffee Obsession across the street or Maison Villatte on Main Street.)

7.4 Cross Woods Hole Road. This is a heavy traffic area, especially in summer, and Massachusetts law requires that cyclists dismount and walk bicycles in all crosswalks.

7.9 Pass Salt Pond Scenic Vista.

8.3 Cross Elm Road. Oyster Pond, with turtles, swans, and rabbits, is on your right.

8.6 Cross Surf Drive (Beach Road). There are gorgeous views of Vineyard Sound and Martha's Vineyard in the distance.

9.2 Cross Fay Road.

9.9 Wooden Bikeway Bridge (over Nobska Road).

10.4 Scenic view of Little Harbor.

10.6 Turn around in Woods Hole at the Steamship Authority parking lot (the official start of the Shining Sea Bikeway) to return the way you came.

21.2 Arrive back at the parking lot in North Falmouth to finish the ride.

RIDE INFORMATION

Local Events and Attractions

Bourne Farm and Salt Pond Bird Sanctuary: 6 N. Falmouth Hwy., North Falmouth; (508) 548-8484. Hike or walk your dog through the bird sanctuary and historic farm. The annual Pumpkin Day in October is great for kids, with pick-your-own pumpkins, pony rides, hayrides, face-painting, kayaks and paddleboats, moonwalks, and crafts.

Woods Hole Science Aquarium: 166 Water St., Falmouth; (508) 495-2001; aquarium.nefsc.noaa.gov. A very small but excellent public aquarium that displays about 140 species of marine animals found in Northeast and Middle Atlantic waters. It's also the oldest aquarium in the US. Free.

Woods Hole Oceanographic Institute: 15 School St., Woods Hole, Falmouth; (508) 289-2252; whoi.edu. WHOI (pronounced "hooey") perhaps needs a little updating, but the Ocean Science Exhibit Center is great. See *Alvin*, the little submarine that allowed the researchers here to explore the *Titanic*.

Marine Biological Laboratories: 7 MBL St., Woods Hole, Falmouth; (508) 548-3705; mbl.edu. Best for adults and older children, they have fascinating tours led by knowledgeable guides, but you have to reserve early. Walk among the world's most brilliant scientists and learn how sea life is affecting medical research far beyond the sea.

Woods Hole Film Festival: P.O. Box 624, Woods Hole, Falmouth; (508) 495-FILM; woodsholefilmfestival.org. Yearly film festival, an eight-day event at the end of July through the start of August. Founded by Judith Laster and Kate Davis, the festival shows a hundred films from seven hundred submissions from emerging independent filmmakers, emphasizing New England (and Cape Cod) filmmakers.

Restaurants

Pie in the Sky Bakery and Internet Cafe: 10 Water St., Woods Hole, Falmouth; (508) 540-5475. Coffee, more coffee, sandwiches, baked goods, pastries, croissants, outdoor umbrella dining. Watch the people go by, connect online, fuel up for the ride back to North Falmouth.

Quicks Hole: 6 Luscombe Ave., Woods Hole; (508) 495-0792. Eat at Beth Colt's restaurant or tavern, quickly becoming a "best place" in Woods Hole to dine or brunch. The water views on the porch overlooking the harbor through French windows are lovely. Try the seared bay scallops.

Village Cafe, Eulinda's Ice Cream: 634 W. Falmouth Hwy., West Falmouth; (508) 548-2486. I love this place. Turn off the Shining Sea Bikeway at Old Dock Road (mile 3.3) and have a great breakfast or lunch, made from fresh and organic ingredients. They have bike racks in back and great coffee. The best breakfast burritos. Eulinda's doesn't have the long lines (yet) and there's plenty of shade at the picnic tables out back. The only drawback: they're not open on Sundays.

Maison Villatte: 267 Main St., Falmouth; (774) 255-1855. When world-class baker Boris Villatte arrived in Falmouth, I felt the hole in my heart (wait, was it in my stomach?) immediately heal. After bringing the most delicious baked concoctions to the P.B. Boulangerie in Wellfleet and then pulling a disappearing act, Monsieur Villatte returns to Falmouth with the best. Paris bakeries have nothing on this place.

Restrooms

There are porta-potties at the start and finish and lots of restaurants in Woods Hole.

Best Bike Rides Cape Cod and the Islands

Tour of Falmouth

This is a fairly challenging road ride, through every village of Falmouth, through hilly forest and countryside inland, and along the Buzzards Bay and Vineyard Sound coastlines. Stretch out your legs a little and enjoy the views. Combine this ride with Ride 3, Villages of Bourne, for a 60-mile ride and explore the entire west coast of Cape Cod in one day.

Start: North Falmouth, on County Road in the dirt parking lot across from Pine Street, just west of the Shining Sea Bikeway North Falmouth entrance.

Distance: 31.4-mile loop

Approximate riding time: 2 hours or more depending on stops

Best bike: Road

Terrain and surface type: Main roads and paved back roads, with some cracks and potholes.

Traffic and hazards: Vehicular traffic that gets busier near Woods Hole, narrower roads with little to no shoulder

Things to see: Old Silver Beach, Falmouth Cliffs, Snug Harbor, West Falmouth, Chapoquoit Beach, Woods Hole, Falmouth Road Race course, Woods Hole Science Aquarium, Woods Hole Oceanographic Institute (WHOI), Marine Biological Laboratories (MBL), Nobska Lighthouse, Vineyard Sound, Surf Drive Beach, Falmouth Inner Harbor (*Island Queen* ferry to Martha's Vineyard), Little Pond, Great Pond, Green Pond, East Falmouth, Coonamessett Farm, Shining Sea Bikeway

Map: *Arrow Street Atlas: Cape Cod including Martha's Vineyard & Nantucket,* p. 50

Getting there: From Route 495/25 and the Bourne Bridge: Go around Bourne Rotary and proceed onto Route 28 South. Take the exit for Route 151 and head west. Cross Route 28A, and continue on County

Road to the dirt parking lot opposite Pine Street on the right. **From Route 6 (and Route 3, points north):** Cross over the Sagamore Bridge and take exit 1C to the Sandwich Road. Turn left (west) at the end of the exit ramp and follow the Cape Cod Canal (should be on the right), heading west to the Bourne Rotary. Exit the rotary onto Route 28 South and exit at Route 151, following the directions to County Road and the dirt parking lot opposite Pine Street (above).

GPS coordinates: N41 38.88' / W70 36.83'

THE RIDE

The Tour of Falmouth is a big loop that goes through every village in town, from North Falmouth to downtown and access to Main Street, into Woods Hole, Nobska, Falmouth Heights, and East Falmouth, then north through Coonamessett and back to the start in North Falmouth. There is so much to see and do on this ride, too much to list, but that's okay because this is a ride for roadies who want a nice, long ride without any stops, but still with some of the best scenery Cape Cod has to offer. With excellent views of the Atlantic Ocean sometimes just a few feet away, ride a good length of Buzzards Bay, with its numerous smaller harbors and coves, and then along Vineyard Sound, with long beaches, gorgeous beachfront homes, and several harbors and marinas. Then this ride pulls away from the water completely on hilly country roads through rural farmland and forest. It can also be combined with Ride 3, Villages of Bourne, for a 60-mile ride that tours the entire west coast of Cape Cod and will leave you exhausted but exhilarated.

Turning right out of the County Road dirt parking lot, the ride takes you quickly to Chester Street and the water's edge at Rand's Harbor and Megansett Harbor. Next, winding Quaker Road takes you to Old Silver Beach (changing facilities, bathrooms, showers), a warmer, more-protected beach than many Atlantic Cape beaches and with gentler surf, perfect for families with children. Over the bridge, take in a view of the nice homes atop Falmouth Cliffs. Cruise around Snug Harbor on Nashawena Street and then take Old Dock Road to Chapoquoit Point at the end of the road with the same name. This is a nice stretch of road with a very long sandy beach, with great views of the Atlantic in front of you and West Falmouth Harbor behind you. The end of Chapoquoit Point is private, so turn around at mile 5.7 of this ride just past the main beach.

Heading back from Chapoquoit Point, cross the Shining Sea Bikeway (Ride 3) and turn right onto the West Falmouth Highway, Route 28A. This road can have more traffic, but is still relatively quiet, especially for a rider used to any city or suburb (but if you want to avoid it, simply take a right onto the Shining Sea Bikeway at mile 6.5 and then turn right at the Palmer Avenue crosswalk to rejoin this ride). As 28A approaches 28, the road climbs a bit, and then turns away back to the coast on Palmer Avenue, then quickly onto Sippewissett Road.

Sippewissett Road is one of my favorite roads to ride on the Cape. It's wooded, hilly, narrow, and offers occasional glimpses of the ocean when looking past some beautiful homes. When you ride the hilly section through the Woods Hole Golf Club, watch out for golf cart crossings and speed bumps—they can catch you off-guard and spell disaster.

From here the road descends into Woods Hole and the traffic suddenly gets very congested, at least in summer. Take a right onto Millfield Street and loop around Eel Pond to Albatross Street. You are now in an international center of ocean and atmospheric science, among Nobel laureates, oceanographic and marine biological scientists, some of the best, if not the best, in the world. They're behind those walls, behind the ivy, with their microscopes, fish tanks, and computers. Ride past the seals in front of the tiny Woods Hole Science Aquarium on the right, operated by the NOAA National Marine Fisheries Service since 1885 (open 11 a.m. to 4 p.m., Tuesday through Saturday, year-round). Then round the corner left onto Water Street, Woods Hole's main drag. Look right for views of the Atlantic, and the Gosnold Islands, Nonamesset, Uncatena, and Naushon Island, visible to the right of Martha's Vineyard. Cross over the Water

Bike Shop

Corner Cycle, 115 Palmer Ave., Falmouth, (508) 540-4195, cornercycle.com

Street drawbridge and turn right toward the Steamship Authority past Coffee Obsession on your right, and watch passengers boarding the ferry to Martha's Vineyard.

The road goes left past the Shining Sea Bikeway, then up a short incline, and if you need a break to rehydrate or eat, the Pie in the Sky Bakery and Internet Cafe is to your left near the top of the hill. Turn right onto Woods Hole Road at the top of the incline, ride less than a block, and make a right onto Church Street. Go over the wooden bridge (avoid the nails and splinters) on Church and follow the road down until it opens up on Nobska Lighthouse off in the distance. This is one of the most photographed locations on Cape Cod. Nobska Point Lighthouse is an active Coast Guard lighthouse built in 1876, and the keeper's house is occupied by the Commander of Coast Guard Sector Southeastern New England. Nobska Light tours are conducted by United States Coast Guard Cape & Islands Division, Auxiliary Flotilla 11-2. Climb up the hill and ride around the lighthouse with great views of Vineyard Sound.

Approaching Nobska Lighthouse on Church Street, Woods Hole

Descend the other side along the shore for a stretch with views of Nobska Point Ledge and Vineyard Sound.

You may have already noticed the big painted numbers on the road starting at Water Street in downtown Woods Hole along this ride, the mile markers for the internationally renowned 7-mile Falmouth Road Race. This ride follows the famous running race all the way to the finish in Falmouth Heights along the pavement with numbers 1 through 6 (mile 7 is the finish and you'll ride over the finish line faster than any world-class marathoner). After Nobska Light, pass under the Shining Sea Bikeway bridge on Nobska Road, and continue straight on Oyster Pond Road through a forested area until it opens up with views of the water to your right. Continue on Surf Drive for a nice long, open stretch before a zig and a zag to go around Falmouth Inner Harbor. Pass the *Island Queen* ferry docks and head into Falmouth Heights, making a 90-degree left on Grand Avenue and ascending to a great view of Martha's Vineyard and Vineyard Sound. After you descend the other side of Grand Avenue (Falmouth Road Race finish), bear right and hug the shore on Menauhant Road and follow this over the Great Pond Bridge, which turns inland, then bends right to cross the long bridge over Green Pond. Pass the Green Pond Marina on the right and turn left on residential Davisville Road, a long, straight stretch of road with many side streets and moderate traffic.

Cross Route 28 (traffic light) onto Old Meetinghouse Road, and the feel of this ride changes dramatically. Now you are entering a rural residential area with farmland that is typical of inland Cape Cod. Crossing over Sandwich Road onto Hatchville Road, retired cranberry bogs and farmland line the road. Hatchville Road goes uphill here with merging traffic from your left, and at mile 28 you can stop at Coonamessett Farm, an organic farm with a membership for picking fruit, vegetables, flowers and ordering poultry or beef as well as your Thanksgiving organic turkey. The chickens here are truly free-range, running through rows and rows of high blueberry where cyclists also get to ride, once a year. In spring, it's strawberry season, where the strawberries are small and sweet. In summer it's raspberries, blueberries, and blackberries, and in the fall it's squashes and cyclocross!

Cyclocross is the United States' fastest-growing sport, a spectator-friendly version of bicycle racing that takes place at Coonamessett Farm, usually in late fall. Cyclocross has been described as "the steeplechase of cycling," with barriers that riders must bunny-hop or hurdle by dismounting and carrying their bicycles, and then remounting to ride on. Cyclocross has been popular in Europe for more than a hundred years, something Tour de France riders did in winter to stay fit. It now has its own national championship in this country, and Louisville, Kentucky, was host to the first UCI World Cyclocross Championships to be held in the United States in 2013. You can watch cyclocross all over New England and the United States, but Coonamessett is the only cyclocross race run on Cape Cod. In fact it's the only bicycle race on Cape Cod. Bring your friends and your cowbells to cheer on the racers. There is rarely a cancellation due to rain or snow.

Riding past Coonamessett Farm, bear left on Sam Turner Road at 28.2 miles, and ride the rolling hills up to Route 151. (My friend Larry Gray, past president of the Cape Cod Cycling Club, suggested an alternate route that avoids riding most of Route 151. Use Thomas B. Landers Road instead of Route 151 by turning around at Coonamessett Farm and taking the second right onto Geggatt Road, then turning right on Thomas B. Landers Road to get to Route 28A. This alternate takes Route 28A north to get to the County Road start/finish of this ride, eliminating the need to ride Route 151.)

Use caution crossing Route 151 from Sam Turner Road at mile 29.6. Farther up the road, at mile 30.7, watch out for cars that will cut you off trying to get past you onto the ramp for Route 28. You may notice mountain bikers on the right here entering the Otis mountain bike trails (see Ride 6). This is the best time to drive defensively. Go under the highway, cross Route 28A (traffic light), continue on County Road past the Shining Sea Bikeway entrance, and return to the parking lot where you began. Epic ride!

MILES AND DIRECTIONS

- **0.0** Ride start. Turn right onto County Road.
- **0.3** Turn left onto Chester Street.
- **1.2** Continue straight on Quaker Road.
- **2.9** Scenic vista of Old Silver Beach and Falmouth Cliffs.
- **4.1** Continue on Nashawena Street.
- **4.7** Turn right onto Old Dock Road.
- **5.1** Turn right onto Chapoquoit Road.
- **5.7** Scenic view and beach stop at Chapoquoit Point. Turn around here and follow Chapoquoit Road back past Old Dock Road.
- **6.5** Cross the Shining Sea Bikeway. (Option: To avoid Route 28A, the West Falmouth Highway, turn right here onto the Shining Sea Bikeway and take a right at Palmer Avenue to continue to Sippewissett Road.)
- **6.6** Turn right onto Route 28A, the West Falmouth Highway.
- **7.7** Turn right onto Palmer Avenue.
- **8.4** Cross Shining Sea Bikeway again.
- **8.5** Turn right onto Sippewissett Road.
- **11.4** Continue straight on Quissett Avenue.
- **13.0** Turn right onto Millfield Street.
- **13.2** Turn left onto Albatross Road.
- **13.4** Turn left onto Water Street.
- **13.5** Continue over the Woods Hole Drawbridge.
- **13.6** Turn right onto Luscombe Avenue. Bear left at Steamship Authority.

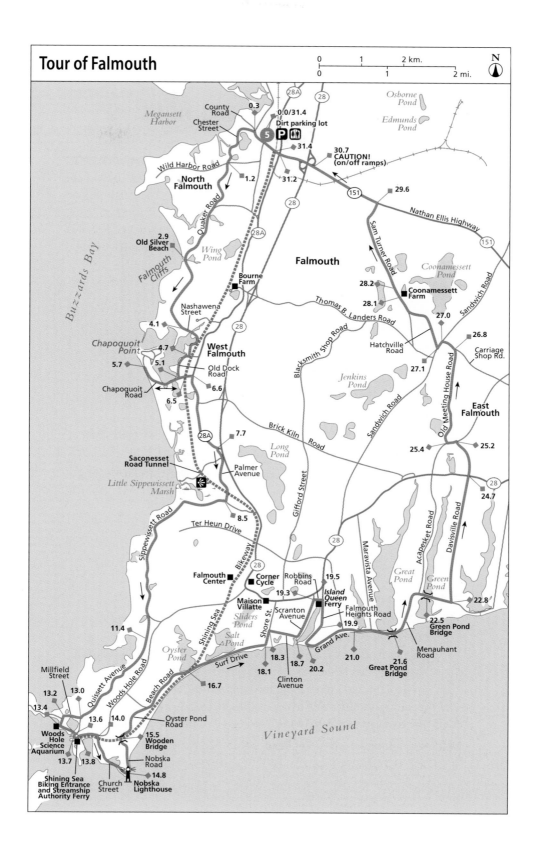

Tour of Falmouth

0   1   2 km.
0   1   2 mi.

N

Osborne Pond

Edmunds Pond

Megansett Harbor

County Road
0.3
Chester Street
0.0/31.4
Dirt parking lot
5 P 🚻
31.4
30.7
CAUTION! (on/off ramps)

Wild Harbor Road
31.2
North Falmouth
1.2

29.6

151
Nathan Ellis Highway
151

Quaker Road

28A

Wing Pond

2.9
Old Silver Beach

Buzzards Bay

Falmouth Cliffs

Bourne Farm

Falmouth

Sam Turner Road

Coonamessett Pond

28.2
28.1
Coonamessett Farm

Sandwich Road

Nashawena Street

28

27.0

4.1
Chapoquoit Point
4.7
West Falmouth
5.1
5.7

Old Dock Road

Thomas B. Landers Road

Hatchville Road

27.1

26.8

Carriage Shop Rd.

Chapoquoit Road
6.5
6.6

Blacksmith Shop Road

Jenkins Pond

27.1

East Falmouth

28A
7.7

Brick Kiln Road

Sandwich Road

Old Meeting House Road

25.4
25.2

Saconesset Road Tunnel

Little Sippewissett Marsh

Palmer Avenue

Long Pond

Gifford Street

28

24.7

8.5

Ter Heun Drive

Sippewissett Road

Bikeway

28

Falmouth Center
Corner Cycle
19.5
Robbins Road
19.3
Maison Villatte
Island Queen Ferry

28

Great Pond

Green Pond

22.8

11.4

Shining Sea Bikeway

Sliders Pond

Salt Pond

Scranton Avenue

Shore St.

Falmouth Heights Road

19.9

Maravista Avenue

Acapesket Road

Davisville Road

22.5
Green Pond Bridge

Menauhant Road

Millfield Street
13.2
13.0
13.4
13.6
14.0

Quisset Avenue

Woods Hole Road

Oyster Pond

Beach Road

Surf Drive

16.7

18.1
18.3
18.7
20.2

Clinton Avenue

Grand Ave.

21.0

21.6
Great Pond Bridge

Woods Hole Science Aquarium
13.7
13.8

Oyster Pond Road
15.5
Wooden Bridge

Nobska Road
14.8
Nobska Lighthouse

Shining Sea Biking Entrance and Steamship Authority Ferry

Church Street

Vineyard Sound

13.7 Pass by Shining Sea Bikeway entrance on your right.

13.8 Turn right onto Woods Hole Road.

14.0 Turn right onto Church Street (becomes Nobska Road).

14.8 View Nobska Lighthouse.

15.5 Continue straight on Oyster Pond Road (Nobska Road continues left).

16.7 Bear right onto Surf Drive.

18.1 Turn left 90 degrees onto Shore Street.

18.3 Turn right onto Clinton Avenue.

18.7 Turn left onto Scranton Avenue.

19.3 Turn right onto Robbins Road.

19.5 Turn right onto Falmouth Heights Road.

19.6 Pass the *Island Queen* ferry docks on your right.

19.9 Bear right onto Grand Avenue.

20.2 Continue on Grand Avenue, which makes a sharp left.

21.0 Bear right (straight) onto Menauhant Road.

21.6 Continue over Great Pond Bridge.

22.5 Continue over Green Pond Bridge.

22.8 Turn left onto Davisville Road, a long straight road with many side streets and moderate traffic for the next 2 miles.

24.7 Cross Route 28 at traffic light and continue straight on Old Meeting House Road.

25.2 Turn left onto Old Barnstable Road.

25.4 Bear right, continuing on Old Meeting House Road.

26.8 Turn left onto Carriage Shop Road.

27.0 Turn left onto Sandwich Road. Heavy traffic.

27.1 Turn right onto Hatchville Road.

28.1 Pass Coonamessett Farm on your right. (Option: Turn around at Coonamessett Farm and take the second right onto Geggatt Road, then turn right on Thomas B. Landers Road to get to Route 28A. This alternate takes Route 28A north to get to the County Road start/ finish of this ride, eliminating the need to ride Route 151. This was a great suggestion made to me by the late Larry Gray, a good friend and beloved President of the Cape Cod Cycling Club for many years.)

28.2 Bear left onto Sam Turner Road.

29.6 Turn left onto Route 151 (Nathan Ellis Highway). Caution! Heavy vehicle traffic.

30.7 Route 28 on/off ramps. Use caution!

31.2 Cross Route 28A. Heavy traffic.

31.4 Turn right into parking lot for ride finish.

RIDE INFORMATION

Local Events and Attractions

Coonemessett Farm: 277 Hatchville Rd., East Falmouth; (508) 563-2560. Explore this partially wind-powered organic farm with the kids, get a membership or one-day pass to pick fresh vegetables, fruits, and flowers. There are chickens, sheep, goats, and llamas, to see, but not for petting. The cafe and store offer sandwiches, drinks, and gifts, and there is ice cream in one of the barns down the hill. Most Novembers, it is the site of Cape Cod's only USA Cycling-sanctioned race, a cyclocross race held on or around Veteran's Day. The beer flows during the race, and there is a fat tire bike race, just for fun. Ride through the blueberries and raspberries!

Nobska Lighthouse: Nobska Road (easier access from Church Street), Woods Hole, Falmouth. Tours are limited and it is suggested that you contact the lighthouse keeper via e-mail at uscgauxwoodshole112@gmail.com if interested. The views are great from anywhere around the lighthouse, and from inside it, if you can arrange a tour. Watch the ferries and sailboats heading to and from Martha's Vineyard here. Good sunset spot.

Falmouth Road Race: Woods Hole to Falmouth Heights, every August. What started out as a small local race has grown into an international event where the world's best runners descend on Falmouth, running 7 miles from Woods Hole to Falmouth Heights. When I first ran the race in 1977 when "Boston Billy" Rodgers won, there might have been a thousand runners at the start. Now there are more than eleven thousand. Don't expect to ride the course during the race (mile 13.5 to mile 20.6 of this ride). Look for the giant mile markers painted on the road. See falmouthroadrace.com.

Woods Hole Science Aquarium: 166 Water St., Falmouth; (508) 495-2001; aquarium.nefsc.noaa.gov. See the listing under Ride 4.

Woods Hole Oceanographic Institute: 15 School St., Woods Hole, Falmouth; (508) 289-2252; whoi.edu. See the listing under Ride 4.

Marine Biological Laboratories: 7 MBL St., Woods Hole, Falmouth; (508) 548-3705; mbl.edu. See the listing under Ride 4.

Woods Hole Film Festival: P.O. Box 624, Woods Hole, Falmouth; (508) 495-FILM; woodsholefilmfestival.org. See the listing under Ride 4.

Restaurants

See also the listings under Ride 4 for restaurants in Falmouth.

C Salt Wine Bar & Grille: 75 Davis Straits, Falmouth; (774) 763-2954. Chef Jonathan Philips has a great wine list to match his innovative and delicious menu. Expensive, and worth it.

Glass Onion: 37 N. Main St., Falmouth; (508) 540-3730. Open for dinner and late-night desserts.

Restrooms

There are porta-potties at the start/finish, Old Silver Beach, Chapoquoit Beach, and the other beaches along the route. Woods Hole has numerous restaurants, and the Steamship Authority has restrooms.

Otis

Heard recently at Otis from a newbie to mountain biking: "Hey, my arms and legs are getting completely cut up by the tree branches on this trail. And there's no way to really ride these rocks. Are you sure we're going the right way?"

Start: Park on Route 151 just east of the on/off ramp to Route 28. This is an unmarked series of trails that have been maintained by New England Mountain Biking Association (NEMBA).

Distance: 8.6 miles, loop and lollipop

Approximate riding time: 2 hours

Best bike: Mountain bike, fat tire bike

Terrain and surface type: Single-track mountain bike trail, with rocks, roots, sand, boulders, some very technical sections (e.g., Graveyard)

Traffic and hazards: Rocks, roots, sand, halfpipe, boulders, jumps, and proximity to Otis Air National Guard Military Base. The northernmost part of this trail empties out onto a main entrance to the base adjacent to the Otis Rotary on Route 28.

Things to see: Mother Nature's challenges, Otis Rotary, Route 28

Map: *Arrow Street Atlas: Cape Cod including Martha's Vineyard & Nantucket,* p. 50

Getting there: From Route 495/25 and the Bourne Bridge: Go around Bourne Rotary and proceed onto Route 28 South. Take the exit for Route 151 and head east (turning right at the end of the exit ramp). There are two parking areas, one immediately on the left after passing under the highway (just after the on-ramp on Route 151), and one a little bit farther on the right. **From Route 6 (and Route 3, points north):** Cross over the Sagamore Bridge and take exit 1C to the Sandwich Road. Turn left (west) at the end of the exit ramp and follow the Cape Cod Canal (should be on the right), heading west to the Bourne Rotary. Exit the rotary onto Route 28 South and exit at Route 151, following the directions to the ride start above.

GPS coordinates: N41 38.61' / W70 36.10'

THE RIDE

Otis is said by some to be the best mountain biking on Cape Cod. It's definitely fun, challenging, and among the best mountain bike trails here.

Otis is named for its proximity to Otis Air National Guard Base in Bourne and Falmouth. This ride's first loop is in Falmouth, but the long lollipop along Route 28 crosses the town line into Bourne and turns around at the Otis Rotary (Route 28 and Connery Avenue, the main entrance to the base). If you do get lost and accidentally find yourself on the Air National Guard property, you may be faced with trouble. If you see what looks like barracks at the end of the trail, simply turn around.

Enter the trail from the small dirt lot, and after 0.1 mile, turn right and ascend to a plateau that doesn't really descend again for 2 miles. Pass a half-pipe at 0.5 mile on your right, and by 1.0 mile you're in an area known as the Graveyard. This ride only does a small part of the Graveyard, on a less technical section of trail, but other options are there for those who wish to have more of a challenge. The Graveyard is about a mile-long strip of big rocks and small boulders that are fit tightly together and require excellent bike-handling skills to avoid stopping or crashing. Less experienced riders get "dropped," or left behind, after trying to negotiate the rocks and roots on this section of trail. If you opt to cross the fire road at the end of the Graveyard there is a rock garden with a "troll bridge" in the woods to the left that makes for some good stunt riding and is popular with local mountain bikers.

At 1.1 miles, turn left onto Star Wars. At 1.4 miles, turn left onto Blue Ribbon, and at 1.8 miles turn right onto the Power Line, which descends and then climbs again halfway to mile 2.5, where the trail turns right and parallels the highway (Route 28) off to the left. For the next 0.5 mile you can hug the highway or take the twisty trail across the sandy trails under the power lines above you, but make sure you make your way back to the

Bike Shops

Art's Bike Shop, 91 County Road, North Falmouth, (508) 563-7379, artsbikeshop.com
Bike Zone, 13 County Road #3, North Falmouth, (508) 563-2333, bikezone capecod.com
Corner Cycle, 115 Palmer Ave., Falmouth, (508) 540-4195, cornercycle.com

Over a rock ledge and through the woods at Otis, Falmouth

highway (Route 28). Head north along the highway and at mile 4.1, bear right at the fork onto the Cosmos Trail. Follow this as it ascends to the right and then descends toward the Otis Rotary, which is visible at mile 5.2. Go down the embankment, turn left, and hug the road, passing underneath the power lines again. Look for a trail entrance into the woods, ahead to your right, and bear left with Route 28 on your right now. This is the Moose Tracks trail, which stays parallel to the highway for about a mile and then retraces your route for another mile. At mile 7.8, bear right and stay close to the highway, then enter the Hare & Hound at mile 8.1. Follow the highway back to the start. Continue to optional parking across the street at mile 8.6 to finish if you parked there.

After I had ridden Otis for more than 2 hours on a hot day in August, I was completely spent, but very satisfied. The trails at Otis will leave you feeling that way.

MILES AND DIRECTIONS

0.0   The trail starts at the dirt parking lot to the east of the on/off ramp for Route 28 on Route 151 (westbound lane), just west of the Falmouth Animal Hospital. Enter the trail over a small bump.

0.1   Turn right.

0.5   Ride up and over the halfpipe on your right.

0.9   Enter the Graveyard Trail. This is a more technical section.

1.1   Turn left onto Star Wars Trail.

1.4   Turn left onto Blue Ribbon Trail.

1.8   Turn right onto the Power Line Trail.

2.5   Turn right and head north, adjacent to the highway (Route 28).

4.1   Turn right onto the Cosmos Trail.

5.2   Go down the embankment and hug the paved road, turning left. Ride under the power lines and look for the return trail entrance with the Otis Rotary to your right.

5.3   Enter the Moose Tracks Trail with the highway (Route 28) off to your right. Hug Route 28 for a couple miles.

7.8   Bear right at the fork.

8.1   Enter the Hare & Hound.

8.5   The trail ends. Cross Route 151 to parking lot across the street if you parked there.

8.6   Optional parking lot on Route 151.

RIDE INFORMATION

Local Events and Attractions

Coonamessett Farm: 277 Hatchville Rd., East Falmouth; (508) 563-2560. Explore this partially wind-powered organic farm with the kids. Get a membership or one-day pass to pick fresh vegetables, fruits, and flowers. There are chickens, sheep, goats, and llamas to see, but not for petting. The cafe and

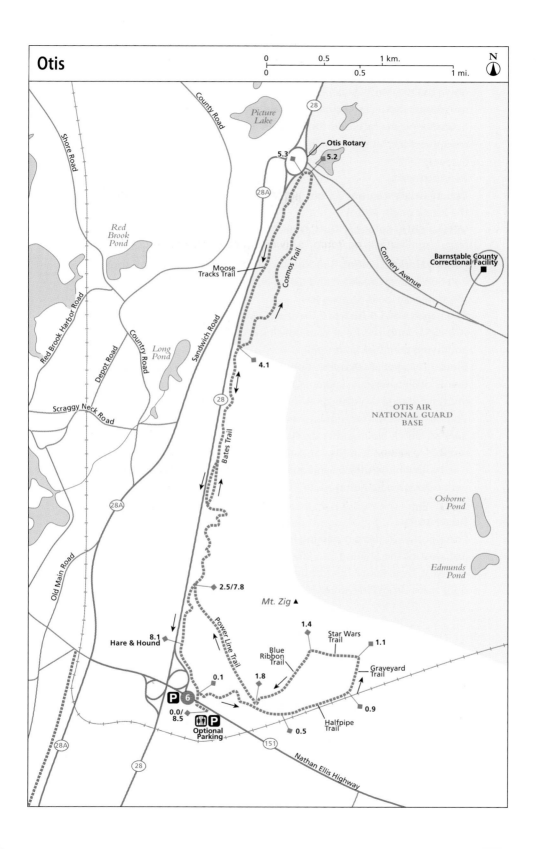

Otis

0   0.5   1 km.
0   0.5   1 mi.

N

Shore Road

County Road

Picture Lake

28

Otis Rotary
5.3
5.2

28A

Moose Tracks Trail

Cosmos Trail

Connery Avenue

Barnstable County Correctional Facility

Red Brook Pond

Red Brook Harbor Road

Depot Road

Country Road

Long Pond

Sandwich Road

4.1

OTIS AIR NATIONAL GUARD BASE

Scraggy Neck Road

28

Bates Trail

28A

Osborne Pond

Old Main Road

Edmunds Pond

2.5/7.8

Mt. Zig ▲

1.4

Power Line Trail

Hare & Hound
8.1

Star Wars Trail
1.1

Blue Ribbon Trail

Graveyard Trail

0.1
1.8
0.9

P 6

0.0/ 8.5

Halfpipe Trail

0.5

Optional Parking

28A

151

28

Nathan Ellis Highway

store offer sandwiches, drinks, and gifts, and there is ice cream in the barn down the hill. Most Novembers, it is the site of Cape Cod's only USA Cycling-sanctioned race, a cyclocross race held on or around Veteran's Day. The beer flows during the race, and there is a fat tire bike race, just for fun. Bring your mountain bike, fat tire or cyclocross bike.

Restaurants

Courtyard Restaurant & Pub: 1337 County Rd., Bourne; (508) 563-1818. See the listing under Ride 3.

Village Cafe, Eulinda's Ice Cream: 634 W. Falmouth Hwy., West Falmouth; (508) 548-2486. See the listing under Ride 4.

Laura's Home Cookin': 440 Nathan Ellis Hwy. (Route 151), Mashpee; (781) 760-6088. Great breakfast and lunch, homemade donuts, and hash. Don't let the strip-mall looks deceive you.

The Lanes Bowl & Bistro: 9 Greene St., Mashpee Commons, Mashpee; (774) 228-2291. Table service at your bowling scoring table. Kids will love the pizza and trying their luck at ten-pin.

Bleu: 10 Market St., Mashpee Commons, Mashpee; (508) 539-7907. The chef/owner of Bleu, Frederic Feufeu, who grew up in the southwest coast of France in Cholet (Stage 4 of the 2008 Tour de France), feels right at home on Cape Cod. His dishes will feel right at home with you. He trained at Les Sorbets culinary school in Noirmoutier-en-l'Île, and left the Rainbow Room via several notable restaurants in New York City for Cape Cod. Try the apple and frisée salad with white truffle oil and quince jam, or the roasted mallard duck breast with pomegranate honey glaze. The wine list is exceptional.

Restrooms

Porta-potties at the dirt parking lot on County Road, across from Pine Street, just west of the Shining Sea Bikeway North Falmouth entrance. Take Route 151 West, cross Route 28A, continue on County Road. The parking lot is on the right across from Pine Street.

Cotuit and Mashpee

Ride the "five fingers of Cotuit" and stop at several scenic viewpoints along Cotuit Bay and Popponesset Bay. Head over to Mashpee and Mashpee Commons, have a cup of coffee, and relax before returning to Lowell Park in Cotuit. Catch the best baseball players in the NCAA Cape Cod Baseball League at a game in summer.

Start: Lowell Park (Cotuit Kettleers baseball field) parking lot, Cotuit

Distance: 22.3 miles, multiple out-and-backs and one lollipop

Approximate riding time: 2 hours

Best bike: Road

Terrain and surface type: Mostly main roads and paved back roads, with some brief dirt sections and one short stretch of slippery wooden dock

Traffic and hazards: Vehicle traffic, sometimes heavy, a highway crossing (Route 28) where bikes must be walked, a rotary with heavy vehicle traffic, shopping district, slippery docks at Cotuit Bay

Things to see: Lowell Park, home of the NCAA Cape Cod Baseball League Cotuit Kettleers, Mosquito Yacht Club, Sampson's Island, Ropes Beach, Cotuit Fresh Market (the "Coop"), Cotuit Town Docks and Landing, Riley's Beach, Loop Beach, Oregon Beach, Rusty Marsh Pond, Prince Cove (which feeds the North Bay), Santuit River, Crocker Neck, Shoestring Bay, Popponesset Bay, Mashpee River, Mashpee Commons

Map: *Arrow Street Atlas: Cape Cod including Martha's Vineyard & Nantucket*, p. 12

Getting there: From Route 28 in Cotuit or points east on Cape Cod: Take Route 28 North (heading west) to Main Street in Cotuit. Turn left on Main Street and go 1.2 miles to Lowell Avenue. Turn left immediately into Lowell Park. **From the Mashpee Rotary and points west on Cape Cod:** Take Route 28 South (heading east) from the rotary and turn right on Main Street in Cotuit. Travel 1.2 miles on Main Street and turn left on Lowell Avenue. Turn left immediately into Lowell Park. From Route 6 (Mid-Cape Highway), take exit 2 and go south on Route 130. Turn left on Route 28, then turn right on Main Street in Cotuit. Travel 1.2 miles, turn left on Lowell Avenue, and turn left immediately into Lowell Park.

GPS coordinates: N41 37.49' / W70 26.11'

THE RIDE

This scenic road ride starts at Lowell Park baseball field, home of the NCAA Cape Cod Baseball League's Cotuit Kettleers baseball team. If you're here in June, July, or early August, catch a game. The quality of play on the fields of the Cape Cod Baseball League (CCBL) is as good as anything in Major League Baseball, and it should be. One of every seven major leaguers playing today also played in the CCBL before getting called up to the majors. In 2013, a record total 257 former Cape Cod Baseball Leaguers populated the Major League. The best thing about the Cape League is that it's free to watch (or whatever you want to donate). As you start this ride out of Lowell Park and the Cotuit Kettleers field of dreams, know that the Cape League has been on Cape Cod since 1885, as old as the first pneumatic bicycle tire and chain-driven bicycle. You can ride your bike to any one of ten CCBL baseball fields on Cape Cod, including this one.

Turning left out of Lowell Park, the route makes a right turn on Putnam Avenue and then descends down Old Shore Road (one-way) to Ropes Beach on Cotuit Bay. Ropes Beach is home to the Mosquito Yacht Club, which offers sailing classes and has hosted yacht races for more than a hundred years. It is the oldest junior yacht club in the United States. The "Cotuit Mosquito," now known as the Cotuit Skiff, is a 14-foot sailboat that has sailed Cotuit Bay as long as there have been yacht races here. As you ride by, look for the fleet of Cotuit Skiffs in the bay, with their four-sided, gaff-rigged mainsails, but with no jib. Make a right turn on Old Shore Road back up to Main Street and turn left. The ride heads back to the bay by turning left on Oceanview Avenue, to Loop Beach, just past Riley's Beach. For Riley's Beach, just turn left onto Cross Street at mile 1.3, from Oceanview Avenue. Now loop back to Main Street on Oceanview Avenue, turn left on Main Street, and follow it to its end at Oregon Beach, secluded by tall marsh grass. This is a gorgeous, white-sand beach off the beaten path with a clear view of Sampson's Island and the Mass Audubon Wildlife Sanctuary, accessible only by boat. Turn around again and head back toward town on Main Street.

Prince Cove, Cotuit

I would probably have never known about these beautiful beaches if not for Rob Miceli, head of the Cape Cod chapter of the Massachusetts Bicycle Coalition (MassBike). He lives in Cotuit and runs guided tours of this region of Cape Cod, and he calls this route "the five fingers tour" because it takes you to four of the best beaches in Cotuit: Ropes, Riley's, Loop, and Oregon in Cotuit (the fingers), with the option of going to Mashpee Neck and Shoestring Bay Beach in Mashpee (the thumb).

Take a right on Main Street and then a right on Oyster Place, and ride down the hill to the Town Dock. Ride right up to the wooden dock and walk out to the end, and take in a breath of fresh, salt air. When I last did that, I thought this would be a good place to hang out all day. Return to Main Street and turn right. Take another right on Putnam Avenue and then right on Old Post Road. The ride is heading north now, and you'll stop at Handy Point and finally Prince Cove, lovely spots in the quaint Cape Cod village of Cotuit, both with views across the waterways that feed Cotuit Bay. Do a 180-degree turn on Old Post Road and head back to Cotuit Center again. This is a nice stretch of road among tall pines. Continue on Putnam to Main and take a right on School Street at 11.1 miles. The Kettle-Ho Restaurant is on the corner here. If you need a break, this is good stop for lunch, with local seafood and lobster rolls. The name Kettle-Ho comes from the original currency used to pay for

the village of Cotuit. According to tradition, Myles Standish, *Mayflower* pilgrim, apparently cut a deal with the Wampanoag Native Americans to purchase Cotuit for the price of one "great brass kettle, seven spans around, and one broad hoe." So, the Kettle-Ho Restau-

Bike Shops

Corner Cycle, 115 Palmer Ave., Falmouth, (508) 540-4195, cornercycle.com
Poppin' Wheelies, 681 Falmouth Rd. (Route 28), #12A, Mashpee, (508) 419-6267, poppinwheelies.net

rant and the Kettleers baseball team are present-day reminders of early European and Native American interaction.

The next part of this ride heads out along the southwest of Cotuit, by the Santuit River and Shoestring Bay to the west, past the Crocker Neck Conservation Area to the east, and out to Popponesset Bay, fed by both the Santuit River and the Mashpee River. Crocker Neck Conservation Area spans ninety-seven acres, with 1.5 miles of town-maintained hiking trails out to the Popponesset Bay and Pinquickset Cove. This is a great place for a rest stop, with picnic tables among the dense grove of white pines offering shade on a hot summer day. The ride heads past Crocker Neck, then returns to School Street via back roads through a residential area. Turn left on School Street and ride to the Mashpee town line, where the road becomes Quinaquisset Avenue. There is the option to head out to Mashpee Neck and Shoestring Bay Beach by taking a left on Mashpee Neck Road at mile 16.5, but the ride continues into Mashpee on Quinaquisset Avenue.

At the end of Quinaquisset Avenue, riders should dismount and walk their bicycles across Route 28, as there is a No Left Turn sign. Turn left (walking) on Route 28, then remount and turn right (up the hill) on Old Barnstable Road. Cross Great Neck Road and turn left on Great Hay Road. Take the second left into a parking lot before the end of Great Hay Road. There are two main parking lots here, both with entrances to the bike trail. Look for the entrance to a bike path on the far right end of the parking lot. Turn left onto the bike path and make a quick right, which will end on Frank E. Hicks Drive (police station to your right, fire station across the street). If you get lost, the Mashpee Police and Fire Departments, Mashpee Senior Center, and Boys & Girls Clubs of Mashpee are all nearby. This bike path is hidden, and there are three entrances to it from two parking lots, but it's a very short loop trail, and there will be lots of help just a short distance away. If you end up at Zoe's Pizza, turn around and then keep bearing left on the bike path. Take the bike path to Frank E. Hicks Drive and turn left. Head for the traffic light and crosswalk. Rob Miceli tells me that this tiny bike path has a great future, and is slated to connect this location in Mashpee with the Shining Sea Bikeway in Falmouth by 2019.

Cross the Route 151 crosswalk and turn left on Steeple Street to explore Mashpee Commons. Eat breakfast or lunch or stop for coffee at Starbucks and be sure to park your bikes across the street at the circular bike rack. Head back to Cotuit via Route 151 and the Mashpee Rotary. This is perhaps one of the more dangerous places to ride on Cape Cod for cyclists. Please use caution, and yield to vehicles and bicycles that are already in the rotary as per Massachusetts state law. Turn right at Quinaquisset Avenue, enjoy this longer stretch of road, then turn left on Main Street in Cotuit and follow the ride back to Lowell Park where it began. If you like, first stop for an ice cream at the Cotuit Fresh Market (formerly known as the Coop) on Main Street, as people have been doing at this old market for more than a hundred years. Cotuit is the quintessential quaint little Cape Cod town.

MILES AND DIRECTIONS

0.0 Start at Lowell Park parking lot and turn left onto Lowell Avenue.

0.1 Turn right onto Putnam Avenue.

0.2 Bear left and descend Old Shore Road to Ropes Beach. Look for the fleet of Cotuit Skiffs.

0.5 Turn left onto Main Street.

0.9 Turn left onto Oceanview Avenue.

1.3 Option to turn left on Cross Street for Riley's Beach, at the end of Cross Street.

1.5 Pause at a scenic view of Cotuit Bay on Loop Beach. Loop back up to Main Street.

1.6 Turn left on Main Street.

Cotuit and Mashpee

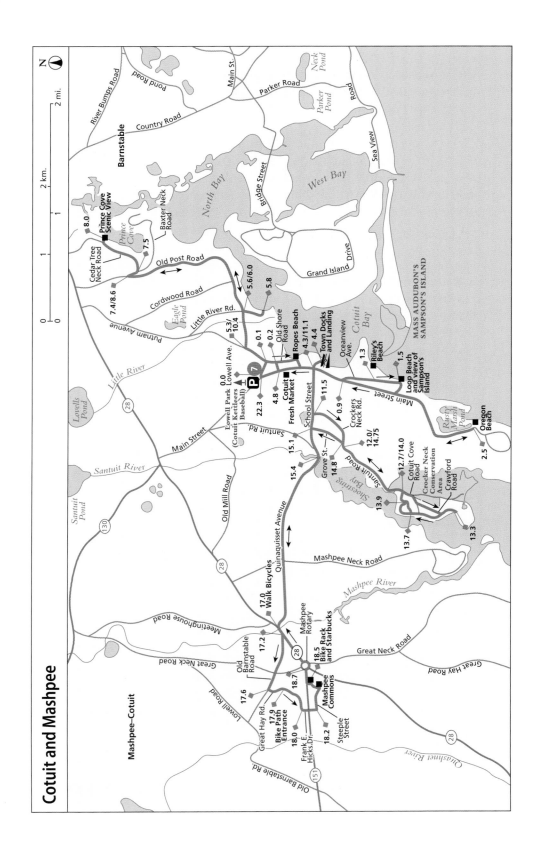

N

0   1   2 km.
0   1   2 mi.

Barnstable

River Bumps Road
Pond Road
Main St.
Country Road
Neck Pond
Parker Road
Parker Road

Prince Cove Scenic View **8.0**
Prince Cove
7.5
Baxter Neck Road
Cedar Tree Neck Road
North Bay
Bridge Street
West Bay
Sea View

7.4/8.6
Cordwood Road
Old Post Road
Putnam Avenue
Eagle Pond
Little River Rd.
Little River Road
5.6/6.0
5.8
Grand Island
Drive

Lovells Pond
28
Little River
Lowell Ave. **5.3/10.4**
Old Shore Road
0.1
0.2
Ropes Beach **4.3/11.1**
Town Docks and Landing **4.4**
Oceanview Ave.
Cotuit Bay
1.3
Riley's Beach **1.5**
MASS AUDUBON'S SAMPSON'S ISLAND

Lowell Park (Cotuit Kettleers Baseball) **0.0**
P
Cotuit Fresh Market
22.3
4.8
School Street
11.5
Crockers Neck Rd.
0.9
Loop Beach and view of Sampson's Island
Main Street
1.5

Santuit River
Santuit Pond
Main Street
Old Mill Road
Santuit Rd.
15.1
Grove St.
15.4
Crocker Neck Road
12.0/14.75
Cotuit Cove Road
12.7/14.0
Crocker Neck Conservation Area
13.9
Crawford Road
Rushy Marsh Pond
Oregon Beach
2.5

130
Old Barnstable Road
14.8
Shoestring Bay
Santuit Road
13.7
13.3

Quinaquisset Avenue
Mashpee Neck Road
Mashpee River

17.0 Walk Bicycles
Meetinghouse Road
Great Neck Road
Great Hay Road
Great Neck Road

28
17.2
Old Barnstable Road
17.6
Mashpee Rotary
28
Bike Rack and Starbucks **18.5**
Great Neck Road
Great Hay Road

Mashpee-Cotuit
Lowell Road
17.9
Bike Path Entrance
18.7
Mashpee Commons
18.0
Frank E. Hicks Dr.
18.2
Steeple Street

151
Old Barnstable Rd.
28
Quashnet River

2.5 Go to the end of Main Street and turn around at Oregon Beach, hidden from view at first by a dense stand of marsh grasses. Head back to town on Main Street.

4.3 Turn right onto Oyster Place (Cotuit Town Dock).

4.4 Head down to Cotuit Town Dock Scenic View. Use caution on slippery dock. Turn around and head back up to Main Street.

4.6 Turn right on Main Street.

4.9 Turn right onto Putnam Avenue.

5.3 Turn right onto Old Post Road.

5.6 Turn right onto Little River Road.

5.8 Stop at Handy Point Scenic View.

6.0 Turn right onto Old Post Road.

7.4 Turn right onto Baxter Neck Road.

7.5 Turn left onto Cedar Tree Neck Road.

8.0 Turn right down to Prince Cove (scenic view).

8.1 Turn left onto Cedar Tree Neck Road.

8.5 Turn right onto Baxter Neck Road.

8.6 Turn left onto Old Post Road.

10.4 Turn left onto Putnam Road.

10.8 Turn left onto Main Street.

11.1 Turn right onto School Street.

11.5 Turn left onto Crockers Neck Road.

12.0 Take left (bear left) onto Santuit Road.

12.7 Bear left onto Cotuit Cove Road.

12.9 Turn left onto Crawford Road.

13.1 Continue onto Clam Shell Cove Road.

13.3 Turnaround point (Ryefield Point).

13.4 Stay on Clam Shell Cove Road.

13.7 Bear left onto Clam Shell Point Road.

13.9 Turn left onto Clam Shell Cove Road.

14.0 Take left onto Santuit Road.

14.7 Bear right onto Crockers Neck Road.

14.8 Turn left onto Grove Street.

15.1 Turn left onto School Street.

15.4   Continue on Quinaquisset Avenue (entering Mashpee).

17.0   Turn left onto Route 28 and walk bicycle across the road. Caution, heavy traffic!

17.2   Turn right onto Old Barnstable Road.

17.6   Turn left onto Great Hay Road.

17.9   Entrance to bike path.

18.0   Turn left onto Frank E. Hicks Drive.

18.1   Cross Route 151 (crosswalk with button).

18.2   Turn left onto Steeple Street.

18.4   Turn left on Market Street.

18.5   Bicycle parking (across from Starbuck's Coffee).

18.6   Turn right onto Route 151.

18.7   Mashpee Rotary (yield to vehicles in rotary).

18.8   Turn right onto Route 28.

19.2   Turn right onto Quinaquisset Avenue.

21.7   Turn left onto Main Street.

22.2   Take right onto Lowell Avenue.

22.3   Turn left into Lowell Park lot (ride end).

RIDE INFORMATION

Local Events and Attractions
Cotuit Center for the Arts: 4404 Falmouth Rd. (Route 28), Cotuit; (508) 428-0669. A hidden gem, offering a variety of educational programs, performances, and exhibitions, including art exhibitions, theatrical productions, music performances, workshops, and community events.

Mashpee Wampanoag Powwow: Barnstable County Fairgrounds, 1220 Nathan Ellis Hwy. (Route 151), Falmouth; (508) 477-0208. Held during the weekend nearest to July 4, the annual Powwow is a traditional celebration of Mashpee Wampanoag culture featuring Native American dancing, drumming, games, food, art, jewelry, wampum, gifts, crafts, and clothing. For more information, contact the Mashpee Wampanoag Tribal Council, 483 Great Neck Rd. South, P.O. Box 1048, Mashpee, MA 02649. Try playing the traditional "fireball," soccer with a flaming ball made of leather strips soaked in whale oil and wound tightly around each other.

Cahoon Museum of American Art: 9 North St., Mashpee Commons, Mashpee (temporary location) and 4676 Falmouth Rd. (Route 28), Cotuit (permanent location under renovation); (508) 428-7581. Works by Ralph Cahoon, Martha Cahoon, Ralph Blakelock, William Bradford, James Buttersworth, John J. Enneking, Alvan Fisher, Levi Wells Prentice, and William Matthew Prior. Special exhibitions of American art are a regular phenomenon. Gift shop.

Mashpee Wampanoag Museum: 414 Main St., Mashpee; (508) 477-9339 (Museum Building), (508) 477-0208, ext. 101 (Tribal Historic Preservation Office). Small but worth the trip, as it is the only museum devoted solely to the history and culture of the Wampanoag. On display are tools, baskets, hunting and fishing implements, weapons and domestic utensils, and a large diorama of an early Wampanoag settlement.

Restaurants

Also see the listings under Ride 6 for restaurants in Mashpee.

Cotuit Fresh Market: 737 Main St., Cotuit; (508) 428-6936. Also known as the Coop, it's a great place for ice cream, groceries, drinks, and sandwiches that's been around for more than a century.

Kettle-Ho Restaurant and Tavern: 12 School St., Cotuit; (508) 428-1862. It's a great place to drink with college kids after a Cotuit Kettleers baseball game. Great chowder. Ask about Cotuit oysters. If there is a downtown Cotuit, this must be the place.

Wicked Restaurant and Wine Bar: 680 Falmouth Rd., Mashpee; (508) 477-7422. Burgers and thick-cut fries, pizza, the way they should be. Try the Caribbean mahi-mahi or organic Scottish salmon.

Restrooms

At the Lowell Park start/finish in Cotuit, and at Mashpee Commons, Mashpee

8

Trail of Tears

A diverse mountain bike course with fast, rolling sections, a few difficult climbs and fast descents, over a variety of terrain and varied vegetation. There are 1,200 acres to ride here in West Barnstable, with a few of them over the town line into Sandwich. With the recent closure of a shooting range, a few old trails that were closed may reopen. With easy, moderate, and difficult trails over single-track and double-track fire roads, there is something for everybody.

Start: 1590 Race Ln., Marstons Mills, West Barnstable Conservation Area, Barnstable

Distance: 8-mile cloverleaf loop

Approximate riding time: 2 hours

Best bike: Mountain bike, fat tire bike

Terrain and surface type: single-track, dirt fire roads, grassy path, soft sand, roots, rocks, and rock gardens

Traffic and hazards: Hunters (in season), trail runners, hikers, other mountain bikers, rocks, roots, soft sand, and a shooting range. If it's winter, cross-country skiers and fat-tire bike riders. The firing range in the northwest corner of Trail of Tears (not far from Scott Rock) was closed in late 2012 and may or may not reopen until a vote in 2015. Hunting is still permitted during hunting season, however, so mountain bikers beware!

Things to see: Scott Rock, Field of Dreams, Dube Rock, Walker Lookout Platform, Barnstable's highest elevation, Humpty Dumpty (no, really), Mystic Lake (take the Cow Tunnel Trail off the Danforth Trail), Cape Cod Airfield, biplanes and skydivers overhead, and a lot of well-maintained trails.

Map: *Arrow Street Atlas: Cape Cod including Martha's Vineyard & Nantucket*, p. 8

Getting there: From Route 6 (Mid-Cape Highway), take exit 5 and head south on Route 149 and immediately come to a small rotary. Continue on Route 149 South by bearing right at the fork with Osterville Road, then continue all the way to a second rotary with Cape Cod Airfield (grass runways) on the right. Turn right on Race Lane past the airfield and follow it for just under 2 miles. You'll see the sign West Barnstable Conservation Area and parking lot in the woods on your right, where Farmersville Road intersects with Race Lane.

GPS coordinates: N41 41.16' / W70 25.73'

THE RIDE

The Trail of Tears has 22 miles of single-track mountain biking trails through 1,100 acres in the West Barnstable Conservation Area, and can be accessed from 1590 Race Ln. (at Farmersville Road) in Marstons Mills, the start of this ride. Parking is also available on the Service Road (parallel to Route 6) near exit 5, on Route 149 at Popple Bottom Road, on Race Lane at the Cow Tunnel Trail across from Marstons Mills Airfield, and on Crooked Cartway, off Race Lane just east of this entrance. The ride I've mapped through the Trail of Tears is a big four-leaf-clover loop that has easy, moderate, and advanced trails for all rider abilities. It covers only one third of the available trails. Feel free to get lost on the remainder of them. Trail of Tears has some steep sections, but even though they are short, and not as technical as other rides in this book, like Otis (Ride 6) or Cliff Pond Killer Loop (Ride 19), they are a fun, up-and-down rollercoaster of a ride.

The Trail of Tears was originally a 9-mile enduro motorcycle trail in the 1970s. In the 1980s two mountain bike riders, Art Hastings and Doug Jordan, first rode the trails here and named them the Trail of Tears, due to the difficulty of those steep and very difficult

Bike Shops

Eastern Mountain Sports, 1513 Iyannough Rd., Hyannis, (508) 362-8690, ems.com
Bike Zone, 323 Barnstable Rd., Hyannis, (508) 775-3299, bikezonecapecod.com
Sea Sports, 195 Ridgewood Ave., Hyannis (508) 790-1217, capecodseasports.com

motorcycle trails that left them bruised and battered. The trails have been expanded and modified greatly since then by the hard-working members of the Cape Cod chapter of the New England Mountain Bike Association (NEMBA), which has maintained the trails for over two decades, working closely with the Barnstable Conservation Commission and the Barnstable Land Management

The trailhead on Race Lane, Marstons Mills, Barnstable

Committee. NEMBA has done a great job marking many of the numerous trails with signs to keep riders from getting lost in the forest. According to NEMBA, the Trail of Tears forest is unique, with beech, red oak, sassafras, white pine, and holly for shade, and fern, bayberry, green briar, spirea, and low-bush blueberry for ground cover. It's a beautiful set of trails with several different landscapes.

This ride starts at the far end of the parking lot at the Pain Train Station and passes under the Trail of Tears sign just after the entrance to the trail. The first trail is the Big Ring Trail, which is relatively flat and easy, so you can ride in the big chain ring here. Turn right onto the Flats Trail, also relatively flat and easy. It's a nice warm-up and intro for 1.5 miles, and after crossing Popple Bottom Road, the trail gets harder and starts to climb, just after turning left onto the Walker Point Trail. At mile 2.0, enjoy the views west of Lawrence Pond in Sandwich from the Walker Lookout Platform. The platform was built by five members of NEMBA who were awarded a grant for the project, in honor of Steven D. Walker, an avid Cape Cod mountain biker and friend of NEMBA.

My first intro to the Walker Lookout Platform and the Trail of Tears was with the president and vice president of NEMBA, Michael Dube and Perry Ermi. This ride was the most fun I'd ever had on a bicycle, made better by the cooling rain on that hot summer day. It was exhilarating! It had some challenging stretches, some easy stretches, and everything in between. Up and down and up and down, a serious challenge to the cardiovascular system. The terrain varied from woods to ferns to soft sand and rock platforms, with a couple steep descents and tough climbs.

Fortunately, the vast majority of the trails at "ToT" were not that muddy or wet, because drainage is exceptionally good here, making the riding enjoyable in almost any weather. This is the place to go for mountain biking if it's wet on Cape Cod and you're determined to ride in the rain.

From the Walker Lookout Platform, the trail heads up to Barnstable's Highest Point (mile 2.5) at 232 feet above sea level, and remains on a plateau, turning left on the Northridge Trail, left on Crocker Road, and then right on the Trail of Tears North Trail, in the northeast part of this clover-shaped route. Opposite the entrance to the North Trail, pay respects to the memory of Scott L. Fenner, another cycling advocate and passionate mountain bike rider, whose name is engraved on a large rock. Scott enjoyed the thrill of a good jump and never passed up a ride. Continue onto the North Trail and at mile 3.9 is a fairly steep and quick descent that levels off and crosses Crooked Cartway, then turns right onto Cape Cod Pathways Trail and turns right again, ascending to the Trail of Tears South Trail.

At mile 4.6 turn left onto the Humpty, a series of rollers among ferns and forest for a short stretch, then through the Field of Dreams. Make a hard right at Dube Rock (named for the President of NEMBA) and follow the Dube Rock

Trail over a flat stretch until it plunges at 5.5 miles to Popple Bottom Road. Ride for a stretch on Popple Bottom Road, turn right, and then turn right again into another descent to the Danforth Trails, which skirt the northern and western borders of the Cape Cod Airfield. Follow Danforth and turn right onto Crocker Road. Turn left onto the "C-O-MM and Get It" Trail to complete the last leaf of this four-leaf clover. (C-O-MM stands for "Centerville-Osterville-Marstons Mills" and this section is on C-O-MM fire district property.) Head back to Farmersville Road, a grassy dirt straightaway that slopes gently downhill (but don't crash here like I did), and finally turn right into the parking lot where the ride started.

Remember: hunting is allowed in the West Barnstable Conservation Area (in season), subject to current rules and regulations. Check the Town of Barnstable website for current information. And always wear your safety orange at Trail of Tears during hunting season. And look up once in a while. In addition to biplanes, skydivers are sometimes seen overhead, with parachutes opened for landing at the adjacent Cape Cod Airfield.

MILES AND DIRECTIONS

0.0 Enter the trail start at the far left of the parking lot (the Pain Train Station) at 1590 Race Ln. This is the start of the Big Ring Trail, under the wooden sign that reads Trail of Tears.

0.7 Turn right onto The Flats trail.

1.0 Cross Old Mill Road and continue on The Flats trail.

1.5 Cross Popple Bottom Road.

1.6 Turn left into the Walker Point Trail and climb.

2.0 Stop at Walker Lookout Platform and enjoy the view of Lawrence Pond in Sandwich.

2.3 Enter the Primal Scream Trail and climb some more.

2.4 Turn sharply right.

2.5 This is the highest elevation in Barnstable, at 232 feet. Begin Northridge Trail.

2.7 Continue straight on the Northridge Trail (on the right is Arseback descent to No Brakes and Car Wash).

3.3 Continue on Northridge Trail (or turn right for No Brakes).

3.35 Turn left on Crooked Cartway and continue on Crocker Road.

3.5 Turn right onto Trail of Tears North Trail. Pay regards at Scott Rock Memorial.

Trail of Tears

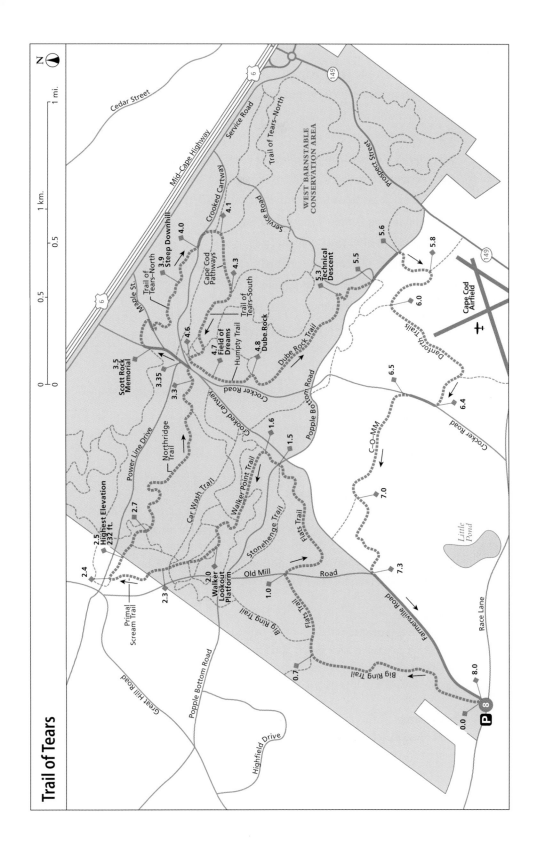

3.6 Turn right and cross Maple Street (dirt road).

4.0 Cross Crooked Cartway and pass under the power lines.

4.1 Turn right onto the Cape Cod Pathways Trail.

4.3 Turn right onto Trail of Tears South.

4.6 Turn left at Redemption Hill onto the Humpty Trail.

4.7 Continue through the Field of Dreams.

4.8 Turn right at Dube Rock onto the Dube Rock Trail.

5.5 Turn left on Popple Bottom Road (dirt road).

5.6 Turn right onto the Danforth Trails.

5.8 Turn right and continue on the Danforth Trails.

6.0 Turn left and continue on Danforth Trails.

6.3 Turn right and continue on Danforth Trails.

6.4 Turn right on Crocker Road (dirt road).

6.5 Turn left onto the "C-O-MM and Get It" trail.

7.0 Turn left at fork.

7.3 Turn left at Crooked Cartway and make an immediate right at the fork onto Farmersville Road.

8.0 Turn right to finish at parking lot.

RIDE INFORMATION

Local Events and Attractions
Cape Cod Airfield: 1000 Race Ln., Marstons Mills (Barnstable); (508) 428-8732. Take a biplane ride, a skydive, or attend flight school at an airfield that dates back to the 1920s, with more than eighty acres of daisy-filled field, three grass intersecting runways, two hangars, and an old windmill. The airfield was once used as a training field for the Army Air Corps.

Restaurants
The Mills Restaurant: 149 Cotuit Rd., Marstons Mills (Barnstable); (508) 428-9814. Great breakfast and lunch spot that has changed ownership several times recently. The new owners appear to have it down, winners of a best breakfast award and lots of great reviews.

Restrooms
There are no public restrooms at the Trail of Tears.

Osterville-Centerville Loop

A nice little ride through the villages of Osterville and Centerville, with a few hills and scenic views of Nantucket Sound and the bays around Osterville. Make it a beach trip, shopping trip, or leisurely ride.

Start: Osterville Bay School (now closed), First Avenue, Osterville

Distance: 10.9-mile loop

Approximate riding time: 1 hour

Best bike: Road

Terrain and surface type: Paved busy roads, paved quiet roads, with some rough patches and potholes

Traffic and hazards: Busy main roads and downtown areas of Osterville and Centerville especially in summer, impatient drivers, potholes, sand at the side of the road, golfers and pedestrians crossing from the Wianno Yacht Club

Things to see: Osterville Center, West Bay, Dead Neck Island, Grand Island, Nantucket Sound, Wianno Yacht Club, East Bay, Dowse's Beach, Bumps River Bridge, Long Beach, Main Street in Centerville, Four Seas Ice Cream

Map: *Arrow Street Atlas: Cape Cod including Martha's Vineyard & Nantucket*, p. 13

Getting there: From Route 6 (Mid-Cape Highway), take exit 5 and head south on Route 149. Go around the rotary, continue on Route 149, then bear left onto Osterville Road. Turn left onto Race Lane and make an immediate right onto the Osterville-West Barnstable Road. Follow it all the way to its end, crossing Route 28, to Main Street in Osterville. Turn left on Main Street, go through town, and bear right onto Wianno Avenue. Turn left on West Bay Road, left again on First Avenue, and turn left into the parking lot of the old Osterville Bay School.

GPS coordinates: N41 37.53' / W70 23.12'

9

THE RIDE

This ride starts from the center of Osterville, which was shortened from Oysterville allegedly because of a misspelling on a map. Osterville is one of seven villages of Barnstable, and has a lively downtown for its size, with restaurants, a health food store, a specialty market, ice cream shop, hardware store, and several shops and services. It is surrounded by natural beauty, including forest, marshes, and seashore, and is also known for its gorgeous oceanfront estates. Turn right out of the parking lot on 1st Avenue, turn left on West Bay Road, and descend to Eel River Road. Eel River is shaded, with twists and turns and a couple of hills, and makes you want to explore some of those hidden houses on both sides of the road. If you're here on a Thursday night, be careful of the "A" group of riders belonging to the Cape Cod Cycling Club based in Hyannis and Falmouth on their weekly Thursday night ride. Come to the end of the road, which rises, and turn right on Sea View Avenue, with views of the Eel River, an extension of West Bay. Pass by some very large homes and at the end of the road gaze across the inlet to Dead Neck Island and Grand Island, also known as Oyster Harbors, a gated community with a private golf course. On the other side of Oyster Harbors is Cotuit Bay (Ride 7). Turning around, ride the long stretch that is Sea View Avenue, past beautiful homes perched on the bluffs with views of Nantucket Sound on the right. The exclusive and historic cedar-shingled Wianno Club is on the right, its eighteen-hole golf course to the left. The current clubhouse was built in 1888 as the new Cotocheset Hotel after a fire in 1888 burned the old hotel to the ground. The Wianno Yacht Club purchased the hotel in 1916. Watch out for golfers and club members at the crosswalk.

Turn left onto Wianno Avenue, then right on East Bay Road down some rough pavement, past Dowse's Beach on the right. The road then bends left 90 degrees, where you can take in spectacular views of East Bay on the right. Roses line the road, with wooden docks stretching out to sailboats and other sea craft anchored in the bay. East Bay Road is rough in spots as it rounds a corner and past the view of the bay, now obscured by trees and more beautiful landscaped homes. At the end of East Bay, turn right onto Main Street. Road cyclists are often seen along Main Street in Osterville, but it remains a busy road where traffic can be heavy and not always friendly. Enjoy the downhill over the bridge at Bumps River into Centerville, then climb South

Bike Shops

Eastern Mountain Sports, 1513 Iyannough Rd., Hyannis, (508) 362-8690, ems.com
Bike Zone, 323 Barnstable Rd., Hyannis Port, (508) 775-3299, bikezonecapecod.com
Sea Sports, 195 Ridgewood Ave., Hyannis (508) 790-1217, capecodseasports.com

The East Bay from East Bay Road, Osterville

Main Street up a hill, down again, and up to a four-way intersection with traffic lights, the intersection of South Main, Craigville Beach Road and Main Street in Centerville. Turn left at the traffic lights onto Main Street (or head 100 feet straight to Four Seas Ice Cream on your left, where you can sit on a swivel stool at the soda counter and enjoy some of Cape Cod's best homemade ice cream). Pass the 1856 Country Store and refuel with cold drinks, then head up Main Street past historic homes, inns, and churches.

Turn left at Henry Place and immediately left on Park Avenue, and then make a quick right on Bumps River Road. Bumps River descends around an old cranberry bog on your right, climbs and turns left, then descends again past a pond on your right. It again climbs, this time a little steeper, bending left at the top of the climb past Lumbert Mill Road. After a gradual descent, Bumps River Road appears to end at a stop sign. Turn left here, and Bumps River Road continues, but turn left again on Starboard Lane. Make a quick right on Old Mill Road, which climbs gradually. There's not much to look at here, but it's good exercise over a long stretch of road, which descends back to Main Street in Osterville. If you want to tour downtown, turn right here and stop at Fancy's Market on the left for great sandwiches made-to-order, hot or cold drinks, a great selection of wines, and gourmet foods. Otherwise, continue the ride and cross Main Street onto East Bay Road again. You could stay straight and revisit East Bay Road (if you just haven't had enough ocean), retracing the route. Otherwise, turn right on Bates Street, a quiet residential street, and climb gradually back to town. Turn right on Wianno Avenue, then left at West Bay Road, and left on 1st Avenue back to the parking lot where the ride started. If you haven't already, take a little tour of downtown Osterville. It's a great little village to walk or ride, with lots of shops and places to eat.

MILES AND DIRECTIONS

0.0   This ride starts in the parking lot of the former Osterville Bay School. Turn right on 1st Avenue.

0.1   Turn left onto West Bay Road.

0.3   Turn left onto Eel River Road.

1.3   Turn right onto Sea View Avenue.

2.1   Turn around at the end of Sea View Avenue. There are great views of West Bay, Dead Neck Island in Cotuit, and the Atlantic.

4.0   Turn left onto Wianno Avenue.

4.2   Turn right onto East Bay Road and pass Dowse's Beach on the right.

4.4   Make a 90-degree left turn and continue on Sea View Avenue.

5.0   Turn right onto Main Street.

6.3   Cross the bridge with great views of the Bumps River to the left, Centerville Harbor, Long Beach, and the Atlantic Ocean to your right.

7.2   Turn left at intersection onto Main Street, Centerville (traffic lights), or head up Main Street a little to Four Seas Ice Cream.

7.3   Visit the 1856 Country Store for cold drinks to go.

7.6   Turn left onto Henry Place and left again on Park Avenue.

7.7   Turn right onto Bumps River Road.

Osterville–Centerville Loop

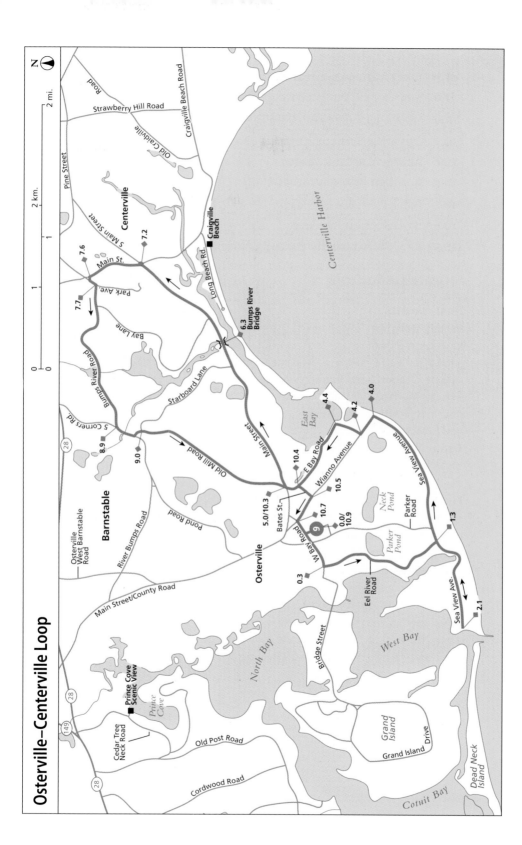

8.9 Turn left at stop sign and continue on Bumps River Road.

9.0 Turn left onto Starboard Lane.

9.0 Make a quick right onto Old Mill Road.

10.3 Cross Main Street onto East Bay Road.

10.4 Turn right on Bates Street.

10.5 Turn right on Wianno Avenue.

10.7 Turn left on West Bay Road.

10.8 Turn left on 1st Avenue.

10.9 Turn left back into the parking lot to finish.

RIDE INFORMATION

Restaurants
Earthly Delights: 15 W. Bay Rd., Osterville; (508) 420-2206. Tommy and Mary have been providing excellent take-out food to Osterville for years now. It's a small place with a few bar stools inside and a nice covered porch with a few tables outside. Delicious food, lots of choices, excellent for vegans and vegetarians.

Fancy's Market: 699 Main St., Osterville; (508) 428-6954. Great deli for lunch, gourmet foods, fresh fruits, and veggies. Good wine and beer selection. Fast and friendly.

Osterville Village Cafe: 3 Wianno Ave., Osterville; (508) 428-1005. Great breakfast and lunch, with an old-fashioned lunch counter but surprisingly varied menu. Large portions and friendly, service-oriented staff.

Five Bays Bistro: 825 Main St., Osterville; (508) 420-5559. The decor is urban, the food excellent for a special evening out. The last time my wife and I had dinner here, we sat outside in summer at one of the few outdoor tables under the stars. Romantic place.

Four Seas Ice Cream: 360 S. Main St., Centerville; (508) 775-1394. Lines out the door in summer speak to the popularity of this 1934 establishment. It looks like you've arrived at somebody's summer cottage, but then the old-fashioned soda fountain with spinning stools is directly in front of you. Homemade ice cream, the best on Cape Cod, made daily. First Lady Jacqueline Kennedy liked the fresh peach so much she had it delivered to the White House. Sandwiches, including lobster salad.

Restrooms
No public restrooms. You'll probably have to patronize one of the restaurants in Osterville or Centerville in a pinch.

Centerville to Hyannis

This is an out-and-back that is also a connector for bicycle commuting to and from Hyannis. Craigville Beach is one of the most popular beaches on Cape Cod, and this ride can be used to get from public transportation in Hyannis to Craigville. Bostonians can travel on the Cape Flyer *train from South Station and get away to Craigville Beach, Kalmus Beach, or Veteran's Park Beach, or check out the Kennedy Summer White House in Hyannis Port.*

Start: Centerville Public Library, 585 Main St., Centerville, or at the parking lot for Four Seas Ice Cream, 360 S. Main St., Centerville

Distance: 11.4 miles, out-and back

Approximate riding time: 1 to 2 hours, depending on stops

Best bike: Road

Terrain and surface type: Paved busy roads, paved quiet roads, with some rough patches and potholes

Traffic and hazards: Busy main roads especially in summer, impatient drivers, potholes, sand at the side of the road, especially along Craigville Beach Road when it's been windy

Things to see: Centerville, Craigville Beach, Hyannis Port, Kennedy Compound, Hyannis Harbor, Lewis Bay, Kalmus Park Beach, Veteran's Park Beach

Map: *Arrow Street Atlas: Cape Cod including Martha's Vineyard & Nantucket*, p. 14

Getting there: From Route 6 (Mid-Cape Highway) and Cape Cod Canal, take exit 5, turn right at the end of the ramp, go around the rotary, and continue on Route 149 South. Turn left onto Osterville Road at the fork, go to the end, and turn left on Race Lane. Turn right on Old Stage Road, cross Route 28 and continue on Old Stage Road to the intersection with

Park Avenue on the right and Main Street on the left. Continue straight on Main Street past the 1856 Country Store on the left, passing Church Hill Road. The library is on the left.

GPS coordinates: N41 38.63' / W70 20.81'

THE RIDE

This ride starts from the village of Centerville, at the Centerville Library parking lot (optional parking at Four Seas Ice Cream), heads down Craigville Beach Road, and rounds the left-bending corner to Craigville Beach, a wide expanse of beach where several big events are held during the year. Pass by the long beach with a clam shack on the left in summer, and the beach house to the right. The road bends left at the end of the beach, then up a slight incline to the right. At the top of the incline, ride a long straightaway out of Centerville and into Hyannis Port over rolling hills. Bear right to continue on Craigville Beach Road, and although it looks like a right-hand turn, it isn't. Smith Street continues to the left, but don't go left. Turn right on Scudder Avenue (more like a merge) and climb the steeper hill into Hyannis Port, passing the Hyannis Port Golf Club on your right. This neighborhood is its own little world, a village within a village, with its own post office, convenience store, golf course, yacht club, beach club, and two churches.

Hyannis Port is not one of the seven villages of Barnstable, but it could be, as it appears to be its own distinct entity. This is definitely a summer neighborhood, with most of its five hundred summer residents gone in the winter. President John F. Kennedy played here as a child with his brothers and sisters in summer. Continue on Scudder Avenue, then turn right on Irving Avenue, and then left on Hawthorne Avenue, a steep, short descent with a great ocean view. Turn left again on Dale Avenue, which goes past the Hyannis Port Beach Club on the right, then bends left up a hill past the Kennedy Compound, the famous summer residence of President John F. Kennedy and Senators Robert and Edward Kennedy.

As you ride past the six-acre Kennedy Compound to your right, you see a group of relatively modest Cape homes, far from some of the huge castles

Bike Shops

Eastern Mountain Sports, 1513 Iyannough Rd., Hyannis, (508) 362-8690, ems.com
Bike Zone, 323 Barnstable Rd., Hyannis Port, (508) 775-3299, bikezonecapecod.com
Sea Sports, 195 Ridgewood Ave., Hyannis (508) 790-1217, capecodseasports.com

A seagull walks Craigville Beach, Centerville

built in other Cape Cod locations, or the mansions on Martha's Vineyard and Nantucket. There is no Camelot-sized kingdom here, and everyone in this neighborhood appears relaxed, used to the tourists, tour buses, and cyclists riding past.

Ride past Marchant Avenue on the right and turn right on Irving Avenue, going past the Kennedy Compound's back yard on the right. Turn left on Iyanough Avenue past the Hyannis Port Yacht Club, with a great view of Hyannis Harbor and the beach, then turn right on Washington Avenue, which turns into Hyannis Avenue. Turn right on Ocean Avenue and descend past the

Ocean Avenue Beach, cross the bridge over the inlet to the marsh, bend left, and ride the incline past Sea Street Beach on the right. Merge with Sea Street on the right and make an immediate right on Gosnold Street, a long straight road that descends into a sharp right turn onto Estey Avenue. Ride over the hills toward the ocean here, turn left on Hawes Avenue, and look off to the right for views of Hyannis Harbor and Nantucket Sound. Hawes Street bends left past Kalmus Park Beach and turns into Ocean Street past a marsh on the left and then through more residential neighborhood. At mile 5.6, turn right into the driveway to Veteran's Park Beach, where there are restrooms, picnic tables, and a nice beach with views of Lewis Bay and Great Island in Yarmouth, across the bay. After resting and exploring, turn around and retrace your route back to the start.

On Thursday nights during summer (and spring and fall as long as there's daylight until 7 p.m.), the Cape Cod Cycling Club has a weekly Thursday Night Ride leaving from Veteran's Park Beach. The Thursday Night Ride comprises four ride groups, from beginners all the way up to serious competitors, with ride leaders assigned to provide guidance and assistance for each group. The Cape Cod Cycling Club (or C4) is Cape Cod's largest cycling club, a nonprofit organization whose mission statement is "all kinds of cycling for all kinds of people." Members participate in many fundraising activities and charity events, especially the Last Gasp and the Best Buddies Challenge. The club also hosts cookouts, parties, and group rides, which are very much social events that foster life-long friendships. The club's website is capecodcycle.com, but much of the communication happens on their Facebook page. The Thursday Night Ride starts at 5 or 6 p.m. (depending on time of year and daylight) and the route is essentially this ride in reverse, added to Ride 9, or a variation of it. If you can bike Rides 9 and 10 in this guidebook back to back without too much trouble, you're more than ready to join C4 on Thursday nights.

MILES AND DIRECTIONS

0.0 Start at the parking lot of the Centerville Public Library or the Four Seas Ice Cream parking lot on South Main Street.

0.5 Pass Craigville Beach on the right—an optional parking lot, but a beach sticker is required from 9 a.m. to 5 p.m. in summer.

2.3 Bear right at the fork with Smith Street and stay on Craigville Beach Road.

2.5 Merge with Scudder Avenue and bear right.

2.9 Turn right onto Irving Avenue.

3.0 Turn left on Hawthorne Avenue.

Centerville to Hyannis

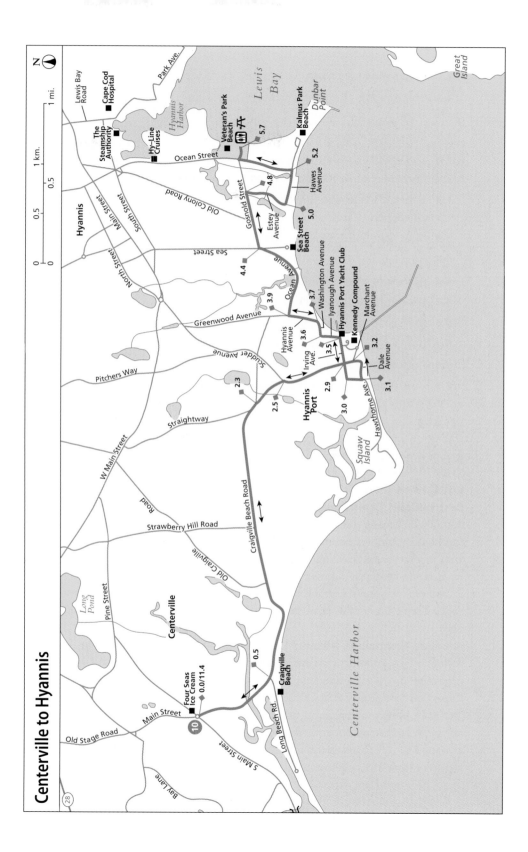

10

3.1 Turn left on Dale Avenue.

3.2 The Kennedy Compound on Marchant Avenue (private) is on the right.

3.3 Turn right on Irving Avenue.

3.5 Turn left on Iyanough Avenue.

3.6 Turn right on Washington Avenue.

3.7 Bear left as the road turns into Hyannis Avenue. Hyannis Harbor is to the right.

3.9 Turn right onto Ocean Avenue.

4.4 Turn left and merge with Sea Street.

4.4 Turn right onto Gosnold Street.

4.8 Turn right on Estey Avenue.

5.0 Turn left on Hawes Avenue.

5.2 Turn left on Ocean Street. Kalmus Park Beach is on the right.

5.6 Turn right into Veteran's Park Beach.

5.7 Turn around at Veteran's Park Beach parking lot on Lewis Bay and return the way you came.

11.4 Arrive back at the start.

RIDE INFORMATION

Local Events and Attractions

Best Buddies Challenge: (800) 718-3536; bestbuddieschallenge.org. Ride 100, 50, or 20 miles, run a 5K with Olympic gold medalist Carl Lewis, or walk 5K for the Best Buddies organization, devoted to improving the lives of people with intellectual disabilities. Meet NFL quarterback Tom Brady at the finish. Founded by Anthony Kennedy Shriver, the son of Eunice Kennedy Shriver, founder of the Special Olympics, and Sargent Shriver, founding director of the Peace Corps. Every May, from Boston to Craigville Beach, the hard, but fun, way!

Kennedy Compound, Hyannis Port: The Kennedy Summer White House. Always try to remember that this is someone's home and neighborhood. Their private road is Marchant Avenue, off Dale Avenue.

Cape Cod Symphony Orchestra: 1060 Falmouth Rd., Suite A, Hyannis; 508-362-1111. Wow, are they good. Conductor Jung Ho Pak has breathed new life and an incredible amount of energy and power into this orchestra. They need a venue worthy of their talent, so support their efforts to build a new performing arts center on Cape Cod.

Restaurants

Four Seas Ice Cream: 360 S. Main St., Centerville; (508) 775-1394. See the listing under Ride 9.

Centerville Pie Company: 1671 Falmouth Rd., Centerville; (774) 470-1406. I'm sure Oprah put this place on the map. Breakfast, lunch, and amazing pies.

Naked Oyster Bistro & Raw Bar: 410 Main St., Hyannis; (508) 778-6500. From the oyster farming Bordeaux town of Archachon, France, comes chef-owner Florence Lowell, who encourages you to relax, eat, and drink in her vibrant, buzzing French Bistro.

Brazilian Grill: 680 Main St., Hyannis; (508) 771-0109. Try the Brazilian BBQ!

Spanky's Clam Shack and Seaside Saloon: 138 Ocean St., Hyannis; (508) 771-2770. The best Hyannis clam shack. Fish & chips, lobster rolls, fried seafood, clam chowder.

Pizza Barbone: 390 Main St., Hyannis; (508) 957-2377; pizzabarbone.com. Delicious pizza baked at 1,000 degrees in its handcrafted Stefano Ferrara oven, built from the rock and ash of Mount Vesuvius. Try the pistachio-pesto pizza and gourmet desserts, ingredients from its rooftop garden.

Restrooms

Restrooms are available at Craigville Beach and Kalmus Beach and at Veteran's Park Beach.

Hyannis to the Cape Cod Rail Trail

This out-and-back ride can also be used as a commuter ride between South Dennis and Hyannis, and gives riders arriving to Hyannis by train, plane, or ferry the opportunity to get to the Cape Cod Rail Trail (CCRT) without a car. This route was chosen to provide the safest route from Hyannis to the Lower and Outer Cape, and there is the option to ride the sidewalk on the more dangerous roads. Until the CCRT extension is constructed, this is definitely one of the safest ways to go, albeit not the most scenic. Once you get to the CCRT, you might never want to turn back.

Start: Veteran's Park Beach, Hyannis

Distance: 19.6 miles, out-and-back

Approximate riding time: 2 hours

Best bike: Road

Terrain and surface type: Paved roads

Traffic and hazards: Busy main roads, especially in summer, sand in the road, congestion by the Ocean Street docks, with vehicles parking and backing up

Things to see: Veteran's Park Beach and Recreation Area (public restrooms), Ocean Street Docks, Cape Cod Hospital, Lewis Bay, Sandy Pond Recreation Area, Dennis-Yarmouth Regional High School, Bass River, Wilbur Park, CCRT in South Dennis

Map: *Arrow Street Atlas: Cape Cod including Martha's Vineyard & Nantucket*, p. 15

Getting there: From points west and the Cape Cod Canal: Take Route 6 (Mid-Cape Highway) to exit 6 and turn right at the bottom of the ramp on Iyannough Road (Route 132). At the Barnstable Airport Rotary, exit the rotary onto Barnstable Road and follow it all the way to Main Street in Hyannis. Cross Main Street and continue on Ocean Street to Veteran's

Park Beach. **From points east on Cape Cod:** Take Route 6 to exit 7, turn left at the end of the ramp onto Willow Street, and follow Willow Street south past Camp Street. Continue straight on Yarmouth Road to Route 28. Cross Route 128 and continue on Yarmouth Road to Main Street. Turn right on Main Street, then left on Ocean Street. Pass the docks on the left and continue to Veteran's Park Beach on the left.

GPS coordinates: N41 38.42' / W70 16.70'

THE RIDE

This ride has been mapped to get riders from busy Hyannis to the Cape Cod Rail Trail, which starts in South Dennis and ends in Wellfleet, with a connecting branch called the Old Colony Rail Trail (OCRT) that goes from Harwich to Chatham. Eventually, a CCRT expansion will extend the 22-mile trail westward from South Dennis to Hyannis in two phases, first west to Yarmouth, and then to Hyannis. The extension has been twenty years in the making, and reports are that the project will be completed by 2016 or 2017, since Phase I (3.7 miles) to Peter Homer Park in South Yarmouth is finally going out to bid as of this writing (according to a *Cape Cod Times* article, "Cape Rail Trail Extension Gets Put on Track," July 8, 2014, by Christine Legere). And since Cape Cod has three main problems in summer—too many vehicles, too little parking, and too much exhaust pollution—more bike paths and lanes are necessary.

Until then, this Best Bike Ride from Ocean Street in Hyannis to the CCRT entrance in South Dennis is one of the safest and most direct routes to connect to the trail and the Lower and Outer Cape from Hyannis.

The new *Cape Flyer* passenger train service from Boston transports cyclists from Boston to Hyannis over the Cape Cod Canal Railroad Bridge on weekends in summer. And although there is a connecting bus to the Outer Cape from Hyannis, many cyclists will

Bike Shops

Eastern Mountain Sports, 1513 Iyannough Rd., Hyannis, (508) 362-8690, ems.com
Bike Zone, 323 Barnstable Rd., Hyannis Port, (508) 775-3299, bikezonecapecod.com
Sea Sports, 195 Ridgewood Ave., Hyannis (508) 790-1217, capecodseasports.com
Barbara's Bike & Sport Equipment, 430 Route 134, South Dennis, (508) 760-4723, barbsbikeshop.com

want to ride and explore the places along the way without having to ride a bus (after having just spent two hours on a train from Boston). So this is

A stretch of the Cape Cod Rail Trail

the best ride to get you from Hyannis to the CCRT, and from there you can ride to *every* town on the Lower and Outer Cape (Dennis, Brewster, Harwich, Chatham, Orleans, Eastham, Wellfleet, and Truro) except Provincetown (we're working on it), by paved bicycle trail.

Turn right onto Ocean Street out of Veteran's Park Beach and ride past the restaurants, outdoor bars, and bustle of the Ocean Street Docks, where the Hy-Line and the Steamship Authority run ferries to Martha's Vineyard and

Nantucket year-round. Be careful of cars pulling in and out of metered parking spaces and lots along the road here. Pass a lovely renovated park on your right, the Michael K. Aselton Memorial Park, cruise down South Street with views of Lewis Bay to the right, and past the Cape Cod Hospital on your left. The route makes several turns through this coastal residential neighborhood, with houses of all shapes and sizes, some quite run down and some majestic and beautifully landscaped. Turning left onto Park Avenue gives one last view of the bay before zig-zagging on several back roads to Baxter Avenue in Yarmouth, a half-mile stretch ending at Route 28. Turn right on Route 28, ride with heavy traffic for just a short way, get into the left lane, and turn left on Town Brook Road.

Turn right onto Buck Island Road, a 2-mile stretch where you can ride the wide sidewalk on the left if you've had enough of traffic. But there is a wide space on Buck Island Road between the fog line (in case you didn't know, that white line on the right side of roads is formally known as the "fog line") and the shoulder, so riding the road is fairly safe. Buck Island Road is the road locals take year-round to avoid Route 28 traffic, so don't give the secret to just anybody. The drivers are typically friendlier than on Route 28, which often backs up and gridlocks in South Yarmouth. Along Buck Island Road, there are a few parks and ponds, called "kettle ponds," with swimming, hiking and other recreation, mostly hidden from view. Sandy Pond Recreation Area is the first one on the left after turning onto Buck Island Road, and there are restrooms available there. Horse Pond Conservation is farther up the road on the left, very much off the beaten path and hard to find, but good for hiking if you want to get lost. And it's easy to get lost there (not recommended for children).

Buck Island Road dead-ends into Winslow Gray Road, and turning left leads to a traffic light across Forest Road. At the end of Winslow Gray Road, descend and turn left on Long Pond Drive. This Long Pond Drive (almost every town on the Cape has a Long Pond Drive) is narrow, with rolling hills, and turns past Long Pond, barely visible in places on the right. Take a right on Station Avenue (the other end of Station Avenue is exit 8 on Route 6) and then a quick left on Regional Avenue past the Dennis-Yarmouth Regional High School tennis courts and football field on the left. Cross Main Street and continue on Sheridan Road. Take a left on Highbank Road past the Bass River Country Club on your right, go over an easy climb, then bear right and descend to the Bass River Bridge (town line) and enter Dennis. There are usually (not always) porta-potties in Wilbur Park just before the bridge, but you're so close to the CCRT you'll probably make it to a porta-potty there. Cross Old Main Street and merge with Upper County Road, then stop at the very busy intersection with Route 134. Turn left on 134, and look for the entrance to the CCRT on the right.

A refurbishing of this parking lot is also in the works with the expansion project, but there is usually enough parking here (if you start this ride in reverse). If not, there is also parking in the neighboring Barbara's Bike & Sport Equipment in the strip mall just before the CCRT entrance on the right. Say hello to Barb, who has been there many years, and who also rents bikes in Nickerson State Park in Brewster. Turn around and return the way you came to finish the ride.

MILES AND DIRECTIONS

0.0 This ride starts at Veteran's Park Beach.

0.1 Turn right onto Ocean Street.

0.8 Pass the Ocean Street docks on your right, and turn right on South Street.

1.2 Turn right on Lewis Bay Road.

1.2 Make an immediate left on Willow Street.

1.4 Turn right on Bayview Street.

1.6 Turn left on Somerset Street.

1.7 Turn right on Highland Street and make an immediate left onto Park Avenue.

2.0 Turn left on Glenwood Street.

2.1 Turn left on Harbor Road.

2.2 Turn left on Wendward Way.

2.3 Turn right on 2nd Road.

2.3 Make an immediate left on Harbor Road.

2.4 Turn left onto Baxter Avenue.

2.9 Turn right onto Route 28 (heavy traffic).

3.1 Turn left on Town Brook Road.

3.4 Turn right on Buck Island Road. There are traffic lights at Higgins Crowell Road and again at West Yarmouth Road.

5.4 Turn left on Winslow Gray Road. Cross Forest Road (traffic lights) and continue on Winslow Gray Road.

6.1 Turn left on Long Pond Drive.

7.0 Turn right on Station Avenue.

7.1 Turn left on Regional Avenue and pass the Dennis-Yarmouth Regional High School (tennis courts) on your left.

7.6 Cross Main Street and continue on Sheridan Road.

Hyannis to the Cape Cod Rail Trail

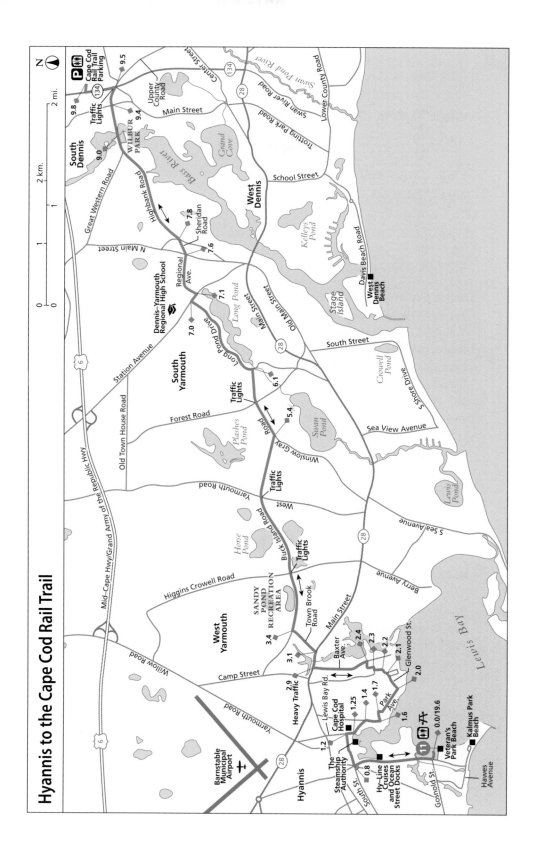

7.8 Turn left on Highbank Road. The Bass River Golf Course is on the right. Be glad you're wearing a helmet!

9.0 Pass Wilbur Park and cross the Bass River.

9.4 Turn right and merge with Upper County Road. Cross the Bass River Bridge into South Dennis.

9.5 Turn left onto Route 134 at the traffic lights (heavy traffic).

9.8 Turn right into the CCRT parking lot (free parking). Turn around and return the way you came.

19.6 Finish the ride in the Veteran's Park Beach parking lot.

RIDE INFORMATION

Local Events and Attractions

Veteran's Park Beach, John F. Kennedy Memorial, and Korean War Memorial: 480 Ocean St., Hyannis; (508) 790-9885. There are two memorials at the start of this ride. The John F. Kennedy Memorial is not to be confused with the John F. Kennedy Museum, below.

John F. Kennedy Museum Foundation: 397 Main St., Hyannis; (508) 790-3077. A small museum at the old Town Hall in Hyannis, a more family-oriented and personal rather than political legacy here, describing the Kennedy family connection with Cape Cod. The Cape Cod Baseball League Hall of Fame is also located here.

Restaurants

Spanky's Clam Shack and Seaside Saloon: 138 Ocean St., Hyannis; (508) 771-2770. See Ride 10 for description.

Caffe Gelato Bertini: 20 Pearl St., Hyannis; (508) 778-0244. Italian gelato delizioso!

Naked Oyster Bistro & Raw Bar: 410 Main St., Hyannis; (508) 778-6500. See Ride 10 for details.

Brazilian Grill: 680 Main St., Hyannis; (508) 771-0109. See Ride 10 for details.

Red Cottage Restaurant: 36 Old Bass River Rd., South Dennis; (508) 394-2923. Homemade breakfast and lunch served by the same family for 30 years. A local staple with all styles of crepes and egg dishes, open 7 days (5 in winter), year-round.

Restrooms

There are restrooms at Veteran's Park Beach, at the Ocean Street docks, at Sandy Pond Recreation Area in Yarmouth, and at the South Dennis end of the CCRT.

Sandy Neck Fat Tire Dune Ride

You'll need a fat tire bike for this ride (or a mountain bike, but you'll need to stay closer to the water, on the harder sand or rocky parts of the beach), the perfect bicycle for riding the sand dunes. Sandy Neck Beach Park is one of the few places with a fat tire bike policy. An unforgettable experience. If you're in great shape, ride to the end of this 6-mile-long peninsula to see the historic lighthouse, dune shacks, and cottages where a small community of people lives.

Start: Sandy Neck Beach Park (main gate, hikers' parking lot), 425 Sandy Neck Rd., West Barnstable

Distance: 5.2-mile loop

Approximate riding time: 1 hour (lighthouse option will take 3 hours)

Best bike: Fat tire bike

Terrain and surface type: Hard sand, deep sand, soft sand, very soft dune trail, gravel

Traffic and hazards: Vehicles on beach; soft, deep dune sand; high tide; deer

Things to see: Cape Cod Bay, Sandy Neck trails, Sandy Neck Beach, Sandy Neck Lighthouse, the cottage community, Great Marsh, Barnstable Harbor and Islands, ospreys, shorebirds, and other flora and fauna including deer

Map: *Arrow Street Atlas: Cape Cod including Martha's Vineyard & Nantucket*, p. 9

Getting there: From Route 6A, turn onto Sandy Neck Road in Sandwich and drive to the park gatehouse at 425 Sandy Neck Rd., in West Barnstable. From Route 6 (Mid-Cape Highway), take exit 4 and drive north on Chase Road. Continue on Old County Road, then turn left on

Howland Lane. Turn left (west) on Route 6A, then right on Sandy Neck Road to the gatehouse.

GPS coordinates: N41 44.12' / W70 23.09'

THE RIDE

Sandy Neck is a beautiful barrier beach peninsula on Cape Cod Bay with 4,700 acres of dunes, coastal forest, and marsh enclosing Barnstable Harbor. And you might not even know it's there, driving down Route 6A in Sandwich past a small sign for Sandy Neck. You have to drive through the town of Sandwich to get to this West Barnstable Beach, as Sandy Neck falls within the Town of Barnstable, so don't let the Entering Sandwich sign keep you from getting there. Just a short drive down Sandy Neck Road, less than a mile, a world of outdoor activity awaits. Sunbathe, swim, run, walk, hike the trails, horseback ride, or ride a bike on this very long stretch of beach and dune. That's right, ride a bike, a *fat tire* bike. With a fat tire bike, or "fatty," ride the dune trails and along the beach at Sandy Neck on squishy, 4-inch wheels and tires designed for sand. You can rent fat tire bikes at local bike shops on Cape Cod or bring your own, and Sandy Neck is one of the best places to demo and try them out. The park is maintained by the Town of Barnstable and has welcomed fat tire bike riders since they started riding here a few years ago, and since Sandy Neck allows cars and other vehicles on a separate off-road vehicle (ORV) beach, it probably wasn't a stretch to allow fat tire bikes when they first showed up.

Regulations say fat tire bike riders must use the Access Trail entrance (where cars drive off-road), just past where it's marked with Do Not Enter and Access by Permit Only signs to keep drivers who are looking for a beachfront parking lot from going into the ORV beach entrance. Riders may also enter on the Marsh Trail next to the gatehouse. After that, the rules are simple: stay on open, marked trails, including the Access Trail or Marsh Trail, which run parallel to one another and are connected by a series of numbered trails. Both trails extend from the main park road all the way to the end of the Sandy Neck peninsula, Beach Point. So there are several miles of beach and dune riding. The Town of Barnstable Sandy Neck Beach Park website (town.barnstable.ma.us/sandyneckpark/default.aspx) has a page for fat tire bikes, and fat tire bike riders should check here for any updated information. Go to the "Beach Status" page and look for "Fat Tire Bikes" to see what trails are open or any other news. When I rode Sandy Neck to map this ride, some of the beach was closed due to piping plover nesting, a controversial subject on Cape Cod, where several

Trail 2 from the beach at Sandy Neck Beach Park, West Barnstable

beaches have been closed to protect the plovers and other endangered species (and consequently protect the beach). Most of the time, all the trails at Sandy Neck are open, but even when partly closed, there are still miles and miles of dune and beach riding on its many trails.

Starting from the entrance, this ride starts at the gatehouse, along the short, paved bike path or the main paved road to the ORV entrance at 0.2 mile on the right, marked with a Do Not Enter sign. Ride past the air-filling station and along the soft, deep sand another 0.3 mile and you're quickly on the beach, with cars, pick-up trucks, RVs, sunbathers, swimmers, fishermen, horseback riders, and beach combers. Riding soft sand is a challenge, even on a fat bike, but riding in the vehicle tracks here makes it easier. Arrive at the beach on the Access Trail and the riding gets easier. The tides can change the nature of this ride every twelve hours, and every day is a new day in the intertidal zone. Ride in soft, deep sand for a stretch and then find yourself in gravel sections and hard-packed sand nearer the water's edge. Tomorrow it will all be different.

This ride follows the water's edge, then returns on the Access Trail path where vehicles travel, and how close you get to the water's edge depends on the tides. This ride is mapped short due to a closure for plovers at 2.6 miles, but often riders can keep going another 3 miles out to Beach Point, the end of the peninsula. Beach Point can also be accessed by riding the Marsh Trail, which parallels the beach, but on the other side of the dunes from the water's edge. Turn around or keep going, depending on any closures, and ride over the dunes (this ride takes Trail 2) over the dunes to the Marsh Trail. Coming up over the dunes, the view is of the Great Marshes and Barnstable Harbor, with osprey nests jutting upward over the many creeks that flow from the marsh into the harbor. Small islands blend with the mainland off in the distance in the tall marsh grasses and tidal flats.

Bike Shop

Sea Sports, 195 Ridgewood Ave., Hyannis (508) 790-1217, capecod seasports.com

Turn right at the end of Trail 2 to continue this shorter but still challenging ride, or turn left on the Marsh Trail and continue east toward Beach Point. If you take the latter route, be ready for one of the hardest workouts ever! The decision to turn right or left at the end of Trail 2 will be easier after a taste of the soft sand of the dunes on Trail 2. On the Marsh Trail, it's much more difficult in the softer sand than by the water's edge! But turning left on the Marsh Trail gets you to some very tempting sites, including Sandy Neck Lighthouse (now private), a horseback riding trail, and tent camping at Trail 4, and a fishing area at Trail 6 that connects back to the Access Trail and the beach. There is also a forested area on the way out to Beach Point that is a great relief from the heat, when the sun beats down on these dune trails and it starts to feel too much like a scene from *Lawrence of Arabia*. Find another world at Sandy Neck by turning left, toward its end at Sandy Neck Lighthouse.

Turn right and enjoy the ospreys flying high and letting out their characteristic screeches while you navigate the dunes in the easy gears. Heading

Sandy Neck Fat Tire Dune Ride

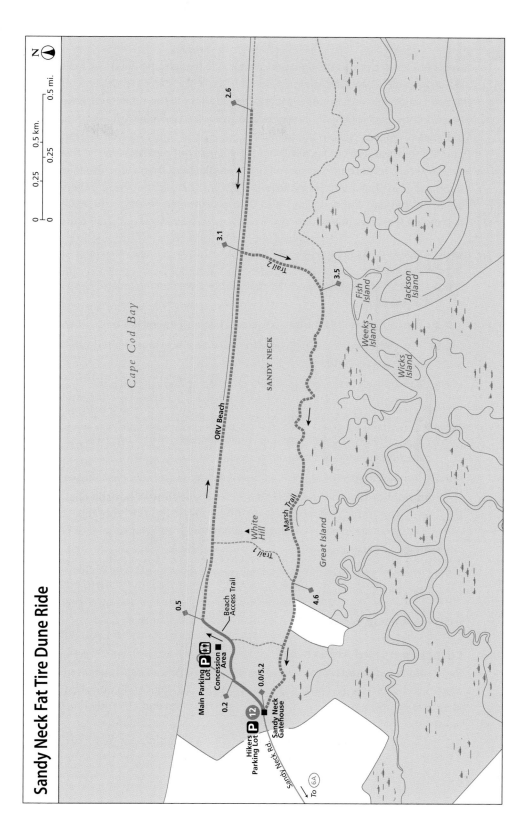

west here, it's all dune to the right and all marsh to the left, and Cape Cod feels like an incredibly beautiful foreign place. The Marsh Trail can have stretches of deeper sand that are hard to negotiate, but traveling in the dune buggy tire tracks left by park rangers is a nice trick to make it easier. On this section of the Marsh Trail there's a big bump in the road, a small sandy hill that is great practice for those new to fat bike riding. If you can get over this hill the first time without dismounting, you're a better fat bike rider than I am. After the bump, ride past Trail 1 and finish the ride at the park ranger's gatehouse. There are restrooms and a concession stand by the swimming beach at the main parking lot (past the ORV entrance).

MILES AND DIRECTIONS

0.0   Start this ride at the Sandy Neck Entrance Gate parking lot and head for the beach.

0.2   Turn right onto the motor vehicle and bicycle entrance.

0.5   Turn right onto the ORV Beach. The hard sand and gravel at low tide make for easier riding.

2.6   Turn around at the beach closure point (temporary piping plover nesting). If the beach is open, and you have the energy, ride as far as you want. Otherwise, turn around.

3.1   Turn left at Trail 2 sign. This is very difficult riding in soft sand. The fat tire bike should have very good, deep tread.

3.5   Turn right onto the Marsh Trail. This is soft sand and very challenging. If you have it in you, turn left for a very long day and head to Beach Point and Sandy Neck Lighthouse. Add a couple hours to your trip (add another 6 miles out-and-back from here).

4.6   Ride past Trail 1 (sign).

5.2   The ride ends back at the main gate and parking lot for hikers (and fat tire riders).

RIDE INFORMATION

Local Events and Attractions
Sandy Neck Lighthouse: You'll have to keep riding or walking. The current tower was built in 1857, is now privately owned by the Hinckley family, and is lit for private navigation.

Green Briar Nature Center and Jam Kitchen: 6 Discovery Hill Rd., East Sandwich; (508) 888-6870. Smell the jam cooking on stoves or being poured into jars for sale.

Restaurants

Cafe Riverview: 451 Route 6A, East Sandwich; (508) 833-8365. Students from Riverview School serve up a mean breakfast and lunch.

Bee-Hive Tavern: 406 Route 6A, East Sandwich; (508) 833-1184. Historic building serving breakfast, lunch, and dinner, with live music on weekends and "adult ice cream" made with your favorite liqueurs.

Restrooms

There are restrooms at the public beach parking lot, next to the concession building.

13

Barnstable Courthouse to Edward Gorey House

An easy, flat ride through historic Barnstable and Yarmouth Port that rides sections of the "Old King's Highway" (Route 6A) and visits Barnstable Harbor. Start at bustling Barnstable Village, hug the coast of Cape Cod Bay, and end at the home of author and illustrator Edward Gorey (now a museum). Something for everyone in the family, including whale watching.

Start: Barnstable County Courthouse parking lot, Route 6A, Barnstable Village

Distance: 10.0 miles, out-and-back

Approximate riding time: 1 hour or more depending on stops

Best bike: Road bike, hybrid bike

Terrain and surface type: Paved roads, sidewalks

Traffic and hazards: Busy main roads, especially in summer, sand in the road, narrow roads, quieter back roads, pedestrians on sidewalk

Things to see: Barnstable County Courthouse, David Lewis statues, Route 6A or the "Old King's Highway" (historic route), Barnstable Comedy Club, Olde Colonial Courthouse (Tales of Cape Cod), Sturgis Library, Crocker Tavern, Coast Guard Heritage Museum and Old Jail, Barnstable Harbor, Iyannough burial site, Captain Bangs Hallett House, Edward Gorey House

Map: *Arrow Street Atlas: Cape Cod including Martha's Vineyard & Nantucket*, pp. 10–11

Getting there: From Route 6 (Mid-Cape Highway), take exit 6, and head north on Route 132 toward Route 6A. Turn right on Route 6A, and park in the parking lot next to the Barnstable Superior Courthouse.

GPS coordinates: N41 42.06' / W70 18.26'

THE RIDE

Start at the Barnstable Superior Courthouse parking lot for this flat, scenic, and historic ride through Barnstable Village, Cummaquid (a sub-village of Barnstable), and Yarmouth Port. Barnstable Village was once a hotbed of Revolutionary War activity, so take note of two statues of patriots James Otis Jr. and his sister Mercy Otis Warren in front of the four-pillared Superior Courthouse overlooking Main Street. Osterville sculptor David Lewis sculpted these and several other sculptures on Cape Cod, including one of Rachel Carson in Woods Hole, John F. Kennedy and Iyannough in Hyannis, and "The Fisherman" in Bourne. The Otis siblings standing at the start of this ride were born in Barnstable, two of thirteen children, and close friends of George and Martha Washington and John and Abigail Adams. Mercy Otis wrote *History of the Rise, Progress, and Termination of the American Revolution* in 1805, the first history of the American Revolution, which Thomas Jefferson ordered in bulk for his cabinet as required reading. The two phrases "No taxation without representation!" and "A man's home is also his castle" are attributed to James Otis Jr. The start of this ride is also the site of a large protest against a king's order that denied colonists to a jury trial, and 1,500 protestors gathered outside the Olde Colonial Courthouse (now owned by Tales of Cape Cod), led by Otis and Samuel Adams in 1774. The Olde Colonial Courthouse and Sturgis Library, the oldest public library in the United States, are found by heading west (turning left) on Route 6A from the start of this ride. And so is Crocker Tavern, a colonial stagecoach stop and inn (you can tour or even rent this privately owned home) and meeting place for Cape Cod revolutionaries like James Otis and Samuel Adams. Opt to visit these historical sites by making a left on Route 6A (heading west).

For this ride, turn right on Route 6A (heading east) out of the Courthouse parking lot, and pass a general store, restaurants, law offices, and a fire station. Route 6A, or the Old King's Highway, was a Wampanoag footpath before Europeans arrived. *Smithsonian* writer Jonathan Kandell was "tempted to conclude this may be the most appealing stretch of America [he knows]" (*Smithsonian*, April 2005), with 34 miles of historic homes, inns, taverns, churches, and burial grounds, always close to Cape Cod Bay, along this historic route. History is everywhere along this stretch of road, and the strict rules to keep it that way are governed by each town's historic commission. That approach has clearly worked, although perhaps not for bicyclists, since the road is narrow, with cars parked in spaces along the right here. Use caution through this short stretch of historic Barnstable. Turn left on Millway at the traffic lights, or opt to see the Old Jail and the Coast Guard Heritage Museum (by heading straight on Route 6A a few yards more, from the intersection with Millway).

Edward Gorey House, Yarmouth Port

There you can see displays of Coast Guard and maritime history, a working blacksmith shop, and the oldest (wooden) jail in the United States, moved here from Old Jail Lane (cyclists can still ride this road) in 1968. Turning left on Millway, the road goes uphill a little, then down a little, and levels off toward Barnstable Harbor and Mattakeese Wharf on the left. This area of the ride reminds riders of Barnstable's old whaling and farming past. Take a whale watch here some other time with Hyannis Whale Watcher Cruises, one of the best on the Cape, or dine on the patio at Osterville Fish, Too. Go to the end of Millway to enjoy views of Sandy Neck peninsula (Ride 12) and Barnstable Harbor at the town docks. Turn around and take a left on Commerce Road, with a marsh on the right and farmland up the road before the road dead-ends back onto Route 6A.

Turn left back onto Route 6A, where there is often not enough room for both vehicles and bicycles on the road without vehicles needing to cross the centerline, so opt to take the sidewalk here. Along this stretch, take note of a sign marking the site of the grave of the Native American Sachem Iyannough, on the left near Bone Hill Road at mile 2.7. According to a 1937 book by Joseph Berger, *Cape Cod Pilot*, the remains of Iyannough, a copper kettle, and other items were found by a local farmer named Davis in 1860. According to 19th-century historian Amos Otis (*Genealogical Notes of Barnstable Families*), one Patrick Hughes, an Irishman working for Enoch Cobb, was plowing in a field near Great Swamp, about a half-mile from where tradition states Iyannough had his village, and found the remains. In any case, Iyannough was a peaceful leader of the Mattacheese tribe in this area of Cummaquid. He gained the respect of the *Mayflower* Pilgrims by finding John Billington Jr., the first European boy to get lost in the woods of Cape Cod. Iyannough was thought to have died from exposure, hiding in the marshes adjacent to the Old King's Highway, during a time of unrest between Pilgrim Myles Standish and the Wampanoags. The Wianno village of Osterville, the village of Hyannis, and Iyannough Road in Hyannis are all named after this great Wampanoag leader.

Bike Shops

Eastern Mountain Sports, 1513 Iyannough Rd., Hyannis, (508) 362-8690, ems.com
Bike Zone, 323 Barnstable Rd., Hyannis Port, (508) 775-3299, bikezonecapecod.com
Sea Sports, 195 Ridgewood Ave., Hyannis, (508) 790-1217, capecodseasports.com

Turn left on Keveney Lane at mile 3.0 and ride the gentle slope down to a bridge that crosses Mill Creek and Hallet's Mill Pond. To the right is the pond with Anthony's Cummaquid Inn sitting perched above the far end of the pond, and to the left is the marsh and creek flowing out to Barnstable Harbor. It's a very peaceful spot where someone occasionally drops a line in for a fresh catch. Bear right around a bend after the bridge, then turn left on Water Street, which turns into Wharf Lane at mile 3.8 at a 90-degree right bend in the road. To the left here is a hiking trail to Short Wharf Creek. Turn left on Thatcher Shore Road and ride past some lovely homes in this marshland, then turn right on Church Street and back to Route 6A. Turn right, go down the hill, and turn left at the Yarmouth Port Village Green at mile 4.9 (Strawberry Lane), where two homes of interest are located. The first is on the right as you enter the green, the Captain Bangs Hallet House, which looks just the way he left it in the late 1800s, with silks, porcelain, toys, and tea this sea captain would have acquired on his long journeys to China and India.

The second house, also a museum, is the Edward Gorey House, one of my favorite places to visit on Cape Cod. Tony Award winner, illustrator, and author Edward Gorey is perhaps best known for his animations in the introduction to the PBS series *Mystery*, hosted by vampire and actor Vincent Price in the 1980s. Gorey was a prolific illustrator, illustrating books by Samuel Beckett, Lewis Carroll, Charles Dickens, T.S. Eliot, Bram Stoker (apparently Gorey fell in love with *Dracula* at age 5), H.G. Wells, Virginia Woolf, and many others. He also published more than a hundred books, sometimes using pen names that were anagrams of his own name, like Ogdred Weary or D. Awdrey-Gore. He had a large cult following, and his books were very popular, including most notably *The Gashlycrumb Tinies* and *The Doubtful Guest*. Readers of Gorey will remember the former, a macabre tale of twenty-six children who all suffer a ghastly and untimely fate, each one representing a letter of the alphabet. Gorey died of a heart attack in 2000 at age 75, but his legacy remains in this delightful museum that was his home and studio for twenty years.

Turn right onto Route 6A from the Edward Gorey House to go back the way you came, or opt to ride Route 6A back to Barnstable Village, and ride what some believe to be the best stretch of road in the United States. Pass numerous inns and bed-and-breakfasts, historical homes, the Winslow Crocker Georgian home, the Old Yarmouth Inn, the dusty but wonderful Parnassus Book Service (used books), an old soda fountain at Hallet's General Store, excellent Japanese cuisine at Inaho, art galleries, and other sites along the Old King's Highway.

There is also the option to ride the sidewalk if you return via 6A from Edward Gorey House to the Barnstable County Courthouse. The sidewalk travels all the way from Yarmouth Port Village Green to Barnstable Village, along the north or bay side of Route 6A, switching to the south side just before returning into Barnstable Village.

Explore more of Barnstable Village at the end of this ride, on foot or by bicycle. Stop by the Nirvana Coffee Company for organic coffee and grab a bag of Late July tortilla chips. Late July owner Nicole Bernard Dawes is a local from Chatham, daughter of the late Steve Bernard, founder of Cape Cod Potato Chips and the man who brought the "kettle chip" back to prominence. Or refuel at the Barnstable Market next door, with a full deli, bakery, and fresh produce.

Barnstable Courthouse to Edward Gorey House

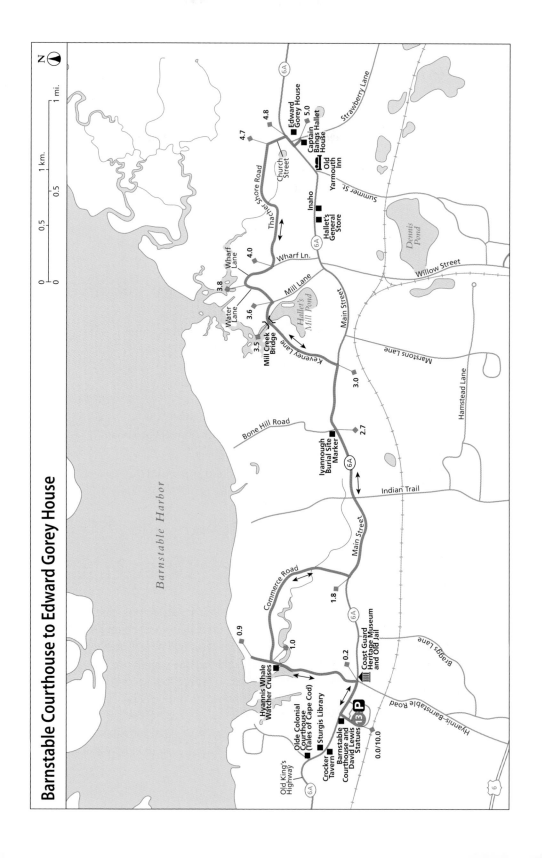

MILES AND DIRECTIONS

0.0   Start the ride at the Barnstable Superior Courthouse parking lot.

0.1   Turn right on Route 6A out of the parking lot.

0.2   Turn left onto Millway at the traffic light.

0.9   Stop at the end of Millway for a view of Barnstable Harbor, then turn around and proceed on Millway.

1.0   Turn left on Commerce Road.

1.8   Turn left on Route 6A.

2.7   Look for the Iyannough grave marker near Bone Hill Road.

3.0   Turn left on Keveney Lane.

3.5   Stop on the bridge overlooking the harbor, Mill Creek, and Hallet's Mill Pond on the right.

3.6   Turn left on Water Street.

3.8   Continue right on Wharf Lane.

4.0   Turn left on Thatcher Shore Road.

4.7   Turn right on Church Street.

4.8   Turn right on Main Street (Route 6A).

4.9   Turn left and bear left around the Yarmouth Port Village Green (Strawberry Lane).

5.0   Visit the Edward Gorey House. Turn around and return the way you came or opt to ride the sidewalk of Route 6A all the way back to the start.

10.0 Arrive back at the start at Barnstable Superior Courthouse.

RIDE INFORMATION

Local Events and Attractions

Hyannis Whale Watcher Cruises: 269 Millway, Barnstable Harbor; (800) 287-0374. Excellent narration by a naturalist and navigated with a captain and crew who clearly know the waters and the whales—by name. A three-hour tour that won't leave you stranded, a Cape Cod must-see experience.

Edward Gorey House: 8 Strawberry Ln., Yarmouth Port; (508) 362-3909. Take a wonderful tour of this illustrator's home. It looks a little creepy, especially when it's raining or dark.

Parnassus Book Service: 220 Route 6A, Yarmouth Port; (508) 362-6420. If you like browsing bookstores, this is one you won't find anywhere else. With new and rare books, and an outdoor book stall where you pay on the honor system, this is a rare find.

Hallet's General Store: 139 Route 6A, Yarmouth Port; (508) 362-3362. A throwback to old Cape Cod, with homemade ice cream and an old-fashioned soda fountain and apothecary. You'll think you're James Stewart in *It's a Wonderful Life*. They don't have a public restroom, though, so I didn't list Hallet's under Restaurants.

Restaurants

Nirvana Coffee Company: 3206 Main St., Barnstable Village; (508) 744-6983. Organic coffees, croissants, scones, muffins, on soft leather chairs and couches packed so tight as to invite friendly conversation. The laptops and tablets keep it quieter than it should be.

Osterville Fish, Too: 275 Old Mill Rd., Barnstable Harbor; (508) 362-2295. BYOB to accompany the fresh seafood, enjoyed on picnic tables outdoors overlooking Barnstable Harbor. The clam chowder is thick and chunky.

The Dolphin: 3250 Main St., Barnstable Village; (508) 362-6610. Hang with the lawyers and judges from across the street. Enjoy the fare and the fireplace by the bar.

Barnstable Restaurant and Tavern: 3176 Main St., Barnstable Village; (508) 362-2355. The steak tips and burgers are legendary, and so are the ghosts and stories about our first president staying here.

Inaho: 157 Route 6A, Yarmouth Port; (508) 362-5522. Best sushi bar on Cape Cod, to match anywhere. Elegant Japanese fare in three rooms, tempura to die for. Extensive sake menu. A fun, relaxed atmosphere.

Old Yarmouth Inn: 223 Route 6A, Yarmouth Port; (508) 744-6341. An old stagecoach stop, serving wayward travelers since 1696, with excellent fare. The huge stone fireplace by the entrance is very nice in winter.

Restrooms

Restrooms are available at the Barnstable County Courthouse complex and at Edward Gorey House in Yarmouth Port (when open), and at the many restaurants along this ride.

This is a fun little mountain bike course, very hilly, with fast sections throughout. You'd never know it was here.

Start: International Fund for Animal Welfare (IFAW) parking lot, 290 Summer St., Yarmouth

Distance: 7.7-mile loop

Approximate riding time: 1 to 2 hours

Best bike: Mountain bike or fat tire bike

Terrain and surface type: Paved busy roads, mostly smooth single-track trails, with lots of winding and hills, and sandy fire road crossings

Traffic and hazards: Busy main road (Willow Street) past ramps for Route 6 near start/finish especially in summer, branches, roots, rocks, occasional motocross riders

Things to see: IFAW headquarters, Willow Street, Route 6, Mother Nature and kettle ponds

Map: *Arrow Street Atlas: Cape Cod including Martha's Vineyard & Nantucket*, p. 92

Getting there: From Route 6 (mid-Cape Highway), take exit 7 and turn north on Willow Street. Turn right on Summer Street and right again into the IFAW parking lot.

GPS coordinates: N41 41.34' / W70 15.29'

THE RIDE

Of all the mountain biking trails on Cape Cod, this is one of the lesser-known trail systems. Willow Street has no trail signs or trailhead marker, and the trailhead starts under the shadow of an interstate highway next to an exit ramp.

Willow Street is another of those Cape Cod mysteries, part of what I call "hidden Cape Cod," where an entire world can open up behind a few trees or down an unmarked dirt path. At Willow Street there are almost 15 miles of winding, hilly trails, with some fast sections and a few tough climbs. The mountain bike trails cross sandy fire roads frequently in this abandoned development that was converted to conservation area. You can cross over the fire roads or ride them. In addition, motocross riders have been using this area for years, so if you hear the engines getting close, be on your guard. This ride is bordered by Barnstable Municipal Airport to the south, Route 6 to the north, Willow Street to the east, and Mary Dunn Road to the west. So, you could get lost, but not for long. And proximity to the roads makes Willow Street a safer ride in case of emergency or injury. Willow Street is fun, with long stretches of smooth single-track on pine needle–covered hard-packed dirt, a few rocks and roots, some technical riding, and a lot of hilly sections near the end of this ride (on the west side trails).

The International Fund for Animal Welfare (IFAW), just down the street from the trail start, has graciously offered their parking lot to mountain bikers through an arrangement with NEMBA. Turn left out of the lot, left again onto Willow Street, go under the highway, and follow the path parallel to the road on the right. It turns right 90 degrees, then crosses active railroad tracks (watch out for trains here) and into the woods. A tenth of a mile later turn left onto Art's Trail, named after mountain bike pioneer Art Hastings, who cut these trails. It's a great introduction to Willow Street. Art's Trail takes a dive down and levels off around a sharp right turn, then has a steep climb around a left turn and then another sharp right turn. It's all over in a half-mile, so you might be tempted to turn around and do it again.

Bike Shops

Eastern Mountain Sports, 1513 Iyannough Rd., Hyannis, (508) 362-8690, ems.com
Bike Zone, 323 Barnstable Rd., Hyannis Port, (508) 775-3299, bikezonecapecod.com
Sea Sports, 195 Ridgewood Ave., Hyannis, (508) 790-1217, capecodseasports.com

From Art's Trail, the trail parallels the highway (Route 6, on the right), takes a couple twists, and then turns around. It first heads south and then east, turning back into a pair of short loops of trail. At mile 1.7, cross a fire road and turn left, head through the woods up an incline, and at mile 1.8 turn left at a fork that quickly descends. This section loops around to where it started, now at mile 2.1. Have a déjà vu moment as you turn left and enter the Automile Trail, which descends with some sharp turns. There's an old, rusted pickup truck here that gave the trail its name, and no one knows how it got there. Rumor has it that somebody used it as shelter for a time, but nobody has been living in it for many years. If you're going the right way, it should be on your right the two times you pass it. Ascend a hill at the end of the Automile, and at mile 2.4 cross a fire road (it's the same one you crossed earlier). Then at mile 2.5, turn left into the Bushwood Trail, where the ride generally flattens out for some fast riding through the bushes. You may "bring home a Christmas tree," but you can really fly in here! The southern end of Bushwood comes very close to the Barnstable Municipal Airport (HYA), where Navy and Army Air Forces flew

The "Automile" trail

antisubmarine patrols during World War II. These days, there are planes flying overhead on their way to Nantucket or Martha's Vineyard, and you may hear them taking off through the trees that border the runways.

If you somehow find yourself at the edge of a pond on Bushwood Trail, turn around. Three larger ponds surround the Bushwood Trail: Lamson Pond to the east, Mary Dunn Pond to the southwest, and Israel Pond to the northwest. Several other smaller ponds dot the perimeter of this trail. The Bushwood Trail then turns right and heads in a twisting pattern north, away from the airport, where it turns left 90 degrees at mile 5.4 and parallels a fire road. Turn right on the Back Nine Trail which climbs up toward the highway (Route 6) along Mary Dunn Road, to the left. Turn right for the home stretch along Route 6, a mile of fast riding with hills and a nice quick descent toward Willow Street. Arrive at the end of the trail, cross the tracks again (look both ways), turn left onto Willow, go back under the highway, and head back to the IFAW parking lot. There is a reserved parking space for your kind of vehicle.

By 2017, if all goes as planned, the Cape Cod Rail Trail will pass very close to the entrance of the Willow Street Trails, possibly even through the trail area, connecting rail trail to mountain bike trail. The only place where mountain bike trail and rail trail intersect now is Nickerson State Park in Brewster. The Otis mountain bike trails are very close to the Shining Sea Bikeway entrance in North Falmouth, (see Rides 4 and 6). The CCRT extension will extend from South Dennis to Yarmouth along the old railroad bed, and then veer off the old tracks to Peter Homer Park on Old Town House Road. Rumors are that it will extend onto Higgins Crowell Road, which intersects with Willow Street very near the start of the mountain bike trail entrance here. One proposed route will take riders through the northern part of the Willow Street mountain bike trail itself as it parallels Route 6. But what will be potentially a small loss for Willow Street mountain bikers will also be a great gain for cycling on Cape Cod, and most of Willow Street will likely remain untouched for mountain biking.

MILES AND DIRECTIONS

0.0 Start this ride at the IFAW parking lot at 290 Summer St. The trailhead is diagonally across the highway.

0.1 Turn left on Summer Street.

0.2 Turn left onto Willow Street and ride under the highway.

0.4 Turn right onto the unmarked trailhead and cross the railroad tracks into the woods.

0.5 Turn left onto Art's Trail.

Willow Street

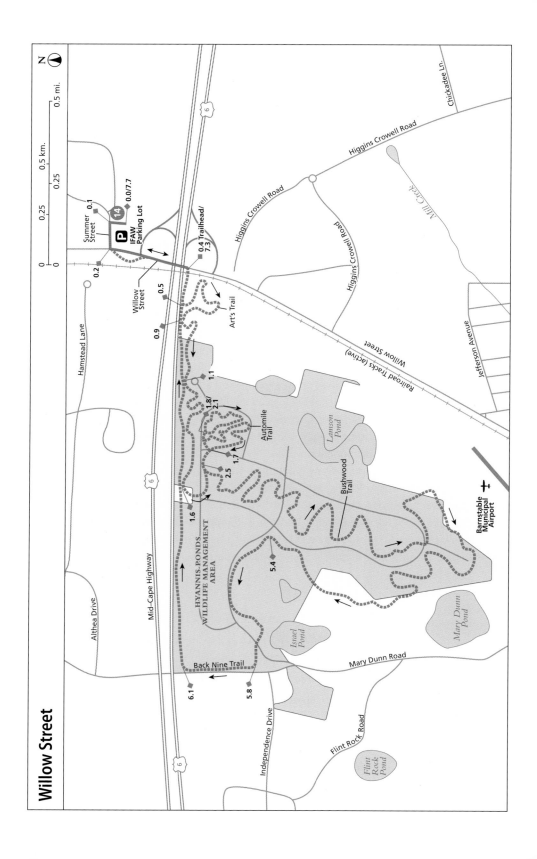

0.9   Turn left.

1.1   Bear left.

1.6   Bear left.

1.7   Turn left.

1.8   Turn left.

2.1   Bear left into the Automile Trail. Look for the rusty pickup truck.

2.4   Cross the fire road.

2.5   Bear left into Bushwood Trail.

5.4   Bear left at the curve.

5.8   Turn right onto the Back Nine Trail (it runs parallel to Mary Dunn Road, off to the left).

6.1   Bear right, head east, parallel to Route 6 to your left.

7.3   Exit the trail, cross the railroad tracks, and turn left on Willow Street.

7.5   Turn right onto Summer Street.

7.6   Turn right into the IFAW parking lot.

7.7   Arrive at the far end of the IFAW parking lot for the end of this ride.

RIDE INFORMATION

Local Events and Attractions
See also the listings under Ride 13.

Gray's Beach (Bass Hole): You can see it from Chapin Memorial Beach (Ride 15), but it's accessible only from Center Street, off Route 6A. Take Willow Street north to Route 6A and head east, past the Edward Gorey House (Ride 13) on Strawberry Lane. Go up the hill past the Colonial House Inn and look for Center Street on the left. Take Center Street to its end and you're there. This is a boardwalk beach that's a hidden gem with restrooms, playground, and picnic tables.

Restaurants
See the listings under Ride 13 for restaurants in Yarmouth Port.

Restrooms
There are no restrooms at Willow Street, so plan ahead. There are restrooms at Peter Homer Park on Old Town Road. Ride your bicycle on Willow Street south to Higgins Crowell Road, turn left on Higgins Crowell Road, and follow that to the bike path that takes you to Peter Homer Park in Yarmouth. The bike path entrance is just past Mid-Tech Drive on the left.

Dennis Bayside Beaches

A hilly ride through Dennis to three calm and beautiful Cape Cod Bay beaches, through charming Cape Cod neighborhoods.

Start: Dennis Senior Center parking lot, on the corner of Route 134 and Setucket Road, Dennis

Distance: 10.5 miles, double loop

Approximate riding time: 1 hour

Best bike: Road bike

Terrain and surface type: Paved roads, hilly sections

Traffic and hazards: Busy main roads, especially in summer, sand in the road, and pedestrians and vehicles entering and exiting the beaches

Things to see: Dennis Senior Center, Bayview Beach, Mayflower Beach, Chapin Memorial Beach, Cape Playhouse, Cape Cinema, Cape Cod Museum of Art, Hokum Rock

Map: *Arrow Street Atlas: Cape Cod including Martha's Vineyard & Nantucket*, p. 39

Getting there: From Route 6 (Mid-Cape Highway), take exit 9B if coming from points east, west, or the Cape Cod Canal, and go north on Route 134 to Setucket Road, Dennis. The Dennis Senior Center is on the (southwest) corner of Setucket Road and Route 134, and there is an entrance to a large parking lot just before the traffic lights at Setucket Road.

GPS coordinates: N41 43.36' / W70 09.52'

THE RIDE

This ride takes you to three beautiful Cape Cod Bay beaches that are sunny and sandy playgrounds in summer but cold and desolate in winter, but where surprises can sometimes be found in the protected waters of the bay. These bayside beaches are gorgeous. If you ride at dusk, you may get lucky and experience a spectacular sunset over the water, as all three beaches face somewhat to the west as well as north. Bayview Beach, Mayflower Beach, and Chapin Memorial Beach give cyclists great views, lots of variety, and access to Cape Cod Bay. At low tide, you can walk for miles on the firm, rippled sand of the tidal flats and search for sea clams, soft shell clams, razor clams, and quahogs (hard shell) and harvest them when shell fishing is in season. In summer, these three beaches can be crowded, but less so as you ride west to Chapin Memorial Beach. Chapin is a longer stretch of beach leading to a dead-end at Bass Hole inlet, the town line between Dennis and Yarmouth. You may even be able to see endangered North Atlantic right whales close to shore. Cape Cod Bay is a favorite waypoint for these endangered whales to feed and nurse their calves, anywhere from Plymouth to Provincetown. So, you might be able to skip the obligatory whale-watch summer cruise if you ride here in winter. More than half of the existing population (there are only five hundred North Atlantic right whales left in the world) has been known to visit Cape Cod Bay in peak migratory season in March and April. So, whether it's summer or winter, this ride has much to offer, and may even surprise.

Start this ride at the Dennis Senior Center, at the southwest corner of Route 134 and Setucket Road in Dennis. If it's a Sunday at 8 a.m., the Cape Cod Cycling Club starts a group here with a typically large group of increasingly faster riders headed to the lower and outer Cape. From the Senior Center, turn left on Setucket Road and say good-bye to them; this ride is far easier, more relaxed, and not nearly as long. Setucket Road passes through a residential neighborhood, and is fairly quiet in terms of traffic. Turn right onto Old Bass River Road and the traffic is much busier. There is a wide sidewalk where cyclists can travel on the right as you ride up Old Bass River Road, so if traffic gives you the jitters, use the sidewalk and watch for pedestrians who use the path frequently year-round. Climb the hill up Old Bass River Road and have a fast descent past Scargo Hill Road on the right. Pass an historic cemetery on the left as you glide down to the intersection with Route 6A.

This is Main Street, the Old

Bike Shops

Barbara's Bike & Sport Equipment, 430 Route 134, South Dennis, (508) 760-4723, barbsbikeshop.com

Dennis Cycle Center, 249 Great Western Rd., South Dennis, (508) 398-0011, denniscyclecenter.com

King's Highway, in an older part of town. This area has a great theatrical history, as the grounds of the Cape Playhouse are just across the street to the right. The Cape Playhouse is the oldest summer professional theater in the

Chapin Beach Road overlooking Cape Cod Bay, Dennis

United States, and for more than seventy years has helped launch the early careers of famous actors including Basil Rathbone, Henry Fonda, Bette Davis, Gregory Peck, Humphrey Bogart, Robert Montgomery, and Shirley Booth. The grounds now also are home to the Cape Cinema, Cape Cod Museum of Art, and the Cape Cod Theater Coalition. There is a lot to do and see along Main Street, including great restaurants, sandwich shops, ice cream, and coffee shops, just in case you want to explore more. This ride also returns to this spot later for a second pit stop.

Cross Route 6A and continue ahead on Hope Lane, which is offset slightly left of where Old Bass River Road dead-ends into 6A. There is an unmarked road to your right that is the sneaky locals' entrance to the Merc (Dennis Village Mercantile) and the Underground Bakery. Pass by another back entrance to the Cape Cod Museum of Art and Cape Playhouse grounds on the right and continue down residential Hope Lane. Make a left on Whig Street and a quick right on Pilgrim Road and wind through quiet back roads to Shore Drive, with its beautiful oceanfront homes overlooking Cape Cod Bay. At the end of Shore Drive on the right is Bayview Beach, with a bike rack, porta-potties and nice white, soft sand. Bayview Beach is popular with families and small children, with lots of kids' bikes parked at the bike racks here. The small, warm tidal pools are a hit with the under-5 crowd. But it's a great beach for everybody.

Turn left onto Bayview Road and then right on Horsefoot Path for nearby Mayflower Beach, which connects to Bayview Beach. Mayflower Beach has a boardwalk, bathrooms, a snack shack, and an outdoor shower. Be happy you're on your bike here in summer, as vehicle parking runs $25 on weekends and often requires a long wait. Turn left on Wade's Way, right on Taunton Avenue, and follow it to Chapin Memorial Beach. Taunton Avenue turns into Dr. Botero Road and then Chapin Beach Road. If the first two beaches are too crowded, Chapin Memorial Beach will give you the chance to get away from the crowds. Chapin has a long stretch of dune-backed quiet beach and offers more of the same fun as the other two beaches, but with fewer people. The sunsets here at low tide are often breathtaking. There are no restrooms or snacks for sale here, but there are porta-potties. You can hop off the bike and walk all the way to the end of Dennis at Bass Hole, which winds around and into the huge marsh you passed earlier on the left.

Turn around in the parking lot and head back to Taunton Avenue past the marsh and bay, then turn right onto Beach Street. Continue down the sloping and hilly Beach Street through a residential neighborhood, and turn left on Whig Street. Retrace your pedal strokes past the Josiah Dennis (for whom the town is named) House on the corner of Whig Street and Nobscussett Road, back to Hope Lane. Stop for refreshments and lunch at the Mercantile, or dinner and tapas at the Harvest Gallery Wine Bar. The Scargo Cafe is across Route 6A and the excellent Fin Restaurant is across the parking lot from Harvest. Cross Route 6A and climb back up Old Bass River Road past Scargo Hill Road.

Turn left on Hokum Rock Road, a long rolling road named for Hokum Rock, a large boulder split into a few pieces on the south side of the road. According to old deeds, the rock is listed as the "Who-come" rock, and legend speaks of an elderly Nobscussett Native American who lived in a cave under the rock asking, "Who come?" when anyone approached. Hokum Rock is now a popular spot for rock climbers to practice bouldering technique, although not very big. It is bigger than Plymouth Rock, and high enough to get hurt if you fall. Look for the whale carved into the side of the rock. Turn right on Route 134 at the end of Hokum Rock Road. If there's time, make a short side trip to Hokum Rock Blueberry Farm by turning left here, where you can pick fresh blueberries in season (typically July to mid-August), just a short walk from the corner of Hokum Rock Road and Route 134. Ride the busy Route 134, or opt to ride the short bike path on the right, back to the Dennis Senior Center at the lights on Setucket Road.

MILES AND DIRECTIONS

0.0 This ride begins at the Dennis Senior Center on Route 134 and Setucket Road.

0.1 Turn left onto Setucket Road.

0.6 Turn right onto Old Bass River Road.

Dennis Bayside Beaches

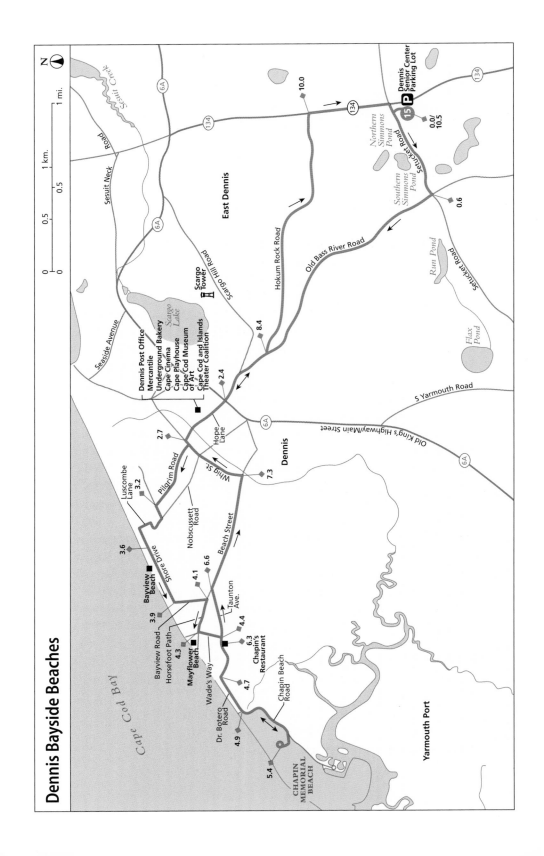

2.4 Cross Main Street (Route 6A) onto Hope Lane.

2.7 Turn left onto Whig Street.

2.8 Make an immediate right on Pilgrim Road.

3.2 Turn left on Nobscussett Road.

3.2 Turn right onto Luscombe Lane.

3.6 Continue straight on Shore Drive.

3.9 Turn left on Bayview Road with Bayview Beach on the right.

4.1 Turn right on Horsefoot Path.

4.3 Turn left on Wade's Way with Mayflower Beach on the right.

4.4 Turn right on Taunton Avenue.

4.7 Turn left on Dr. Botero Road.

4.9 Continue on Chapin Beach Road.

5.2 Bear right at the fork into Chapin Beach parking lot.

5.3 Turn right into the parking lot and circle around.

5.4 Turn left out of the parking lot and follow Chapin Beach Road, then Dr. Botero Road back to Taunton Avenue.

6.3 Pass Chapin's Restaurant and continue on Taunton Avenue.

6.6 Turn right on Beach Street.

7.3 Turn left on Whig Street.

7.7 Turn right on Hope Lane.

8.0 Cross Route 6A and continue on Old Bass River Road.

8.4 Turn left on Hokum Rock Road. Look for Hokum Rock.

10.0 Turn right on Route 134 (busy traffic) and opt to ride the sidewalk if desired.

10.4 Turn right on Setucket Road.

10.5 Turn left into the Dennis Senior Center to finish this ride.

RIDE INFORMATION

Local Events and Attractions

Hokum Rock Blueberry Farm: 1215 Route 134, East Dennis; (508) 385-2768. Open July to mid-August for blueberry picking.

Cape Playhouse: 820 Main St. (Route 6A), Dennis; (508) 385-3911. Experience live theater in the country's oldest professional summer theater. Even Marlon Brando acted here. Since 1927, the "Birthplace of the Stars" (which isn't far off).

Cape Cinema: 35 Hope Ln., Dennis; (508) 385-2503. Art deco theater from 1930, with better films not always shown in the bigger theaters.

Cape Cod Museum of Art: 60 Hope Ln., Dennis; (508) 385-4477. Works by outstanding artists associated with Cape Cod, Nantucket, and Martha's Vineyard, and Southeastern Massachusetts.

Josiah Dennis Manse and Old Schoolhouse: 77 Nobscusset Rd., Dennis; (508) 385-2232. Ride by it or take a tour of the home of the man after whom the town is named.

Restaurants

Chapin's: 85 Taunton Ave., Dennis; (508) 385-7000. Great for the family. Outdoor deck and bar in summer. Valet parking.

Gina's by the Sea: 134 Taunton Ave., Dennis; (508) 385-3213. Classic Italian, a timeless roadside beach restaurant. No reservations. Busy in summer, closed winter.

Village Tea Room at Borsari Gallery: 524 Main St. (Route 6A), Dennis; (508) 385-3434. It's oh, so civilized, with tea and scones, finger sandwiches, and desserts. They have an annual Downton Abbey Tea in November.

Scargo Cafe: 799 Main St. (Route 6A), Dennis; (508) 385-8200. The fireplace, bar, and porch in this historic Dennis sea captain's home are comfy, with a homey side and more modern bistro side depending on your mood.

Harvest Gallery Wine Bar: 776 Main St. (Route 6A), Dennis; (508) 385-2444. Artist and chef/owner Michael Pearson mixes food, wine, music, and art tastefully and deliciously.

Fin: 800 Main St., Dennis; (508) 385-2096. Fine dining in a romantic atmosphere. Downstairs cozy bar. Upstairs quieter dining. One of the best restaurants on Cape Cod.

The Mercantile: 766 Main St. (Route 6A), Dennis; (508) 385-3877. Sandwiches, coffee, deli.

The Underground Bakery: 780 Main St. (Route 6A), Dennis; (508) 385-4700. Excellent bakery and coffee.

Restrooms

Restrooms at the beaches are open in season. There are many restaurants in the area.

Oh No, It's Signal Hill!

This one is for climbers, with a couple of steep hills by Cape Cod standards, including one that might make you gasp, "Oh, no!" Start out in Brewster over a few gentle hills, and take a trip past Cape Cod Bay by Sesuit Harbor as a warm-up before the bigger climbs in Dennis. Opt for the very steep side trip up to Scargo Tower. Start and finish in Brewster, past many historical sites and lots of things to see and do. This ride has just about everything.

Start: Cape Cod Rail Trail parking lot at the intersection of Route 137 and Underpass Road in Brewster

Distance: 19.3 miles, double-ended lollipop

Approximate riding time: 1 to 2 hours, depending on stops

Best bike: Road bike

Terrain and surface type: Paved roads, many hilly sections, including two big climbs on Signal Hill Drive and Scargo Hill Road in Dennis, and an optional short, steep climb up to Scargo Tower from Scargo Hill Road; paved bike (multi-use) path, short section uphill on the CCRT

Traffic and hazards: Busy main roads, especially in summer, sand in the road, narrow roads with narrow shoulders, beach traffic and pedestrians walking to beach, other cyclists and pedestrians on the CCRT in Brewster, dangerous travel on Route 6A in Brewster and Dennis

Things to see: CCRT parking lot at intersection of Route 137 and Underpass Road, Brewster Herring Run, Stony Brook Gristmill, Sesuit Neck, Sesuit Harbor, Corporation Beach, Cape Playhouse, Cape Cinema, Cape Cod Museum of Art, Cape Cod and Islands Theater Coalition, Signal Hill, Scargo Hill, Scargo Lake, Scargo Tower, Brewster General Store, the Bramble Inn and Restaurant, Brewster Ice, CCRT

Map: *Arrow Street Atlas: Cape Cod including Martha's Vineyard & Nantucket*, p. 28

16

> **Getting there:** From Route 6 (Mid-Cape Highway), take exit 10. From points west and the Cape Cod Canal, turn left at the end of the exit ramp toward Brewster (north). From points east, turn right at the end of the ramp. Drive north on Route 124, then turn right on Tubman Road. Turn right on Route 137. The parking lot is a few yards ahead on the right, just after the crosswalk for the CCRT.
>
> **GPS coordinates:** N41 45.13' / W70 04.26'

THE RIDE

"Are there any hills on Cape Cod?" you ask. And the answer is yes or no, depending on where you're from. By Denver or San Francisco standards, the answer is probably no, because there just are not any long climbs for road cyclists on Cape Cod, anywhere. Yes, we have wind in our faces constantly, often very strong in hurricane season, or bitterly cold in winter, and we consider riding into the wind our Cape Cod version of hill training.

But possibly after a few rides along our flat beaches and shorelines, riders might want to challenge themselves on some short climbs. Hills are to be found in most of our towns, from Sandwich to Provincetown, with a surprising number on the Mid and Outer Cape, where one might think it would be flatter the farther one travels out on the sandy hook. The hills are everywhere if you know where to look. The Signal Hill climb is hidden around a short bend in the road and not easily seen from Route 6A. It's one of the steepest long hills on Cape Cod.

This ride starts in Brewster at the Cape Cod Rail Trail free parking lot across from Underpass Road where it intersects Route 137. In summer, say hello to Cap at his hotdog stand and grab a cold drink. If he runs out, try Ferretti's Market across the street on Underpass Road. Turn left on Route 137 from the parking lot and turn left at the fork on Tubman Road. Cross busy Route 124 and continue down Tubman Road, first settled in the 19th century by Irish immigrants named Tubman, whose descendants still live on this road. The road descends sharply then bends right and rolls out to Route 6A. After a very short stretch on this busy main road, turn left on Stony Brook Road.

This area of the Stony Brook Valley is the site of the first grist mill built by the Pilgrims east of Plymouth. It is also known as *Sauquatuckett*, a Nauset Native American sacred site because of the herring that run up the brook from Cape Cod Bay every spring. If it's April, look for seagulls circling around and squawking overhead as they dine on the herring. The Grist Mill offers an interesting tour and it's a great spot for a picnic or hike. Make a hard right just

past the small parking lot and continue on Stony Brook Road. The rest of this road is lined with Quaker history, with the Quaker Burial Ground on the right. Between 1657 and 1667 Quakers fled the town of Sandwich where they were being persecuted by the Puritans. This part of town was originally called Yarmouth, and then Harwich, and, by 1803, Brewster. Ride over the crest of the hill and cross A.P. Newcomb Road at a four-way stop sign. Continue past and up another hill or two and descend down to Route 6A.

Route 6A is a very busy road without enough room for both a cyclist and a car in the same narrow lane. Ride along this flat section into Dennis past Quivett Creek on the right, and turn right at the traffic light onto Bridge Street. Quivett Creek Marsh opens up on both sides of the road for a great view. Turn right onto Sesuit Neck Road past the marsh, through a residential neighborhood on Sesuit Neck, and approach Sesuit Harbor on the right. Tucked behind the marina on the right is the Sesuit Harbor Cafe (mile 6.2), my favorite place for a lobster roll on Cape Cod. Watch the boats going in and out of the harbor at umbrella-covered picnic tables for breakfast, lunch, or dinner (in season). Loop around the neighborhood on Harbor Road and peek through the beautiful seaside homes on the right for a view of Cape Cod Bay. Turn away from the bay on Stephen Phillips Road, past rural farmland and sheep, on Bridge

Brewster General Store, Main Street (Route 6A), Brewster

Oh No, It's Signal Hill!

Street, Mooncusser's Lane, and Winding Way, past the conservation land on the right. Head back to Route 6A via Old Town Lane and Sesuit Neck Road through farmland and cedar-forested neighborhood, and merge with Route 6A on the left. Travel only 0.2 mile, then turn off the highway onto Seaside Avenue on the right. Two optional right turns off Seaside Avenue lead to two beautiful small beaches, Howe's Beach (turn right on Howe's Street) and crescent-shaped Corporation Beach (turn right on Corporation Road). The curve in this natural bay at Corporation Beach forms tidal pools that heat up over the baked sand when the tide rolls out, making for a warm shallow-water bath.

Bike Shops

Rail Trail Bike & Kayak Shop, 302 Underpass Rd., Brewster, (508) 896-8200, railtrailbikeshop.com

Brewster Bike, 442 Underpass Rd., Brewster, (508) 896-8149, brewsterbike.com

There are restrooms and a concession stand here. Find the grassy area and search for hermit crabs. Or save it for when you're not in the mood to attack the hills.

Back on Route 6A, pass the Cape Playhouse on the right and turn right at the post office complex, where there is a group of restaurants all together. The Underground Bakery gets my vote for best coffee and baked goods, the Mercantile for sandwiches, and the Harvest Gallery Wine Bar for dinner and music. You could just stay here and then turn back, but with all that good eatin', you should probably head for the hills and burn a few calories. Get back onto 6A and cross the highway carefully turning left onto Signal Hill Drive, which bends right, and then . . . Oh no! It's only a half-mile stretch of uphill! But it's *steep*. At the top, turn left to get out to Old Bass River Road, where you can opt to descend, turn left on Route 6A, and climb Signal Hill again. For this ride, however, turn right on Scargo Hill Road, a nice steady climb that's not so steep. Over the top of Scargo Hill, descend a little, and opt to ride up a very steep, short hill to Scargo Tower, overlooking Scargo Lake and Cape Cod Bay. There is a spiral staircase inside for an even better view. Descend Scargo Hill Road back onto Route 6A and backtrack all the way to Stony Brook Road in Brewster. Pass the herring run and grist mill in Brewster and turn left just before the end of Stony Brook Road on Brier Lane, which quickly crosses Route 6A. Follow Brier to its end, turn right on Lower Road, and follow it all the way back to Route 6A.

Stop by the Brewster Store (locals call it the "general store") on the left for coffee, pastries, or a morning newspaper. They still sell Coca-Cola in glass bottles and there are rows of candy, gifts, and souvenirs upon entering through the 1866 front doors. Walk down the original church hardwood floors to the penny candy aisle and put a few quarters in the nickelodeon (player piano) and light the place up. Continue along 6A (you can ride the sidewalk here if you want) and pass the Bramble Inn and Restaurant on your left. For thirty years, award-winning chef/owner Ruth Manchester has offered the best gourmet dining experience on Cape Cod, in the French-windowed 1861 house with beautiful gardens and tastefully appointed bed-and-breakfast rooms upstairs.

Continue past Brewster Ice on the left, where Roland "Rolly" Bassett Sr., the "coolest man in town," hauled ice starting in 1949 with a chest freezer and a pickup truck. Turn right on Underpass Road for the final climb of this ride. Stop by Guapo's Shore Shack (in season) on the left for a drink or burrito and eat outside under the grass umbrellas on the deck. Turn right at the crosswalk just past Guapo's orange sign (immediately after the Brewster Post Office) onto the CCRT. Continue climbing the gentle hill past Stony Brook Elementary School, home of the Brewster Whitecaps Cape Cod Baseball League team. Pass the entrances to two bike shops on the left, first the Rail Trail Bike Shop and then Brewster Bike, then arrive at Route 137 with the parking lot ahead on your left. Well done! You can now tell your cycling friends you actually found some decent climbs on Cape Cod.

MILES AND DIRECTIONS

- **0.0** Start the ride at the Route 137 CCRT parking lot.
- **0.1** Turn left on Tubman Road.
- **0.7** Cross Route 124 (Harwich Road) and continue on Tubman Road.
- **1.6** Turn left onto Main Street (Route 6A).
- **1.8** Turn left onto Stony Brook Road.
- **2.4** Pass by Nauset Wampanoag sacred ground and view the Stony Brook Gristmill and the Herring Run.
- **2.5** Turn sharply right and continue on Stony Brook Road.
- **2.8** Pass the Quaker Burial Ground on the right.
- **3.1** Cross A.P. Newcomb Road.
- **4.1** Turn left on Route 6A.
- **5.2** Turn right on Bridge Street.
- **5.4** Turn right on Sesuit Neck Road.
- **6.3** Continue straight on Harbor Road.
- **6.5** Turn left on Stephen Phillips Road.
- **7.0** Turn right on Bridge Street.

Oh No, It's Signal Hill!

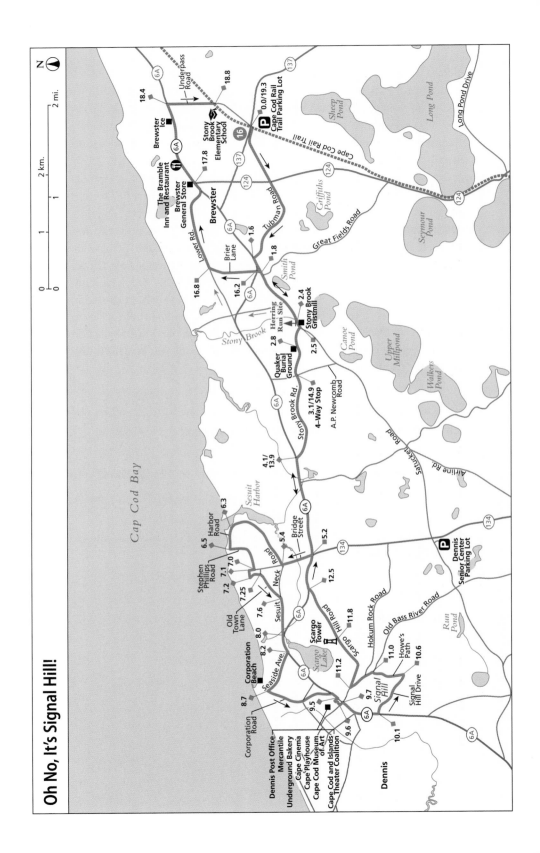

7.1   Turn left on Mooncusser's Lane.

7.2   Turn left on Winding Way.

7.2   Turn right on Old Town Lane.

7.6   Turn right on Sesuit Neck Road.

8.0   Turn right on Route 6A.

8.2   Turn right onto Seaside Avenue.

8.7   Turn left on Corporation Road.

9.4   Turn right on Route 6A.

9.5   Turn right into the Dennis Post Office parking lot.

9.6   Turn left on Hope Lane.

9.7   Turn right on Route 6A.

10.1   Turn left on to Signal Hill Drive. This is a steep climb.

10.6   Turn left on Howe's Path.

11.0   Turn left on Old Bass River Road.

11.2   Turn right on Scargo Hill Road. (Or descend Old Bass River Road, turn left on 6A, and do hill repeats on Signal Hill.)

11.8   Pass Scargo Tower on the left with option to climb the hill to the castle tower for a great view of Scargo Lake and Cape Cod Bay.

12.5   Turn right and merge onto Route 6A.

13.9   Turn right on Stony Brook Road.

14.9   Cross A.P. Newcomb Road and continue straight on Stony Brook Road.

15.5   Turn left at the stop sign and continue on Stony Brook Road.

16.2   Turn left onto Brier Lane.

16.2   Cross Route 6A and continue on Brier Lane.

16.8   Turn right on Lower Road.

17.7   Turn left on Route 6A.

17.8   The Brewster General Store is on your left.

18.4   Turn right onto Underpass Road.

18.8   Turn right onto the CCRT at the crosswalk.

19.3   Cross Route 137 and turn left into the CCRT parking lot.

RIDE INFORMATION

Local Events and Attractions

See also the listings under Ride 15, Dennis Bayside Beaches.

Lobster Roll Cruises: 356 Sesuit Neck Rd., Dennis; (508) 385-6134. Cruise Cape Cod Bay and have a sunset dinner.

Stony Brook Gristmill and Museum: 830 Stony Brook Rd., Brewster. The second mill built in Plymouth Colony, and the herring run made famous by naturalist writer John Hay in *The Run*.

Brewster General Store: 1935 Main St. (Route 6A), Brewster. Penny candy, nickelodeon, Cape Cod books and gifts, hard to find lamp parts. Coffee, donuts, pastries. Walk the creaky wooden floor along the main aisle where hundreds of young Cape Cod couples from long ago walked to say their vows. Say "I do" to the fresh-baked donuts at the end of the aisle.

Cap's Hot Dogs: The CCRT parking lot, Route 137 and Underpass Road, Brewster (start/finish of this ride). Hope he never retires, because the hot dog stand with cold drinks sure hits the spot after a hot summer day of riding.

Restaurants

See also the listings under Ride 15, Dennis Bayside Beaches.

Marshside Restaurant: 28 Bridge St., East Dennis; (508) 385-4010. Great views of Quivett Marsh and consistently good food.

Sesuit Harbor Cafe: 357 Sesuit Neck Rd., Dennis; (508) 385-6134. My favorite place to have a lobster roll on a sunny day, with outdoor picnic table dining by Sesuit Harbor.

Bramble Inn and Restaurant: 2019 Main St. (Route 6A), Brewster; (508) 896-7644. Perhaps the best restaurant on Cape Cod, where multiple award-winning chef Ruth Manchester rules the roost and husband Cliff entertains. Cozy, well-appointed rooms upstairs.

Guapo's Shore Shack: 239 Underpass Rd., Brewster; (508) 896-3338. Eat under the grass umbrellas on the outdoor deck on the CCRT (seasonal).

Breakwater Fish & Lobster: 235 Underpass Rd., Brewster; (508) 896-7080. Eat outside on a picnic table (there aren't many) or take-out. Great local fresh fish and lobster market next to the CCRT.

Restrooms

There are restrooms at the many restaurants and beaches (in-season) along this route. There are no restrooms at the parking area at the start/finish of this ride, but Guapo's on Underpass Road (mile 18.7) has restrooms.

Cape Cod Rail Trail, South Dennis to Nickerson State Park

The Cape Cod Rail Trail runs a total of 22 miles from South Dennis to Wellfleet. This ride takes you only as far as Nickerson State Park in Brewster and back. It's a beautiful paved path past cranberry bogs, estuary, and kettle ponds and through forest, without having to deal with vehicle traffic, except at the many crosswalks. It can be combined with Ride 18 to Wellfleet, or Ride 23 to Chatham via the Harwich Bike Rotary on the Old Colony Rail Trail. This is a great ride for children and families, fairly flat with only gradual climbs and descents.

Start: CCRT parking lot, Route 134, South Dennis

Distance: 21.2 miles, out-and-back

Approximate riding time: 1.5 to 2 hours

Best bike: Road bike, any smooth-tired bike

Terrain and surface type: Paved multi-use path, very gentle hills, crosswalks across busy roads

Traffic and hazards: Many crosswalks across busy roads, stop signs, rail trail traffic, walkers, runners, in-line skaters, other cyclists, skateboarders, occasional horseback riders, small children, animals (deer, coyotes, foxes, squirrels, dogs, low-flying catbirds), some roots (spoke-breakers), bicycle rotary in Harwich, tunnel just before rotary in Harwich

Things to see: Herring River Estuary, active cranberry bogs, Harwich bike rotary and tunnel, intersection with Old Colony Rail Trail, Hinckley's Pond, Long Pond, Seymour Pond, Sheep Pond, Route 137 and Underpass Road parking lot (Cap's hot dogs and cold drinks), Stony Brook Elementary School and tennis courts, Nickerson State Park

Map: *Arrow Street Atlas: Cape Cod including Martha's Vineyard & Nantucket*, p. 41

Getting there: From Route 6 (Mid-Cape Highway), take exit 9A to South Dennis and drive south on Route 134 past Patriot Square Shopping

Center, through two traffic lights, then look for the parking lot entrance to Nickerson State Park CCRT on the left. If you arrive at the traffic light for Lower County Road, you just missed it.

GPS coordinates: N41 41.40' / W70 09.05'

THE RIDE

Running 22 miles to South Wellfleet, the Cape Cod Rail Trail (CCRT) official start is currently on Route 134 in South Dennis, with free parking, restrooms, a bike shop with attached strip mall and parking, and nearby restaurants, grocery stores, and cinema at Patriot Square shopping plaza and Ring Brothers Marketplace. Route 134 is a busy road, but you can leave the traffic behind on this multi-use trail, one of the best bikeways in the United States. It's a multi-use, smooth paved path that has undergone many improvements in the past several years since its original construction from 1978–80 (Dennis to Orleans) and completion to South Wellfleet in 1995. Whether cycling tourist, mountain biker, road cyclist, fat tire biker, or cyclocross rider, or traveling with small children, large groups, or anything in between, the CCRT is an easy way to explore much of the beauty of Cape Cod without having to ride alongside motor vehicles.

This ride maps the first half of the CCRT from South Dennis (with plenty of free parking) to Nickerson State Park in East Brewster. There are mileage markers printed at every 0.1 mile (painted yellow on the asphalt trail) that start in South Dennis and finish in Wellfleet to help give a sense of direction and location. But as an option, start this ride at Nickerson State Park or at any number of other parking spots along the way. There are several great ways to organize a CCRT ride, depending on what activities are the focus of your ride.

Rules for the CCRT are posted at the start of this ride and are worth a read. Massachusetts law also requires riders to stop at all crosswalks and walk their bikes, although cars usually stop for riders who blow past the stop signs.

Start this ride at the main parking lot in South Dennis and proceed through an oak- and pine-covered straightaway. The trail is straight and flat here, crossing Gage's Way, busy Great Western Road, and then Depot Street (bike trail parking available here) into West Harwich and the massive Herring River Estuary, also known as Bell's Neck Conservation Area. It's beautiful here, and you first get the sense of leaving the traffic behind and getting out into nature. This may be the prettiest part of the CCRT, with swans craning their necks in the fresh water off to the right in West Reservoir, which feeds the Herring River and flows out to Nantucket Sound. Opt to turn right onto Bell's Neck Road at mile 1.9 to explore this 250-acre estuary maintained by the Harwich

Through the bike tunnel on the Cape Cod Rail Trail, Brewster

Conservation Trust. It's a dirt road, though, so if you're riding a road bike you'll need good bike handling skills to navigate the softer sections. Fatter tires definitely help here, and cyclocross, mountain, or fat tire bikes are great to explore the marsh trails. Try to spot the elusive black-crowned night heron in spring or summer, or watch the herring run upstream at a ladder built at the west trailhead in April. There are a number of hiking trails in this little-known area of Cape Cod, and maps are available online or at trailheads.

Cape Cod Rail Trail, South Dennis to Nickerson State Park

Next, cross Great Western Road again and ride along an active cranberry bog to your left. Cross Lothrop Avenue and ride to the Harwich Bike Rotary, which connects the CCRT with the Old Colony Rail Trail (OCRT; Ride 23) through Harwich Center to Chatham. Bear right into the rotary and be sure to yield to bicycle traffic in the rotary, going around the rotary to stay on the CCRT (second right around the rotary). Bear left past the entrance to the OCRT toward Brewster and points north. There are park benches and maps of both trails inside the rotary, but no restrooms. Continue along this stretch with another active cranberry bog to the left, and hiking trail to the right, and cross Old Queen Anne Road. Cross over the highway on the "Shirley Gomes Bridge" (yet to be officially named for the Harwich native and state representative who

Directions on the Cape Cod Rail Trail, Nickerson State Park, Brewster

pressed the state for this bridge due to the concerns about public safety) and cross Headwaters Drive past another active cranberry bog on the right as the trail passes through a narrow section of land between the bog and Hinckley's Pond to the left. Cross busy Route 124 past the newly reopened and iconic Pleasant Lake General Store on the left, which was once a train stop and a general store with post office dating back to the 1850s. Ride through a wooded section to Long Pond on your right, where motorboats pull water skiers around and sailboats cruise all summer. The beaches off to the right at Long Pond are private and belong to the houses to the left. Cross 124 again and pass Seymour Pond on the left, where there is a public freshwater beach very popular among cyclists in summer (bike racks and porta-potty available).

Cross Route 124 a fourth time into Brewster and start a long and gradual uphill ride through oak and pine forest. There is a free parking lot on the left here, and a great freshwater pond farther up the trail at the end of Fisherman's Landing Road (turn right and ride down the steep hill to Sheep Pond). Cross Fisherman's Landing Road and continue uphill to Route 137, where there is another free parking lot on the right. Say hello to Cap and get

Bike Shops

Barbara's Bike & Sport Equipment, 430 Route 134, South Dennis, (508) 760-4723, barbsbikeshop.com
Dennis Cycle Center, 249 Great Western Rd., South Dennis, (508) 398-0011, denniscyclecenter.com
Barb's Bike Rentals, 3430 Route 6A, Nickerson State Park, Brewster, (508) 896-7231, barbsbikeshop.com
Rail Trail Bike & Kayak Shop, 302 Underpass Rd., Brewster, (508) 896-8200, railtrailbikeshop.com
Brewster Bike, 442 Underpass Rd., Brewster, (508) 896-8149, brewsterbike.com

a hot dog or cold drink if it's summer. Ferretti's Market is at the corner of Route 137 and Underpass Road across the street and open year-round if it's winter. Cross Route 137 and descend past Brewster Bike on the right, cross the Stony Brook Elementary School (public tennis courts on the right), and pass Rail Trail Kayak & Bike (on the right). At the intersection with Underpass Road, there are a post office and three places to eat, at least one open year-round. Ride through the oak canopy past Underpass Road, ride past a horse farm and stables on the left, then pass the Ocean Edge Golf Course. At mile 9.1, pass an entrance to the golf course and Ocean Edge residential area that is opposite Thad Ellis Road. Thad Ellis Road connects riders quickly to Route 6A and has a sign incorrectly labeled as "Brewster Center" (it's actually Foster Square, and Brewster "Center" is about a mile west of here, considered by most as the division between East and West Brewster with the hub of activity at the Brewster Store). But there are several places to refuel along this part of Route 6A, with a convenience store, pizza, ice cream, a few restaurants, bookstore, hardware store, chocolatier, health food store, and gas station (see Ride 21, Beach Fatty Food Tour).

Continue through the bike tunnel under Ocean Edge ahead (children must scream inside the tunnel for the echo effect), passing by beach plum, blackberry, and grapes that park rangers cut back every year to prevent rapid overgrowth. In September, the smell of grapes is very strong along this stretch, and it's a slight downhill ride that is heavily wooded and fragrant. Pass a large pond barely visible on the right and then a smaller one on the left, and finally a farm on the left where a rooster is constantly crowing. After the farm to the left, cross at Millstone Road cautiously. Judging by the number of skid marks at Millstone Road, cyclists often miss the stop sign here. Be sure to stop and walk bicycles across here as with all crosswalks. Pass through the tall oaks on the other side of Millstone Road and watch out for another root section before mile 10. The tree cover starts to change to white pine as the trail passes the bike rental parking lot on the left (still free). Turn right after a blind corner into the Nickerson State Park main parking lot ($5 parking fee for Rail Trail users).

Enjoy the aroma of baked pine needles in summer. Nickerson State Park, once the private game reserve of the Nickerson family, is one of my favorite places on Cape Cod, and truly one of my favorite places in the world, one I keep coming back to year after year. The CCRT continues to Wellfleet from here (Ride 18), but it's the turnaround point for this ride. Restrooms are available here, as well as picnic tables and bike racks. There is a nearby park store stocked with food, drink, and other essentials (seasonal). The entrance gate at the opposite end of the parking lot is staffed with park rangers who can answer any questions. Public transportation including a bus with a bike rack is also available here. If you're not continuing on to Wellfleet, turn around and retrace your route back to the start.

MILES AND DIRECTIONS

0.0 Start the ride at the CCRT, Route 134, South Dennis parking lot.

0.7 Cross Gage's Way at the crosswalk.

0.8 Cross Great Western Road.

1.3 Cross Depot Street.

1.5 Stop to view the swans in the West reservoir of the Herring River Estuary.

1.9 Cross Bell's Neck Road (dirt road).

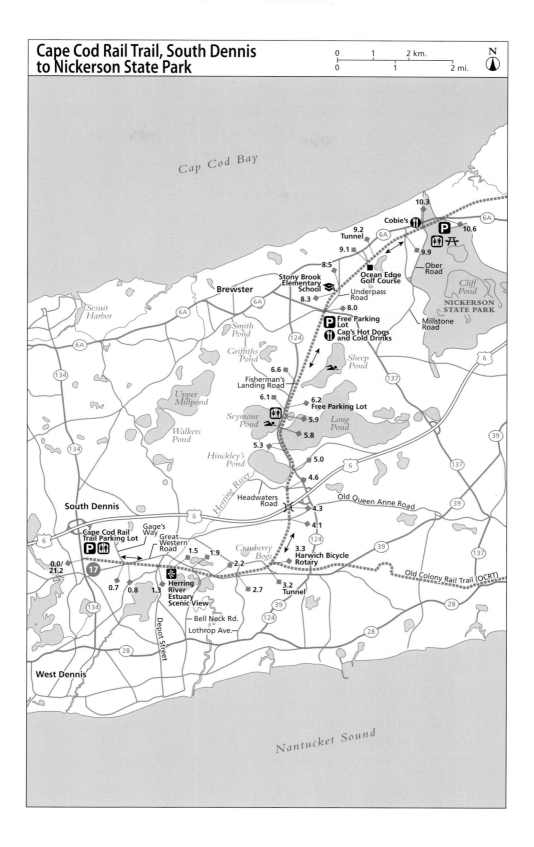

Cape Cod Rail Trail, South Dennis
to Nickerson State Park

0   1   2 km.
0   1   2 mi.

N

Cap Cod Bay

10.3

Cobie's
9.2
Tunnel
9.1

6A

P   10.6

9.9

Ober
Road

8.5

Stony Brook
Elementary
School
8.3

Ocean Edge
Golf Course

Underpass
Road

8.0

*Cliff
Pond*

NICKERSON
STATE PARK

Brewster

6A

P Free Parking
Lot
Cap's Hot Dogs
and Cold Drinks

Millstone
Road

6

*Sesuit
Harbor*

6A

124

*Smith
Pond*

*Sheep
Pond*

*Griffiths
Pond*

6.6

137

6A

Fisherman's
Landing Road

6.1   6.2
Free Parking Lot

5.9

134

*Upper
Millpond*

*Seymour
Pond*

*Long
Pond*

5.8

*Walkers
Pond*

5.3

39

*Hinckley's
Pond*

5.0

134

Herring River

4.6

*Headwaters
Road*

Old Queen Anne Road

6

137

4.3

South Dennis

6

4.1

39

**Cape Cod Rail
Trail Parking Lot**

P

Gage's
Way
Great
Western
Road

1.5 1.9

*Cranberry
Bogs*

3.3
Harwich Bicycle
Rotary

124

39

137

0.0/
21.2

17

2.2

Old Colony Rail Trail (OCRT)

0.7 0.8 1.3

Herring
River
Estuary
Scenic View

2.7

3.2
Tunnel

39

28

134

Bell Neck Rd.
Lothrop Ave.

124

28

Depot Street

28

West Dennis

Nantucket Sound

2.2 Cross Great Western Road.

2.7 Cross Lothrop Avenue.

3.2 Ride through the tunnel (under Main Street).

3.3 Ride around bike rotary (stay to the right) and exit rotary toward Wellfleet.

4.1 Cross Old Queen Anne Road.

4.3 Ride the Rail Trail Bridge over Route 6.

4.6 Cross Headwaters Drive.

5.0 Cross Route 124 (Pleasant Lake Avenue).

5.3 Cross Sequattom Road.

5.8 Cross Route 124.

5.9 Enter Brewster and pass Seymour Pond (swimming). There are toilets and bike racks.

6.1 Cross Route 124.

6.2 Pass a free parking lot on the left.

6.6 Cross Fisherman's Landing Road (Sheep Pond swimming area is down the hill to the right).

8.0 Cross Route 137 (Long Pond Road). There is another free parking lot here.

8.3 Cross Stony Brook Elementary School entrance road.

8.5 Cross Underpass Road.

9.1 Pass Thad Ellis Road on the left and Ocean Edge Golf Course on the right.

9.2 Ride through the tunnel.

9.9 Cross Millstone Road carefully.

10.3 Pass Cobie's on the left and cross Ober Road (cars occasionally cross Rail Trail).

10.6 Arrive at Nickerson State Park main parking lot. Turn around and return the way you came.

21.2 Arrive back at the start at the CCRT parking lot in South Dennis.

RIDE INFORMATION

Local Events and Attractions
Cape Cod Rep Theater: 3299 Main St. (Route 6A), Brewster; (508) 896-1888; caperep.org. Nestled in the woods opposite Nickerson State Park, with indoor

(shows year-round) and outdoor theater, with shows for children and adults. This is the only outdoor theater on Cape Cod, completely renovated in 2013.

Crosby Landing Beach: At the end of Crosby Lane, past the Crosby Mansion. Accessible by crossing Route 6A (just before the main parking lot at Nickerson State Park) at a crosswalk. Use caution if crossing Route 6A here, as cars do not always stop for pedestrians (Massachusetts law requires vehicles to stop at crosswalks).

Linnell Landing Beach: At the end of Linnell Landing Road, off Route 6A opposite Cobie's, accessible from mile 10.3 of this ride, via a paved path (Ober Road). Cross at the crosswalk.

Restaurants

See Ride 21 for a list of restaurants also nearby.

Ring Brothers Marketplace: 485 Route 134, South Dennis; (508) 394-2244. On the pricey side, but a great place to refuel, with a huge salad bar and gourmet food bars around the perimeter. Premade frozen or fresh meals, no need to cook. Extensive beer selection, very good wine selection.

Pleasant Lake General Store: 403 Pleasant Lake Ave, Harwich; (508) 430-0020. Closed for two years, it re-opened in late 2014. Local Flavor Lunch & Bagel (formerly on Underpass Rd. in Brewster) has taken over, with excellent sandwiches for riders. Try the panini. Coffee, cold drinks, lobster rolls. Breakfast and lunch, open 7 days. Summer hours 7–5.

Cobie's: 3260 Main St. (Route 6A), Brewster; (508) 896-7021. This is the consummate Cape Cod clam shack, since 1948, with fried delights and ice cream, covered picnic table outdoor seating, and more parking in back. At mile 10.3 of this ride.

Peddler's Bistro: 67 Thad Ellis Rd., Brewster; (508) 896-9300; peddlersrestaurant.com. At mile 9.1 of this ride. No reservations, no credit cards (they take American Express), French cuisine in a place that looks somewhat deserted and covered with an overgrowth of shrubs. Inside, however, *c'est magnifique,* with candlelit tables and crisp white linens in an intimate, romantic setting. It's an authentic French family country bistro, with chef/husband Alain Hasson doing the cooking and wife Beth serving. Excellent French cuisine from a trained Provence chef.

Restrooms

There are restrooms at the start in South Dennis and at the turnaround point of this ride at Nickerson State Park. Porta-potty at the Pleasant Lake General Store. There is also a porta-potty at Seymour Pond (mile 5.9).

Cape Cod Rail Trail, Nickerson State Park to Wellfleet

This beautiful ride begins at Nickerson State Park in Brewster and turns around in Wellfleet, and can be combined with Ride 17 to complete the length of the 22-mile Cape Cod Rail Trail, a 44-mile round trip from South Dennis. Rides 19-22 all start from points along the CCRT or Nickerson State Park in Brewster, and Rides 27-30 and 32 from points along the CCRT in Orleans, Eastham, and Wellfleet. Ride 31 does not branch off the CCRT, but Ride 30 connects to Ride 31 from the CCRT. This is another great ride for children with families, and fairly flat, with only gradual slopes up or down. The tunnels under Route 6A in Brewster and Route 6 in Eastham are the steepest parts of the trail, and smaller children will need supervision. This ride could be called the Gateway to the Outer Cape and Cape Cod National Seashore.

Start: Nickerson State Park main parking lot, Route 6A, Brewster

Distance: 23.0 miles, out-and-back

Approximate riding time: 2 to 3 hours

Best bike: Road bike, hybrid

Terrain and surface type: Generally smooth paved path; very gentle hills suitable for children; paved crosswalks across busy roads; paved main roads and back roads

Traffic and hazards: Narrow blind tunnels (in Brewster and Eastham), many crosswalks at busy roads, stop signs, walkers, runners, in-line skaters, other cyclists, skateboarders, occasional horseback riders, small children, those traveling on the left (breaking CCRT Rule 4), animals (deer, coyotes, foxes, dogs with leashes, squirrels, low flying catbirds), roots (spoke-breakers)

Things to see: Namskaket Creek, Orleans Center, Boat Meadow Salt Marsh, kettle ponds (with swimming and fishing), Cape Cod National Seashore (Salt Pond Visitor Center via Locust Road, Eastham), Marconi Beach, Marconi Wireless Station, access to points north

Map: *Arrow Street Atlas: Cape Cod including Martha's Vineyard & Nantucket*, p. 30

Getting there: By car (from Boston, New York, Cape Cod Canal, and points west): Take Route 6 to exit 11 and head north to Brewster on Route 137N. Take a right on Millstone Road and follow to end. Take a right on Route 6A. Nickerson State Park entrance is on the right. **From points on Outer Cape Cod east of Orleans:** Take Route 6 to exit 12 and take a right on Route 6A (west) at the end of the ramp. Enter Brewster and look for entrance signs to Nickerson State Park.

GPS coordinates: N41 46.51' / W70 01.93'

THE RIDE

At the entrance to Nickerson State Park, riders are at a major hub of all types of cycling on Cape Cod. From this parking lot there are a number of mountain bike trails (see Rides 19 and 20), access to Cape Cod Bay for fat bike riding via Linnell Landing Road (see Ride 21), and a paved bike path great for kids, next to a playground (see Ride 22). If it's Sunday morning, the Cape Cod Cycling Club will whizz by the entrance to this ride around 8:30 a.m. on its way to the Hot Chocolate Sparrow in Orleans to pick up other riders at 9 a.m. They may be a group of four to five riders in winter to a large peloton of thirty or more riders in summer. Join them if you're looking for a fast group ride that typically averages over 20 mph. For the rest of us, this second leg of the Cape Cod Rail Trail (CCRT) is not at all a race. This is vacation and relaxation, with salt air, the scent of pine, and alternating sun and shade for the next 23 miles. Or it is family time, with the kids having one of the biggest adventures of their lives. You will, too.

From the main parking lot adjacent to the Main Entrance (Contact Station) on Route 6A, there is immediate access to the CCRT from the parking lot (northwest corner of lot). This ride first travels east to Orleans Center, and then north through Eastham to South Wellfleet within the boundaries of the Cape Cod National Seashore. It's a gorgeous stretch that takes riders past several kettle ponds and marshes, through thick forest, past coves and creeks, and through the vast area of pristine and protected national park, with its extensive network of sandy fire roads through oak and scrub pine, past miles and miles of sandy beaches that are easily accessible from several points along this trail.

From the main parking lot, the beginning of this ride is at the far end of the lot (northwest corner). Large maps of the park and trails are posted next

Cape Cod Rail Trail turnaround point, Lecount Hollow Road, Wellfleet

to the CCRT entrance on a covered display board next to picnic tables, bike racks, and restrooms. The "Contact Station" (main entrance) has maps, and the friendly park rangers can answer any questions. A very short paved path from the parking lot takes you to the CCRT. Turn right toward Wellfleet, descending immediately into a fairly steep left turn through the tunnel under Route 6A. Bear right out of the tunnel and ride slowly over this section, which is lined with bumps from roots underneath the trail.

Cross and continue past Mitchell Lane and pass an abandoned cranberry bog through the pine and oak forest. Cross Seaview Road and descend slightly into the Namskaket Creek Marsh area, the boundary between Brewster and Orleans. There is a bike rest area on the left with a bench and bike parking (no restrooms). Catch a sunset through the trees here, or just enjoy a panoramic view of a large Cape Cod salt marsh, with wildlife including deer, coyotes, foxes, herons, and other shorebirds. Marshes like this are among the most productive habitats in the world, even when you don't see much going on.

From Namskaket Creek, the trail ascends slightly and appears to come to an end at a residential neighborhood. Continue straight ahead through the neighborhood on Salty Ridge Road, which turns left 90 degrees at mile 1.6 and finally ends at West Road. Turn right onto West Road. It's a busy road, but the CCRT continues along a wide shoulder with ample markings. Please stay to the right. Motorists are very used to bicycle traffic here, but it's a bit scary for smaller children and presents a real problem for children who are wobbly, just inches away from passing cars. Continue on West Road on the bridge over Route 6, and then turn left at the crosswalk at the bottom of the overpass. There is a small paved area with enough room for a family of bicycles at the end of the crosswalk. Walk bikes across and continue on the paved path at the

Bike Shops

Barb's Bike Rentals, 3430 Route 6A, Nickerson State Park, Brewster, (508) 896-7231, barbsbikeshop.com

Orleans Cycle, 26 Main St., Orleans, (508) 255-9115, orleanscycle.com

Idle Times Bike Shop, 29 Main St., Orleans, (508) 240-1122, idletimes bikes.com

Mike's Bike Trail Rentals, 14 Canal Rd., Orleans, (508) 240-1791, cape escapeadventures.com

Idle Times Bike Shop, 4550 Route 6, Eastham, (508) 255-8281, idletimes bikes.com

Little Capistrano Bike Shop, 30 Salt Pond Rd., Eastham, (508) 255-6515, littlecapistranobikeshop.com

Little Capistrano Bike Shop, 1446 Route 6, Wellfleet, (508) 349-2363, littlecapistranobikeshop.com

end of the crosswalk to Orleans Center. Pass the old train depot (covered area on the right), and take a rest or shop Main Street. There is ample bike parking all around, at the bike shops, at the Hot Chocolate Sparrow across the street from the train depot, and in Depot Square Public Parking Lot adjacent to the trail. You can stop and play in Orleans and then turn around for a shorter ride, or continue on to Eastham and Wellfleet.

Cross busy Main Street and ride the gentle downward slope that starts to bend north here toward Eastham. Take care at the crosswalks here as you approach Route 6, then ride over the highway and enjoy the view of traffic below at the Eastham Rotary to the right.

Going over the bridge, the trail flattens out and stays straight for a very long stretch. Pass Boat Meadow Marsh on the left and right, cross Governor Prence Road and Bridge Road, and continue past a few kettle ponds after crossing Samoset Road. At 5.9 miles (distance from Nickerson State Park, not CCRT mileage markers), cross Locust Road with the option to turn right to connect to the Salt Pond Visitor's Center at Cape Cod National Seashore and the Nauset Trail (Ride 30) via Old State Road and the Little Capistrano Bike Shop. Continue past Locust and cross Kingsbury Beach Road, then descend slowly into a blind tunnel under Route 6. The tunnel is visible from both the Kingsbury Beach Road crosswalk and the Old Orchard Road crosswalk, which lie on both sides of the tunnel. But children or people with poor bike-handling skills should walk their bikes down the hill from either crosswalk so they don't lose control. There is a center line painted in the tunnel that should never be crossed, of course, and lots of signage on both sides. But crashes still happen, so use caution.

Pass Arnold's Restaurant on the left after the crosswalk on Old Orchard Road, and then continue on a long straightaway that crosses Brackett and Nauset Roads. Descend gradually for 2 miles past a Cape Cod National Sea-shore forest on the right. Just past a small pond on the right, the path starts to incline slightly for a mile and then crosses Marconi Beach Road. There is the option to turn right here to explore Marconi Beach and Marconi Wireless Station, site of the first trans-Atlantic wireless communication between the US and England in 1903. The station is more of a platform with unobstructed views of the Atlantic Ocean atop a 40-foot cliff above the outer beach, and you can stand there and put most of America behind you. Marine radio trans-missions at Marconi Station included news and telegrams for passengers of the shipwrecked *Lusitania*, distress calls from the *Titanic* in 1912, and a mes-sage between President Roosevelt and King Edward VII in 1903. The station closed in 1917.

Marconi Beach is at a separate location south of the station, and has a hiking trail, the Atlantic White Cedar Swamp Trail. The 1.5-mile trail has white cedar and red maple mixed in with scrub oak and pine, all mixed in with the low-ground heath shrub. Hikers forget they're close to a vast expanse of ocean beach as they hike through the swampy trail on boardwalk and single-track. The optional ride to either the beach or the station (take the right fork to the beach) adds a few miles but is well worth it.

Cross Marconi Beach Road and descend past one of the narrowest parts of the Cape Cod peninsula at Blackfish Creek to the parking lot in South Wellfleet. The South Wellfleet General Store, a bike shop, a small bakery, and a French restaurant and bakery are all here. The P.B. Boulangerie on Lecount Hollow Road around the corner from the parking lot is not to be missed. Sample the award-winning food at the bakery, sit by the outdoor fire pit in the cooler shoulder seasons, close your eyes, listen to the steady stream of French music and radio, and pretend you're riding in Le Tour de France. Then wake up and turn around to retrace your pedaling all the way back to Brewster. There is the option to connect to other rides from the parking lot here (see Rides 29 and 32), if your legs will carry you.

MILES AND DIRECTIONS

0.0   Start the ride at Nickerson State Park main parking lot.

0.05 Turn right toward Wellfleet out of main parking lot.

0.1   Ride through the tunnel under Route 6A.

0.2   Cross Mitchell Lane.

0.8   Cross Seaview Road.

1.1   Pass Namskaket Creek bike rest area (bike rack, no restrooms).

1.5   The paved bike path ends. Continue on Salty Ridge Road.

1.6   Follow Salty Ridge Road as it bends left 90 degrees.

1.7   Turn right on West Road (heavy traffic). Beware of pedestrians and cyclists on the wrong side of the road.

1.8   Ride over Route 6.

1.9   Turn left at the crosswalk onto the paved bike trail.

2.5   Pass Depot Square in Orleans Center.

2.6   Cross Main Street.

2.9   Cross Locust Road with caution.

3.0   Cross Jones Road, then Canal Road.

3.2   Ride over Route 6 and Rock Harbor Road on the Rail Trail bridge.

4.5   Cross Governor Prence Road.

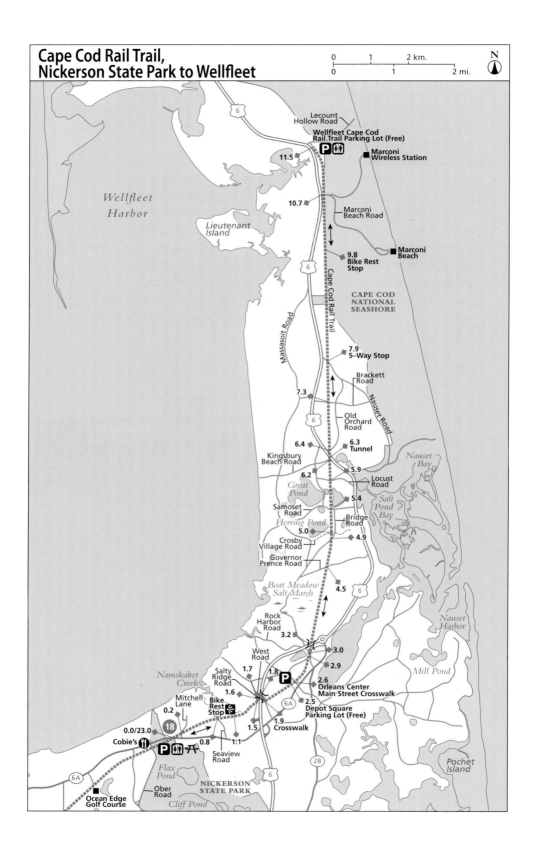

0   1   2 km.
0   1   2 mi.

Lecount
Hollow Road

Wellfleet Cape Cod
Rail Trail Parking Lot (Free)

P

11.5

Marconi
Wireless Station

10.7

Marconi
Beach Road

Wellfleet
Harbor

Lieutenant
Island

9.8
Bike Rest
Stop

Marconi
Beach

Massasoit Road

Cape Cod Rail Trail

CAPE COD
NATIONAL
SEASHORE

7.9
5–Way Stop

Brackett
Road

Nauset Road

7.3

Old
Orchard
Road

Nauset
Bay

6.4

6.3
Tunnel

Kingsbury
Beach Road

5.9

Locust
Road

Salt
Pond
Bay

6.2

Great
Pond

Samoset
Road

5.4

Herring Pond

Bridge
Road

5.0

4.9

Crosby
Village Road

Governor
Prence Road

Boat Meadow
Salt Marsh

4.5

Nauset
Harbor

Rock
Harbor
Road

3.2

3.0

West
Road

2.9

Mill Pond

1.7

1.8

P

2.6
Orleans Center
Main Street Crosswalk

Namskaket
Creek

Salty
Ridge
Road

1.6

2.5
Depot Square
Parking Lot (Free)

Mitchell
Lane

0.2

Bike
Rest
Stop

1.5

1.9
Crosswalk

0.0/23.0

18

Cobie's

0.8

1:1

Seaview
Road

P

Flax
Pond

Ober
Road

NICKERSON
STATE PARK

Ocean Edge
Golf Course

Cliff Pond

Pochet
Island

4.9   Cross Bridge Road.

5.0   Cross Crosby Village Road (dirt road).

5.4   Cross Samoset Road.

5.9   Cross Locust Road (or turn right to connect to Cape Cod National Seashore, Salt Pond Visitor Center, and Coast Guard Beach via Salt Pond Road).

6.2   Cross Kingsbury Beach Road.

6.3   Ride through the tunnel under Route 6 with caution!

6.4   Cross Old Orchard Road.

7.3   Cross Brackett Road.

7.9   Cross Nauset Road at the five-way stop.

9.8   Stop for a scenic view at the bike rest stop (no restrooms).

10.7 Cross Marconi Beach Road and the entrance to Marconi Wireless Station and Marconi Beach.

11.5 Arrive at the Wellfleet CCRT parking lot (free) on Lecount Hollow Road. Return to start.

23.0 Arrive back at the Nickerson State Park parking lot.

RIDE INFORMATION

Local Events and Attractions
See also the listings under Ride 17.
Marconi Wireless Station and Beach: Turn right at mile 10.7 of this ride to see the site of the first wireless trans-Atlantic communications by Guglielmo Marconi. The *Titanic* sent distress calls to this station, to no avail.
Maguire's Landing Beach: At the end of Lecount Hollow Road.

Restaurants
See also Ride 17 and Ride 21 for more restaurant suggestions.
Hot Chocolate Sparrow: 5 Old Colony Way, Orleans; (508) 240-2230; hot chocolatesparrow.com. A weekly Sunday pit stop for a fast group bike ride out of Dennis; also a hub for cycling on the Outer Cape. Homemade chocolate, yes, but also coffee, sandwiches, ice cream, and free wireless.
Rock Harbor Grill: 18 Old Colony Way, Orleans; (508) 255-3350. Tasty entrees, brick oven pizza, and tapas menu, with big screen TV at the fun bar. A newcomer that's crowded because it's excellent.
P.B. Boulangerie and Bistro: 15 Lecount Hollow Rd., Wellfleet; (508) 349-1600. At the end of the CCRT, chef Phillipe Rispoli creates French deliciousness

served by a French-speaking staff. The attached bakery has lines out the door, with cyclists in full kit parked by the fire pit. The bike racks, with French music and deck dining, make it a cyclist's destination.

Van Rensselaer's Restaurant and Raw Bar: 1019 Route 6, Wellfleet; (508) 349-2127. Always busy, this seasonal family-owned restaurant has served consistently excellent food for more than forty-five years. Fresh locally caught seafood, great menu selection.

Restrooms

There are restrooms at the start/finish and turnaround point of this ride. There is a porta-potty at Depot Square in Orleans Center (mile 2.5) and one at Brackett Road in Eastham (mile 7.3).

Cliff Pond Killer Loop

This is a difficult mountain bike ride on unmarked trails through the oak and pine forests of Nickerson State Park. Exceeding lactate threshold, red-lining, or bonking (use your favorite term) should be no problem as you circle Cliff Pond on the single-track and fire road trails, riding through the nether regions of the park. Find a friend to ride with who knows the trails; you'll have a good story to share after this ride. Then cool off in Cliff Pond after you're done. Killer ride!

Start: Nickerson State Park, Fisherman's Landing parking lot

Distance: 7.5-mile loop

Approximate riding time: 1 to 2 hours

Best bike: Mountain bike, fat tire bike

Terrain and surface type: Single track, sandy bridle paths, dirt roads, some paved path and road

Traffic and hazards: Hikers, horseback riders, other mountain bikers, branches, roots, rocks, steep sections near Cliff Pond, vehicle traffic on park roads and parking lots

Things to see: Deer Park Road, Fisherman's Landing at Cliff Pond, Grassy Nook Pond, Little Cliff Pond, Eel Pond, Higgins Pond, Flax Pond

Map: *Arrow Street Atlas: Cape Cod including Martha's Vineyard & Nantucket*, p. 30

Getting there: From Route 6 (Mid-Cape Highway) and points west and the Cape Cod Canal: Take exit 12 and turn left at the end of the exit ramp on Route 6A. **From points east on Route 6:** Take exit 12 and turn right at the end of the ramp. Drive 1.5 miles on Route 6A (west) past the Brewster town line and turn left into Nickerson State Park in Brewster. Drive past the gatehouse on the left 1.8 miles to Fisherman's Landing on Deer Park Road (the main park road). Turn left into Fisherman's Landing (dirt road) and park in the dirt parking lot. If that lot is full, park in the main parking lot by the gatehouse and ride 1.8 miles to the start.

GPS coordinates: N41 45.34' / W70 01.83'

THE RIDE

You'd never know Nickerson State Park has some of the best single-track mountain bike riding on Cape Cod. It isn't advertised much. This mapped ride is one of the better rides in the park. I had what they call a "being in the zone" ride experience here, a "shredding the gnar" experience through a tunnel of concentration and sweat, riding over mostly smooth track with very little rock, a fair number of roots, and a lot of up and down. It is a killer loop that is very challenging, especially when ridden fast.

Start out at Fisherman's Landing or park in the main parking lot (or bike rental parking lot) and ride Deer Park Road to the start of this ride. Fisherman's Landing is a popular spot in Nickerson State Park for swimming and fishing, where boats get launched onto Cliff Pond. The parking area is on dirt among the trees, and there aren't many spaces. Start riding onto an unmarked trail on the east end of the parking lot, with Cliff Pond to your left. The trail ascends and then it's an up-and-down series of hills for the 1.5 miles. The single-track here is narrow, with some smooth parts and some roots, but no rocks. At mile 1.7, the trail splits, and turning right, follows Little Cliff Pond on the left. At mile 2.3 the single-track turns left into Area 7 and then turns to cross the main park road, Deer Park Road, and does a short, fun, hilly loop close to Route 6 through a dense stand of pine, and back to Area 7. Opt to skip this short side loop, but miss out on the fun!

At mile 3.7 turn right onto single-track and then turn left 90 degrees at mile 3.8, heading to Higgins Pond Road, a dirt road. Turn left and ride Baker's Pond Road around Eel Pond and then Higgins Pond on the right. Enter single-track at mile 4.7 and then hug Higgins Pond, veering left with Little Cliff Pond to the left. At mile 5.2, turn right on Flax Pond Road (paved) and turn immediately right on the sandy dirt Higgins Pond Road. At the top of the climb here, turn left onto single-track at mile 5.4 and wind back through some twists and turns, descending after a sharp left turn to Flax Pond Road. Cross Flax Pond Road and continue descending to a flat stretch with Flax Pond to the right. Just

Bike Shops

Orleans Cycle, 26 Main St., Orleans, (508) 255-9115, orleanscycle.com
Idle Times Bike Shop, 29 Main St., Orleans, (508) 240-1122, idletimes bikes.com

Nickerson State Park Entrance, Main Street (Route 6A), Brewster

after the pond, start a long climb back to Deer Park Road, turn left, and follow on its descent back to Fisherman's Landing. Turn off Deer Park Road at mile 7.1 with a steeper descent to the parking lot. If you survive this ride in one piece without getting lost, it will be an accomplishment. Learn the pond geography, learn what camping area you're in, take this book with you, and you'll likely have a far better experience. I'll keep coming back to Nickerson State Park as I have since I was a young boy, only this time to keep exploring.

Cliff Pond Killer Loop

MILES AND DIRECTIONS

0.0   Start this ride at Fisherman's Landing in Nickerson State Park.

0.6   Turn left on Deer Park Road (the main park road).

0.7   Turn left off Deer Park Road and ride around Grassy Nook Pond.

1.3   Turn hard left and head back toward Cliff Pond. Stay between Area 6X and Cliff Pond.

1.4   Turn right at the beach and hug the edge of Cliff Pond on the left. Stay between Area 6 and Cliff Pond.

1.7   Bear right around Little Cliff Pond (on the left).

2.1   Cross the road.

2.2   Make a 90-degree left turn.

2.3   Cross Area 7 paved road.

2.5   Turn right onto Area 7 dirt road.

2.6   Cross Deer Park Road.

2.8   Make a 90-degree right turn into a steep downhill.

3.0   Ride a short uphill to a dirt road and turn right.

3.1   Cross Deer Park Road.

3.4   Turn right on Area 7 paved road.

3.6   Turn left on Area 7 dirt road.

3.7   Turn right 90 degrees off the road onto single-track.

3.8   Turn left 90 degrees.

3.9   Turn left.

4.0   Turn left onto Baker's Pond Road (dirt road and steeper climb) and follow the dirt road around Eel Pond and Higgins Pond (both on the right).

4.7   Turn right 90 degrees onto single-track and keep Little Cliff Pond on your left.

5.2   Turn right onto Flax Pond Road (paved surface).

5.2   Make an immediate right onto Higgins Pond Road (dirt and sand road).

5.4   Turn left onto single-track.

5.7   Bear left.

5.8   Bear right.

5.9   Turn left 90 degrees.

Cliff Pond Killer Loop

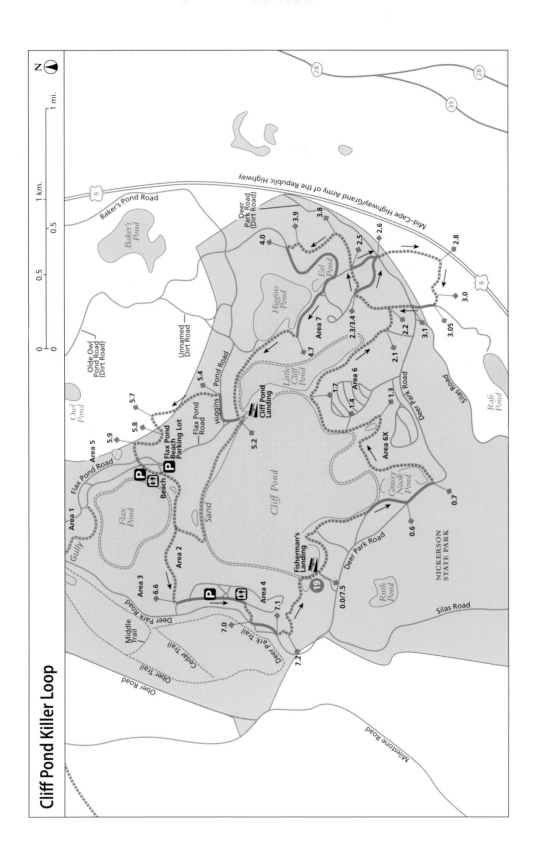

5.9 Cross Flax Pond Road (paved).

6.6 Turn left 90 degrees into Area 4 and stay parallel to Deer Park Road on your right. Keep climbing.

7.0 Continue along Deer Park Road.

7.1 Turn left off Deer Park Road onto single-track and a steep descent.

7.2 Make a sharp left turn and ride another steep descent.

7.5 The ride ends at Fisherman's Landing parking lot.

RIDE INFORMATION

Local Events and Attractions
See the listings under Rides 17and 21.

Restrooms
Restrooms are available at the main entrance parking lot of Nickerson State Park, in Areas 3 and 4, and at the Park Store on Deer Park Road.

Flax Pond–Owl Pond Loop

This is an easy mountain bike ride through another section of Nickerson State Park, but this one connects to the Cape Cod Rail Trail. I like a cyclocross bike for this ride, but a mountain bike or fat tire bike can handle it easily. Flax Pond is a great fresh-water swimming area, and you can ride this loop and start or finish there as an option.

Start: Nickerson State Park bicycle rental parking lot, Route 6A, just west of main parking lot

Distance: 5.5-mile loop

Approximate riding time: 1 hour

Best bike: Mountain bike, fat tire bike, cyclocross bike

Terrain and surface type: Hilly single-track, sandy fire road double track, paved path, paved park road

Traffic and hazards: Cape Cod Rail Trail traffic at the start and finish with pedestrians, children, and other riders; sandy trail sections, sandy dirt roads, roots, and vehicle traffic on Deer Park Road and occasionally on dirt roads; hikers on the single-track and bridle paths

Things to see: Nickerson State Park, Flax Pond, Owl Pond, Cliff Pond, Cape Cod Rail Trail

Map: *Arrow Street Atlas: Cape Cod including Martha's Vineyard & Nantucket*, p. 30

Getting there: From Route 6 (Mid-Cape Highway) and points west and the Cape Cod Canal: Take exit 12 and turn left at the end of the exit ramp on Route 6A. **From points east (Provincetown, Truro, Wellfleet, Eastham) on Route 6:** Take exit 12 and turn right at the end of the ramp. Drive 1.6 miles on Route 6A (west) past the Brewster town line and just past the Nickerson State Park main entrance. Look for a brown sign with white lettering on the left that says Cape Cod Rail Trail Parking Area (with a bicycle and horseshoe engraving), and turn left into the parking lot for the start of this ride.

GPS coordinates: N41 46.49' / W70 02.09'

THE RIDE

This ride is a short cyclocross or mountain bike route that takes riders on a challenging course through pine and oak forest, along a fresh water beach, around a few ponds, over sandy climbs, and down fast descents through Nickerson State Park and Brewster. It starts at the Cape Cod Rail Trail (CCRT; bike rental) parking lot at Nickerson, and travels through the northern part of Nickerson State Park and adjacent forested neighborhoods. This one is fun because it takes you through a lush pine forest, hugs the north and east shores of Flax Pond, and then travels along the beach at Cliff Pond before heading out of the park property and onto some sandy dirt roads past Baker's Pond and Owl Pond. It then crosses busy 6A and heads through a nice residential neighborhood and returns via the CCRT in Brewster. It's a quick, but challenging ride, something you could squeeze into an hour. Or you could take it slow and stop for a swim or at the many places along the way for a picnic. Or both.

The ride starts by turning right out of the bike rental parking lot onto the CCRT. Don't forget to look left when riding down the paved path from the parking lot. Ride just a short way and look for an unmarked, sandy entrance to single-track on the left. This is a well-worn trail and isn't too hard to find. Ride this trail south toward the power lines, going over a sandy little bump, and then descend and bend right to a sandy section under the power lines at 0.3 mile. Cross a sandy double-track, ride uphill a few feet, and bear left along a rooty section that hugs the dense stand of pines to the right. Descend slightly and turn right 90 degrees into the pines, jumping over a big log at mile 0.4. Turn left onto the paved bike path and wind through this pine forest, where there is an old burial ground on the right just after hitting the pavement. Ride to mile 0.5 and cross Deer Park Road, then make an immediate right turn onto single-track, descend a short steep section, and stop before crossing the paved road.

Bike Shops

Orleans Cycle, 26 Main St., Orleans, (508) 255-9115, orleanscycle.com
Idle Times Bike Shop, 29 Main St., Orleans, (508) 240-1122, idletimesbikes.com

Paved bike path connecting mountain bike trails, Nickerson State Park

20

Cross Flax Pond Road carefully, continue on the trail on the other side of the road, and turn left 90 degrees. Look at the trail ahead, which dips down and then climbs up to Area 1. Ride it hard and gain momentum up the hill into the Area 1 campsite, then turn right onto a paved road that heads slightly uphill. Turn left into a campsite (make sure there's nobody around) and head up a steep little hill to the top at mile 0.8 with great views of Flax Pond to the right. Descend the chute, turn left onto pavement, and then turn right at mile 0.9 onto the Area 1 paved road that runs parallel to Flax Pond Road with Flax Pond to the right. At the end of the paved road where the road turns to the left (mile 1.0), continue straight off-road onto a wide trail that ascends slightly through the woods straight ahead. Follow this down a mild slope, veer left, then right, and ascend a little. Make a sharp left turn at mile 1.2 up to a smaller parking lot in Area 5. Turn right out of the parking lot onto Flax Pond Road, descend, and turn right into the bigger parking lot for Flax Pond Beach at mile 1.3. There are restrooms up the short incline to the right (seasonal).

At the northwest corner of the parking lot, just left of the path that takes you up and over to the beach (past the restrooms on the right), a steep single-track trail goes uphill. Take it. It's just to the left of the paved walkway to the beach. Follow the trail with Flax Pond to the right and head uphill, turning left at mile 1.6 and climbing to the top before descending to Cliff Pond on the other side. At 1.7 miles turn left at the bottom of the descent, and hug the shoreline of Cliff Pond along the beach. There is a parallel trail above you in case the water level is high. Follow Cliff Pond and ride some freshwater beach or go for a swim. Follow Cliff Pond's shore until the landing (with parking lot) where Cliff Pond meets Little Cliff Pond. Facing the landing below, turn around, and ride past the parking lot on Flax Pond Road.

Turn right onto an unmarked dirt road, which is Higgins Pond Road. Ride uphill to mile 2.8 and turn left on an unmarked dirt road. Get to the top of the climb and start a quick descent to mile 3.1, where you turn left on another unmarked dirt road, Baker's Pond Road. This road is a fast, fun descent but there is occasional vehicle traffic here. The descent continues into a sharp left turn onto Olde Owl Pond Road at mile 3.4 and keeps descending until Olde Owl Pond levels off. Olde Owl Pond dumps you into Owl Pond Road, a paved road in a residential neighborhood. Bear right and descend the pavement to Route 6A, and cross onto Seaview Road. Continue down residential Seaview Road, turn left onto the CCRT, and recover along the paved path from a quick but challenging workout, back to the start.

Flax Pond–Owl Pond Loop

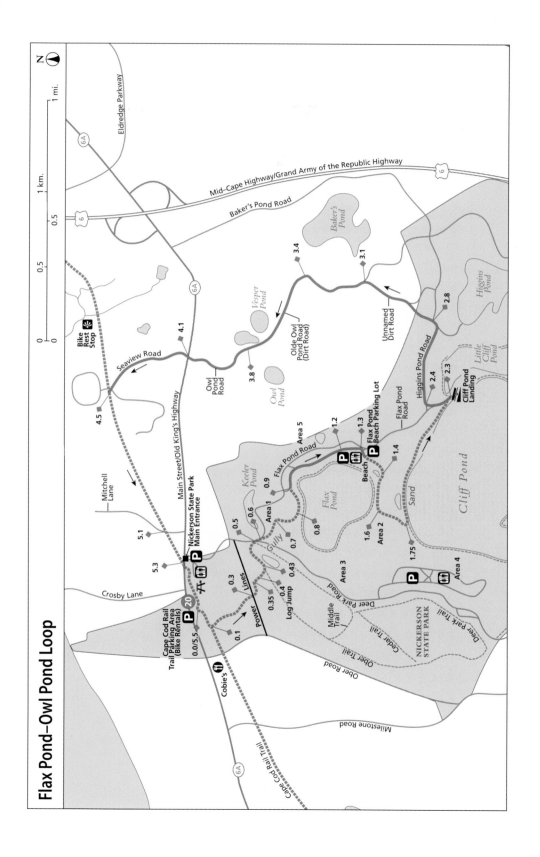

MILES AND DIRECTIONS

0.0 Begin this ride at the CCRT parking lot (off Route 6A west of the main entrance to Nickerson State Park).

0.0 Turn right onto the CCRT.

0.1 Turn left onto a sandy single-track, unmarked trail.

0.3 Ride through a sandy section under the power lines.

0.35 Make a 90-degree right turn into the woods.

0.4 Jump over the log, bunny-hop it, or dismount and remount if you're on a cyclocross bike.

0.43 Turn left turn onto the paved bike path.

0.5 Bear left and cross Deer Park Road.

0.6 Turn right off the paved bike path and stop at Flax Pond Road. Cross carefully and be ready to turn left.

0.62 Cross Flax Pond Road with caution.

0.65 Turn left into the downhill gully.

0.7 Turn right at the top of the climb onto a paved road.

0.8 Turn left off the pavement and up the hill onto a single-track path.

0.9 Turn right onto the paved road that parallels Flax Pond Road through Area 1.

1.0 Ride straight ahead off the pavement past a campsite to the right onto a wide trail.

1.2 Turn left up to a parking lot and then right onto Flax Pond Road.

1.3 Descend right into the Flax Pond Beach parking lot.

1.35 View Flax Pond (there are seasonal restrooms here).

1.3 Turn around and exit northwest corner of lot. Then turn right onto uphill single-track.

1.4 Make a 90-degree right turn.

1.6 Bear left and ride a steeper uphill section.

1.7 Descend the hill to the edge of Cliff Pond.

1.75 Turn left facing Cliff Pond and hug the shoreline.

2.3 Turn right onto Flax Pond Road and enter the parking lot.

2.3 View Cliff Pond and Little Cliff Pond Landings, then turn around.

2.4 Turn right onto Higgins Pond Road (a sandy, dirt road), and climb.

2.8 Turn left off Higgins Pond Road onto an unnamed dirt road.

3.1   Turn left onto Baker's Pond Road (dirt road).

3.4   Turn left onto Olde Owl Pond Road (dirt road).

3.8   Ride onto Owl Pond Road (paved surface).

4.1   Cross Route 6A and continue on Seaview Road.

4.5   Turn left onto the CCRT.

5.1   Cross Mitchell Lane.

5.3   Ride past the Nickerson State Park main parking lot on the left.

5.5   Finish this ride at the CCRT parking lot.

RIDE INFORMATION

Local Events and Attractions
See Rides 17 and 21 for attraction and restaurant listings.

Restrooms
There are restrooms just a short walk or ride from the parking area at the start/finish of this ride. There are also restrooms at Flax Pond Beach (mile 1.3).

21

Beach Fatty Food Tour

This is another fat tire bike ride, but unlike Sandy Neck (Ride 12), it can be done on a mountain bike or cyclocross bike. This ride depends on having a low tide, a Cape Cod phenomenon best experienced on Cape Cod Bay. Riding the tidal flats at low tide in Brewster is not be missed, and opens up an entirely new cycling experience, as the slope into the bay is gradual and the tidal flats extend for miles. The views and sense of openness are wonderful here, and you can see all the way to Provincetown on a clear day.

Start: Linnell Landing Beach

Distance: 5.0 miles, out-and-back

Approximate riding time: 1 to 2 hours, depending on hunger

Best bike: Fat tire bike, mountain bike, cyclocross bike

Terrain and surface type: Beach, deep sand, soft sand, tidal flat (hard sand and smooth gravel), paved back road, paved sidewalk along busy Route 6A, and paved multi-use path (CCRT)

Traffic and hazards: The incoming tide (it's slow), high tide (you will ride through water), pedestrians on sidewalks, side streets with vehicle traffic crossing the sidewalk on Route 6A

Things to see: Linnell Landing Beach, Cape Cod Bay, the Brewster flats, Ocean Edge Resort and Golf Club, Ellis Landing Beach, a variety of restaurants, the Cape Cod Rail Trail, and more restaurants

Map: *Arrow Street Atlas: Cape Cod including Martha's Vineyard & Nantucket*, p. 30

Getting there: From the Cape Cod Canal and points north and west: Take Route 6 (Mid-Cape Highway) to exit 11 and head north to Brewster on Route 137 North. Take a right on Millstone Road and follow it to its end to Route 6A. Take a right on Route 6A, pass Cobie's (clam shack) on the right, and take an immediate left on Linnell Landing Road. **From**

points on Outer Cape Cod: Take Route 6 to exit 12 and take a right onto Route 6A (west) at the end of the ramp. Enter Brewster, pass the Nickerson State Park main entrance on the left, and turn right onto Linnell Landing Road.

GPS coordinates: N41 46.93' / W70 02.29'

THE RIDE

This is the kind of ride you probably did as a kid and should probably spend a lot more time doing. Loafing around, we used to call it. Loitering, sometimes. Using your bike to actually go somewhere and do something as transportation. Not just to ride, but to see and be seen about town and visit people, mingling with the locals. In this case, eating with the locals. Brewster has some of the best dining experiences on Cape Cod. The Beach Fatty Food Tour also connects to the Cape Cod Rail Trail (CCRT) quickly, with nearby Nickerson State Park, which has all types of bike riding and fresh water beaches. It also connects quickly and safely to the ocean from the CCRT (via connector Linnell Landing Road, which connects to the CCRT via Cobie's Restaurant and Nickerson State Park), passes by the Ocean Edge Resort and mansions, and passes by several restaurants ranging from inexpensive to expensive, all within a 2.5-mile stretch.

"Fatty" has three meanings here: It is slang for a fat tire bike, refers to the abundance of fatty food along this ride, and it is a ride that has great potential to make you fatter. It's a gastronomic tour of a stretch of Brewster that really should not be missed, and a very relaxing ride. Many of the restaurants on this ride are closed for the winter months, but many are not. This ride *must* be timed for low tide, which occurs at least once during daylight, year-round. In summer it could be ridden twice during the day (on a day when there are two low tides during daylight). It's a ride best done on a hot summer day or nice evening with a great sunset, when you're hungry, and you can get back before nightfall. Beach sand riding can work up an incredible appetite and thirst. Suffer in softer sand or cruise on the firmer sand of the tidal flats, depending on preference, and make it as hard or easy a workout as you want. Then reward yourself with a few tasty calories.

Start this ride at Linnell Landing Beach parking lot, or opt to start at one of the two Nickerson State Park parking lots on Route 6A. It is a short, safe, and easy ride from Nickerson State Park and the CCRT to Linnell Landing Beach if you opt to park at Nickerson. Simply ride to points west on the

Fat tire bike rest stop on Cape Cod Bay tidal flats, Brewster

CCRT from either parking lot (main parking lot or CCRT parking area), turn right at the paved path to Cobie's Clam Shack from the Rail Trail, cross Route 6A at the crosswalk in front of Cobie's onto Linnell Landing Road, and head down the quiet road to its end on Cape Cod Bay. This would be a dead-end ride for a road bike, but not for a fat tire bike, mountain, or cyclocross bike. A fat tire bike is easiest.

Turn left and head west on the tidal flats, into a spectacular sunset at dusk, or wake up early with your back to the sunrise. This ride is good for breakfast, lunch, or dinner! Ride over the often rippled and colorful sand, get close to any shellfish living beneath your fatter tires, and watch the beach come alive, water squirting upward out of the sand as you ride over these underground creatures. The tidal flats are beautiful, with a rich environment that is mostly invisible beneath the sand, with softshell clams (steamers), the hard-shelled quahogs (including littlenecks and cherrystones), the larger hard-shelled sea clams (found farther out in the bay during a full- or new-moon low tide), and the evasive razor clam. Look for the fast-disappearing horseshoe crab, now being harvested for medical purposes. Watch for endangered North Atlantic right whales in the bay when they're migrating here, a

Bike Shops
Rail Trail Bike & Kayak Shop, 302 Underpass Rd., Brewster, (508) 896-8200, railtrail bikeshop.com
Brewster Bike, 442 Underpass Rd., Brewster, (508) 896-8149, brewsterbike.com

rare but beautiful sight indeed. If you look across the water to the right, you can see Pilgrim Monument in Provincetown jutting out above the horizon far off in the distance. On some lazy summer days you can barely see it in the haze over Cape Cod Bay. You can see the sandy cliffs of Eastham and Great Island in Wellfleet, all much more visible at low tide than high. In summer, you pass by the Cape Cod Sea Camps, where children learn archery, swimming, and sailing. Their fleet of sailboats can be seen to the right, at rest or in action during the day. There is a lot going on here in summer.

On the left at 0.8 mile, pass Ocean Edge Resort. Viewed from here, the resort is a row of really nice condos set back from the dunes. From Route 6A, you see the two large mansions, the home and carriage house of the Roland C. Nickerson family. Nickerson State Park was the Nickersons' private game reserve in the early 1900s. Opt to take a side trip on this ride to see the historic mansions and eat at the Ocean Terrace behind the mansion on the left, with views across Cape Cod Bay. After passing Ocean Edge, veer left onto Ellis Landing at the 1.0 mile point. Take note of the stone wall in front of the houses to the right at Ellis Landing, built to keep the cottages from falling into the bay.

Cape Cod Bay has been receding in the past fifty years, and the flats you've been riding were covered by dunes just a few years ago. The next big storm will wreak havoc along this shoreline. In my time on Cape Cod, I've watched the shoreline recede more than 100 feet.

Ride up the pavement on Ellis Landing Road to Route 6A, past the tightly packed cottages to the right. All the property to the left is Nickerson property or was given to the Town of Brewster by the Nickersons. Turn right on Route 6A at the end of Ellis Landing Road (or opt to turn left to see the mansions), and begin your gastronomic tour. Start with the Hopkins House Bakery on the right, housed in an historic home of an early descendant of Stephen Hopkins, *Mayflower* passenger. The homemade baked goods sell out fast, but if you wait a little, more may be coming fresh out of the oven. Across the street is JoMama's, with sandwiches, bagels, and organic coffee in a pastel-colored, surfer-themed room with a high ceiling and comfy leather couches. Next on the right is J.T.'s Seafood and Ice Cream, where you can order the classic fried clams, oysters, or lobster dinner with homemade ice cream for dessert. Next on the right is Ardeo's, run by the Jamiel family, which has been busy preparing Mediterranean fare for more than thirty years on Cape Cod. Next on the right in Foster Square is Oki Sushi, one of the few take-out sushi restaurants on Cape Cod, and Brewster Pizza, now with a full bar next door.

Cross Route 6A at the crosswalk from Foster Square and continue on Thad Ellis Road. On the left, about halfway up the road, is a run-down cottage overgrown with vegetation, with a small sign in front that reads Peddler's. But looks can be deceiving, as Peddler's Bistro is a hidden gem. Inside is a romantic, candlelit, country dining room. They oddly don't take reservations or credit cards (except American Express), and husband and wife owners (Alain and Beth) prepare and serve everything.

At the end of Thad Ellis Road, turn right onto the CCRT. Ride slightly uphill on the pavement under a canopy of oak and pine to Underpass Road, where the road used to go under a train bridge. On the left, up the hill and across the street are Local Flavor, a good bagel and sandwich shop, and Morello's (formerly Morelli's and Ardeo's) on the trail. Turn right for Guapo's Shore Shack, a fun Mexican takeout restaurant with ample bike racks and deck seating under grass umbrellas. Or try Breakwater Fish & Lobster next door for fresh seafood to take out or eat at the picnic tables out front. Turn around and decide where to eat, but be sure to make it back to the start before sundown. Night riding is forbidden on the CCRT unless commuting. If you time it right, you'll end up at Linnell Landing Beach for a beautiful sunset before the tide rolls in.

Beach Fatty Food Tour

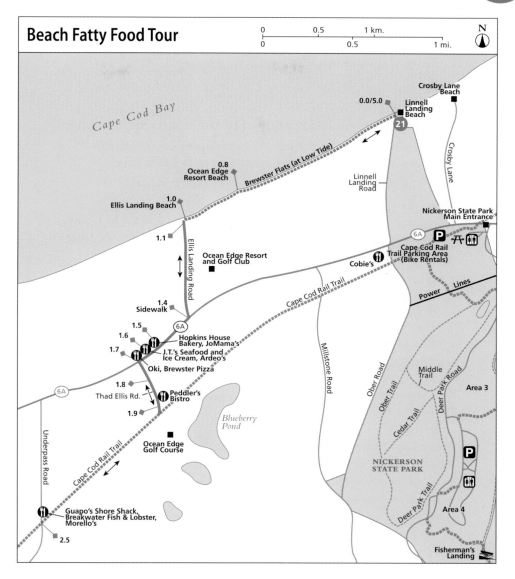

0   0.5   1 km.
0   0.5   1 mi.

N

Cape Cod Bay

Crosby Lane Beach

0.0/5.0   Linnell Landing Beach

21

Brewster Flats (at Low Tide)

0.8 Ocean Edge Resort Beach

Linnell Landing Road

Crosby Lane

1.0 Ellis Landing Beach

Nickerson State Park Main Entrance

1.1

6A   P

Cape Cod Rail Trail Parking Area (Bike Rentals)

Ellis Landing Road

Ocean Edge Resort and Golf Club

Cobie's

Cape Cod Rail Trail

Power Lines

1.4 Sidewalk

1.5

6A

1.6   Hopkins House Bakery, JoMama's

1.7   J.T.'s Seafood and Ice Cream, Ardeo's

Oki, Brewster Pizza

Millstone Road

Ober Road

Ober Trail

Middle Trail

Deer Park Road

Area 3

1.8

6A

Thad Ellis Rd.   Peddler's Bistro

1.9

Cedar Trail

Blueberry Pond

Underpass Road

Cape Cod Rail Trail

Ocean Edge Golf Course

NICKERSON STATE PARK

P

Deer Park Trail

Guapo's Shore Shack, Breakwater Fish & Lobster, Morello's

Area 4

2.5

Fisherman's Landing

MILES AND DIRECTIONS

0.0 Start this ride at the Linnell Landing Beach parking lot at low tide.

0.0 Facing the water, turn left by the water's edge and start riding the tidal flats.

0.8 Pass the Ocean Edge Resort Beach on your left.

1.0 Turn left onto Ellis Landing Beach (Ellis Landing Road).

1.1 Continue on Ellis Landing Road.

1.4 Turn right onto the Route 6A sidewalk. Opt to take a quick left for a short out-and-back to the Ocean Edge Resort.

1.5 Pass Hopkins House Bakery on the right and JoMama's across the street.

1.6 Pass J.T.'s Seafood and Ice Cream and Ardeo's Restaurant on the right.

1.7 Pass Foster Square Mall with Oki Sushi and Brewster Pizza, then cross Route 6A onto Thad Ellis Road and pass by Peddler's Bistro.

1.9 Turn right onto the CCRT at the end of Thad Ellis Road.

2.5 Turn around, or opt to turn right or left onto Underpass Road and stop at a local restaurant for lunch or dinner. Backtrack and return to the start the way you came, or return via the CCRT (a safer choice if you start to run out of sunlight).

5.0 Arrive back at the Linnell Landing Beach parking lot.

RIDE INFORMATION

Local Events and Attractions
See the listings under Ride 17.

Restaurants
Cobie's: 3260 Main St. (Route 6A), Brewster; (508) 896-7021. See the listing under Ride 17.

Ocean Edge Resort and Golf Club: 2907 Main St. (Route 6A), Brewster; (508) 896-9000. There are four places to dine at Ocean Edge: Ocean Terrace, Bayzo's Pub, Linx Tavern, and Shark Bah. The first two are accessible on this ride, the second is reached by driving through the golf course from mile 1.9, and the fourth is only for members and guests. The Ocean Terrace is the place to go for the best view of Cape Cod Bay from any restaurant. Bayzo's Pub is in the basement of one of the mansions, and gets great reviews for service and sandwiches.

JoMama's: 2740 Main St., Brewster; (774) 323-0719. New York bagels, fresh coffee, and deli sandwiches (including panini). Yum.

Hopkins House Bakery: 2727 Main St., Brewster; (508) 896-3450. Baked goods fresh out of the oven by Heather Baxter. Gift shop, antiques, folk art in an historic 300-year-old home (the original built in the late 1600s).

J.T.'s Seafood: 2689 Main St. (Route 6A), Brewster; (508) 896-3355. Fried seafood and ice cream, family-owned, but not just ordinary, with baked seafood dishes and steamed vegetables. Picnic table street-side dining under huge umbrellas, inside dining, and a back porch.

Ardeo's: 2671 Main St. (Route 6A), Brewster; (774) 323-3669. This popular restaurant has made a terrific comeback. Tuscan and Mediterranean fare.

Oki: 2655 Main St., Brewster; (508) 896-8883. Great sushi and Japanese to go, not really a comfortable sit-down place, although there are chairs and tables. Order from the "specials" menu.

Brewster Pizza: 2655 Main St., Brewster; (508) 896-3341. They've expanded to include a bar and restaurant. Good pizza.

Peddler's Bistro: 67 Thad Ellis Rd., Brewster; (508) 896-9300; peddlersrestaurant .com. See the listing under Ride 17.

Guapo's Shore Shack: 239 Underpass Rd., Brewster; (508) 896-3338. Eat a burrito, fish taco, or other Mexican treat outside on the deck under a grass-umbrella-covered picnic table by the CCRT. Bike racks, outdoor bar/tequila shack, fun atmosphere.

Breakwater Fish & Lobster: 235 Underpass Rd., Brewster; (508) 896-7080. See the listing under Ride 16.

Morello's Taverna: 280 Underpass Rd., Brewster; (508) 896-9400. Mediterranean fare with Greek and Italian specialties, on the CCRT.

Restrooms

There are port-o-potties at Linnell Landing Beach (in season) and restrooms at nearby Cobie's and Nickerson State Park (see Ride description above). There also many restaurants along this ride.

Nickerson State Park Kids' Ride

This ride through Nickerson State Park's paved bicycle trails is ideal for older kids on their own bikes or for parents with smaller children in trailers or attachments. There are a few steep hills here, so bike-handling skills are a must. This ride goes to the park playground and store, and can be shortened to avoid the tougher climbs and descents. It also connects to the Cape Cod Rail Trail and many other rides in this book. It's a fun little roller-coaster through Mother Nature, with frog ponds and nearby swimming at Flax and Cliff Ponds.

Start: Nickerson State Park main parking lot, optional parking at CCRT parking area

Distance: 4.0-mile lollipop

Approximate riding time: 1 hour, depending on stops

Best bike: Road, hybrid (with younger kids in trailers or attachments)

Terrain and surface type: Mostly smooth paved bike path through oak and pine forest, with bad roots and bumps in sections (due for repair), with hilly sections, some steep and dangerous for smaller children or those without good brakes or bike-handling skills

Traffic and hazards: Steep hills, vehicle traffic in the main parking lot, park road crossings, bad roots on some of the trails (especially at the start of the ride), other riders, pedestrians on the trails

Things to see: Check in at the Nickerson State Park main gatehouse (the "Contact Station" on the park map) for summer programs and activities in the park, helpful park rangers; Mother Nature, with pine and oak forest, kettle ponds, and wildlife; restrooms and picnic tables at the start and finish; park store for refreshments and camping supplies; playground with picnic tables and restrooms; nearby access to a clam shack, ice cream, and Cape Cod Bay beaches (via Linnell Landing Road); nearby swimming at Flax and Cliff Ponds

Map: *Arrow Street Atlas: Cape Cod including Martha's Vineyard & Nantucket*, p. 30

Getting there: By car (from Boston, New York, Cape Cod Canal and points west): Take Route 6 to exit 11 and head north to Brewster on Route 137N. Take a right on Millstone Road and follow to end. Take a right on Route 6A. Nickerson State Park entrance is on the right. **From points on Outer Cape Cod east of Orleans:** Take Route 6 to exit 12 and take a right on Route 6A (west) at the end of the ramp. Enter Brewster and look for entrance signs to Nickerson State Park.

GPS coordinates: N41 46.52' / W70 01.94'

THE RIDE

Nickerson State Park is one of the biggest, cleanest, and best state parks in the United States, and my favorite in Massachusetts. And this ride gives kids a little of everything the park has to offer. The ride is shaded most of the way, so riding midday under a hot helmet won't be as much of an issue with children. Available are a playground, park store, fresh-water swimming, fishing (ponds are stocked with trout), boating, hiking and mountain biking trails, and picnic areas. The start is also a short ride from Cape Cod Bay for ocean swimming, and Cobie's clam shack with ice cream. The views are wonderful from the higher elevations.

This ride is for older children or those amazing younger bike riders who have experience with brakes and hills, some of them quite steep. For little kids, this can be a frightening bike path, with downhill sections that are steep enough to cause serious injury. With smaller children on their own bikes, it is best to stay on the Cape Cod Rail Trail (CCRT), which is very flat by comparison. The park rangers offer a bike trail map for the 8 total miles of paved bikeways in the park, and riders who want to explore more within Nickerson can opt to continue past the turnaround point of this ride for another 6 miles of paved bike paths (link to other trails at mile 2.0 of this ride). There are even more hills farther into the park, like the one that descends past the fire tower to Fisherman's Landing, or the curvy hills around Ruth Pond.

Start the ride at the picnic tables in the main parking lot ($5 parking fee) adjacent to the restrooms and entrance to the CCRT in the northwest corner of the lot. Alternatively, park at the CCRT bike rental lot, which is free, and ride to this spot. Work your way around the parking lot to Deer Park Road (main entrance or "Contact Station"), turn right, and make an immediate left

Nickerson State Park bike trail, Brewster

onto a gravel path onto the bike path. The Contact Station has a map and can show you the entrance to the bike path if needed. Turn right onto the bike path (the gravel path merges right), and follow the bike path under the power lines where it bends right and crosses Deer Park Road again at mile 0.4. Make an immediate right turn onto the Ober Trail and go through the pine forest, where there is an old burial site on the left. This section of the Ober Trail was closed to road cyclists during 2014 due to large roots pushing up pavement, but plans to repave are in the making. Mountain bikes, cyclocross bikes, and fat tire bikes are all fine here.

Nickerson State Park was once the private game reserve of Roland C. Nickerson, who lived at the mansions now known as Ocean Edge farther west on Route 6A. Nickerson hosted famous guests and hunted and fished here with President Grover Cleveland. And there is still a lot of wildlife here, including foxes, coyotes, deer, squirrels, turtles, frogs, and many types of birds, although hunting is prohibited. The ponds are stocked with trout, and rental boats are available to go fishing, sailing, or kayaking with your kids. It doesn't take long to feel like you're part of the great outdoors, far away from it all.

At mile 0.6, the ride starts climbing onto a plateau for 0.4 mile and passes two connector trails on the left, first the Middle Trail and next the Cedar Trail, so if you need to cut the ride short with the kids for any reason, you can. The top of this first climb might be the last one the kids want to ride, with the "Are we there yet?" questions beginning. Both connector trails take you back to the main park road and parallel trail, and could be just the shortcut needed to the playground or lunch. But hopefully not! Continue to mile 1.8 where

Bike Shop

Barb's Bike Rentals, 3430 Route 6A, Nickerson State Park, Brewster, (508) 896-7231, barbsbikeshop.com

the trail makes a left turn and heads up a shorter but fairly steep hill alongside Joe Long Road. At the top of this hill, the trail makes a 90-degree left turn and on the park map is called the Deer Park Trail, which parallels the main park road, Deer Park Road.

The next half-mile down Deer Park Trail is a gradual descent, a nice break after the first mostly uphill half of this ride. At mile 2.5, turn right off the trail, cross Deer Park Road, and stop by the park store for refreshments or camping items. Pass to the left of the park store and follow the signs into Area 3, where there are restrooms and showers (seasonal). Loop around to the left from the restrooms to the park playground and hang with the kids or have a picnic. The playground, rebuilt in 2010, has a ladders-and-ropes course, lots of swings, and other equipment to climb over a soft wood-chip base, all under the shade of a pine forest. From the playground, cross Deer Park Road and turn right into a very steep downhill, followed by another steep downhill. Use caution here—even walk if it looks like it's going to be too much. Otherwise, enjoy the fast descent, and remember it's a two-way path with curves! There is a sharp right turn at the bottom of this hill, with another sharp left immediately after. Good brakes are essential! At the parking lot, riders can opt to cross Deer Park Road to swim at Flax Pond, at Area 1 or 3. Continue to mile 3.4, cross Deer Park Road, and follow the trail back to the main parking lot where the ride started.

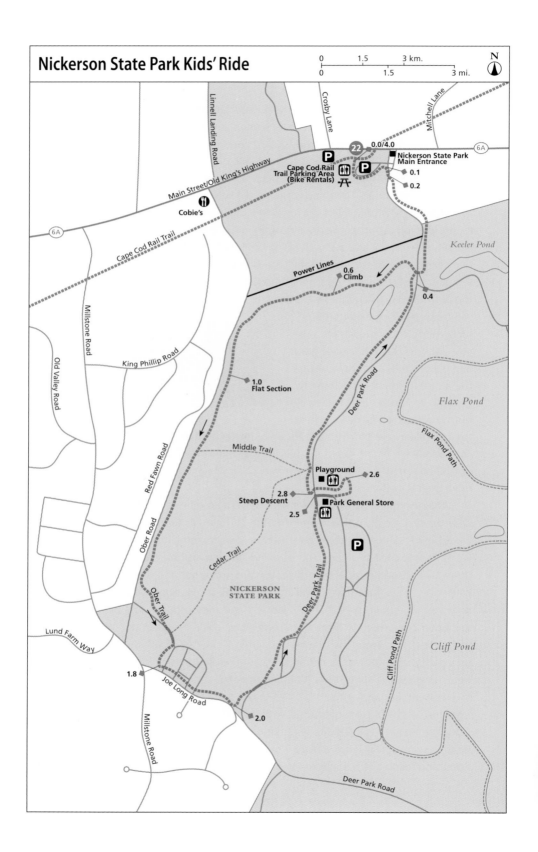

Nickerson State Park Kids' Ride

N

Linnell Landing Road
Crosby Lane
Mitchell Lane
Main Street/Old King's Highway
6A

22   0.0/4.0
■ Nickerson State Park
Main Entrance

P
P
0.1
0.2

Cape Cod Rail
Trail Parking Area
(Bike Rentals)

Cobie's

6A

Cape Cod Rail Trail

Keeler Pond

Power Lines   0.6
Climb

0.4

Millstone Road

Old Valley Road

King Phillip Road

Deer Park Road

Flax Pond

Flax Pond Path

1.0
Flat Section

Red Fawn Road

Middle Trail

Playground   2.6

Ober Road

2.8
Steep Descent

2.5   ■ Park General Store

P

Cedar Trail

NICKERSON
STATE PARK

Deer Park Trail

Cliff Pond Path

Cliff Pond

Ober Trail

Lund Farm Way

1.8

Joe Long Road

2.0

Millstone Road

Deer Park Road

0.0 Start this ride at the picnic tables in the Nickerson State Park main parking lot.

0.1 Turn right onto Deer Park Road (main road) from the main parking lot.

0.2 Cross Deer Park Road onto a gravel path and turn right on the paved bike path.

0.4 Cross Deer Park Road again and turn right onto the paved bike path.

0.6 This is the start of a challenging climb for kids, and younger children should avoid it.

1.0 The trail levels off for a plateaued section.

1.8 Turn left and continue on the trail into an uphill section that parallels Joe Long Road.

2.0 The trail bends 90 degrees to the left at the top of this climb. It is now called the Deer Park Trail, which parallels Deer Park Road.

2.5 Cross Deer Park Road for the park store, restrooms, and playground.

2.6 Circle around by the restrooms past the playground and return to Deer Park Road.

2.8 Cross Deer Park Road and turn right on the bike path. Caution, steep downhill section.

3.4 Turn right and cross Deer Park Road. Trail veers left to return to the main parking lot.

4.0 This ride ends at the Nickerson State Park main parking lot.

RIDE INFORMATION

Local Events and Attractions
Also see the listings under Ride 16 and 17.

Drummer Boy Park and Playground: 773 Main St. (Route 6A), Brewster; (508) 896-9521. Weekly band concerts in summer. Huge grass lawn park by Cape Cod Bay, with playground and picnic tables.

Cape Cod Museum of Natural History: 869 Main St. (Route 6A), Brewster; (800) 479-3867. Bird viewing area, downstairs aquarium, library, osprey nests, and adjacent trail (Wing Island) to Cape Cod Bay. Gift shop, lectures, summer camp program. Great for kids.

Brewster Ladies Library: 1822 Main St. (Route 6A), Brewster; (508) 896-3913. Not just for the ladies, but also gentlemen and children of all ages. A beautiful space, with lots of computers, a teen room, journal reading room, and great children's section. Numerous exhibits, events, and performances. Free WiFi. Part of the Cape Cod and Islands extensive library network CLAMS (Cape Libraries Automated Materials Sharing).

Restaurants

See the listings under Rides 16, 17, and 21 for restaurants in Brewster.

Restrooms

There are restrooms at the main parking lot start/finish, and adjacent to the park playground.

Old Colony Rail Trail, Harwich to Chatham

The Old Colony Rail Trail (OCRT) starts at the Harwich Bike Rotary and connects the Cape Cod Rail Trail to points in Harwich and Chatham. This ride can be started from either end or combined with Ride 17 to make a longer ride, although there is no vehicle parking at the Harwich Bike Rotary (nearby parking at Brooks Park). It's a relatively easy and flat ride, with a few short climbs and descents, good for families and kids.

Start: Harwich Bike Rotary, Harwich Center, from the CCRT

Distance: 16.2 miles out-and-back

Approximate riding time: 1 to 2 hours

Best bike: Road

Terrain and surface type: Smooth paved trail, paved back roads, bike lane on main road

Traffic and hazards: Busy road crossings, bike rotary, where some cyclists and pedestrians go the wrong way, bike lane along George Ryder Road next to Chatham Municipal Airport, some riding on neighborhood roads alongside vehicle traffic, sand in the roads and on the trail

Things to see: Harwich Bike Rotary (no restrooms), Harwich Center, Island Pond Conservation Area (hiking trails), Brooks Park, Monomoy Regional High School, Thompson's Field Conservation Area, Chatham Municipal Airport, White Pond swimming area, Chatham Railroad Museum, Veteran's Field

Map: *Arrow Street Atlas: Cape Cod including Martha's Vineyard & Nantucket*, p. 57

Getting there: Ride to the Harwich Bike Rotary on the CCRT from either South Dennis (Ride 17, mile 3.3) or from points north in Harwich,

Brewster, Orleans, Eastham, or Wellfleet. Or park your car at Brooks Park on Oak Street in Harwich (mile 1.0 of this ride, GPS coordinates N41 41.27' / W70 04.20'). To get to Brooks Park from Route 6 (Mid-Cape Highway), take exit 10 toward Harwich Center on Route 124 South (Pleasant Lake Avenue), turn left on Old Colony Road, and drive to the end on Oak Street. Cross Oak Street into the Brooks Park parking lot directly in front of you. If you start at Brooks Park (mile 1.0), the round-trip distance to Chatham is 14.2 miles.

GPS coordinates: N41 41.32' / W70 05.34'

THE RIDE

The Old Colony Rail Trail (OCRT) is the newest extension of rail trail connecting the Cape Cod Rail Trail (CCRT) to Chatham via Harwich, and was completed in 2004. Starting at the Harwich Bike Rotary, the trail goes east through Harwich Center to Crowell Road in Chatham, and then cyclists can take back roads to Veteran's Field, the Chatham Railroad Museum, and Main Street in Chatham. The trail lies on the old railroad bed that was owned by the Chatham Railroad Company, completed in 1887 as a Chatham connector from Harwich. Rail transportation to Chatham ended in 1937, and the OCRT was the result of the towns of Harwich, Chatham, and the Massachusetts Department of Conservation and Recreation working together.

This ride is more of a connector from the CCRT to Chatham, as there is no parking for vehicles at the Harwich Rotary. There is parking at Brooks Park and Harwich Town Hall, which are both a short ride away on the OCRT, but I decided to map from the bike rotary to connect the CCRT to two more popular Cape Cod destinations, and two rides in this book, Rides 25 and 26. From the OCRT, there is access to Harwich Center and Brooks Park (Ride 25), Monomoy Regional High School and the Harwich Community Center, East Harwich, the Chatham Municipal Airport, Veteran's Field and playground, the Chatham Railroad Museum, and Main Street in Chatham, a beautiful seaside town with its historic lighthouses, inns, harbors and beaches (Ride 26).

Start this ride connecting from any point on the CCRT, at the Harwich Bike Rotary in Harwich. Follow the sign for Old Colony Rail Trail heading east to Harwich Center, and pass by Island Pond Conservation Area, followed by the Island Pond Cemetery, on the left. The trail goes slightly uphill here through the woods. Pass by the Harwich Congregational Church and its cemetery and cross Route 124 at mile 0.8. This is Harwich Center, not to be confused with seaside Harwich Port (Ride 25). Have a great breakfast

Riders on the Old Colony Rail Trail at Brooks Park, Harwich

or lunch at Ruggie's around the corner from here on Main Street. Continue down the trail here, which looks like more of a wide sidewalk than a trail, as it parallels Old Colony Road with many driveway crossings and the Harwich Town Hall on the right. Next, cross Oak Street and through Brooks Park, with a playground, tennis courts, baseball field, and bandstand (optional vehicle parking for this ride is here). The newly built Monomoy Regional High School, Harwich Community Center, and Whitehouse Field are all on Oak

Street to the left, but continue on and cross the busy Route 39 at mile 1.4, walking the crosswalk.

The next stretch of trail heads out of town and away from traffic through the fifty-seven-acre Thompson's Field Conservation Area, a popular hiking area that has a short bike path and a lot of pitch pine forest. The trail is a long straightaway and then does a sharp left turn after entering Thompson's Field, around Harwich Water Department property. At mile 2.3, the trail keeps curving right, but heads downhill quickly. There always seems to be sand at the bottom of this hill, making it somewhat dangerous at high speed. The trail then goes up and bends to the left for another long straightaway to Depot Road. Cross Depot Road at mile 2.9, then Morton Road in South Chatham at mile 3.7 (connect to Ride 25 here) and then Meetinghouse Road (Route 137) at mile 4.0. The OCRT runs very close and parallel to Route 28 here, and two beautiful beaches at the ends of Cockle Cove Road and Ridgevale Road with the same names are easily accessed from Route 28 just east of Meetinghouse Road.

Bike Shops

Barbara's Bike & Sport Equipment, 430 Route 134, South Dennis, (508) 760-4723, barbsbikeshop.com
Dennis Cycle Center, 249 Great Western Rd., South Dennis, (508) 398-0011, denniscyclecenter.com

The trail ascends and starts rolling up and down, passing a field of solar panels on the left, then crossing Sam Ryder Road to George Ryder Road at the end of a long, gentle incline. Turn right on George Ryder road across from the Chatham Municipal Airport. Jump out of planes with Skydive Cape Cod, the only place in New England you can jump over a beach, with 11,000-foot jumps a regular occurrence. You'll be able to see every bicycle ride on Cape Cod and the Islands from up there, guaranteed. Or just watch the planes and try the lemon ricotta pancakes and red flannel hash at the Hangar B Eatery (inside the airport and open for breakfast and lunch). The OCRT travels the downward slope on George Ryder Road in a bike lane, and turns left back onto paved bike path at the crosswalk at mile 5.7. Wind left around the airport, climb up a couple of easy hills, and the paved path ends on Wilfred Road. Continue to the end of Wilfred Road, passing White Pond swimming area on the right through a flat section of residential neighborhood. Cross Old Queen Anne Road at the end of Wilfred Road and continue up the hill on Stepping Stones Road, where the trail is more of a sidewalk. Cross Stepping Stones Road twice, then continue to the end of the OCRT at Crowell Road. The OCRT itself is 7.5 miles long and ends at Crowell Road.

Turn right on Crowell Road and ride a few feet, then make an immediate left up the hill on Tipcart Drive. Turn right at the top of the hill on Hitching Post

Road, then turn left on Depot Road. Finish at the Chatham Railroad Museum across from Veteran's Field, home of the Chatham Anglers Cape Cod Baseball League Team. There is a playground here for kids, and Main Street in Chatham is a short ride away (Ride 26). Turn around to return to the Harwich Bike Rotary and the CCRT, or connect to other points in Chatham.

MILES AND DIRECTIONS

0.0   Start at the Harwich Bike Rotary and follow the sign to the OCRT.

0.6   Cross Island Pond Road (cemetery entrance).

0.8   Cross Route 124 (Pleasant Lake Avenue) at the crosswalk (walk bikes, heavy traffic).

1.0   Cross Oak Street and pass Brooks Park on the right.

1.4   Cross the Route 39 crosswalk (heavy traffic).

1.9   Pass through Thompson's Field Conservation Area. The trail bends to the left.

2.3   Use caution on this downhill section that bends to the right (watch out for sand at the bottom).

2.9   Cross Depot Road.

3.7   Cross Morton Road.

4.0   Cross Route 137 (Meetinghouse Road).

4.7   Cross Sam Ryder Road.

5.4   Turn right onto George Ryder Road (bike lane).

5.7   Turn left at the crosswalk and re-enter the OCRT paved bike path.

6.4   Proceed straight ahead onto Wilfred Road.

7.0   Cross Old Queen Anne Road.

7.1   Cross Stepping Stones Road.

7.2   Cross Stepping Stones Road again.

7.5   The OCRT ends. Turn right onto Crowell Road (for a few feet).

7.5   Turn left immediately on Tipcart Drive.

7.8   Turn right onto Hitching Post Road.

8.0   Turn left Depot Road.

8.1   Arrive at the Chatham Railroad Museum. Turn around to retrace your route to the start.

16.2   Finish the ride at the Harwich Bike Rotary.

Old Colony Rail Trail, Harwich to Chatham

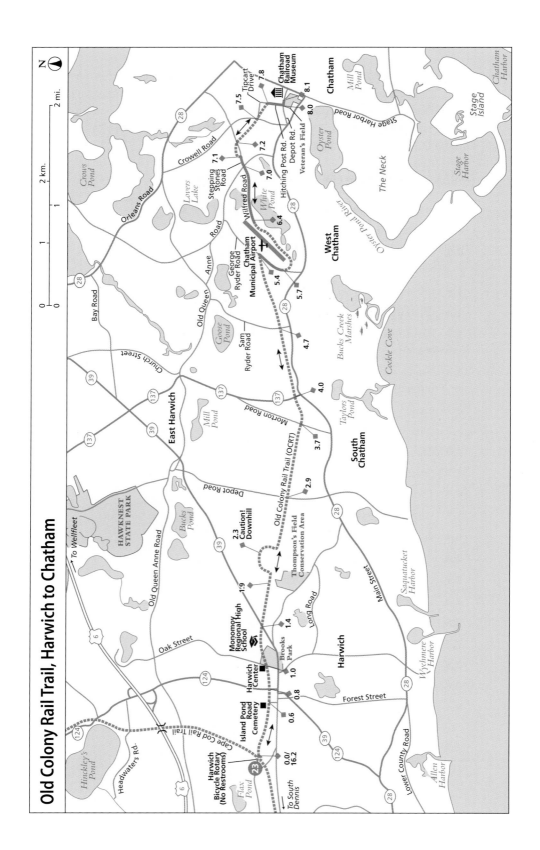

Local Events and Attractions
Skydive Cape Cod (Chatham Municipal Airport): 240 George Ryder Rd., Chatham; (508) 420-5867. Get a new perspective on the beach, and see every ride in this guidebook—all at once!

Chatham Railroad Museum: 153 Depot Rd., Chatham; (508) 945-5100. Attention, railroad buffs! See the interior of a caboose and visit a well-maintained railroad station.

Cape Cod Baseball League: Harwich Mariners, Whitehouse Field, Harwich. Chatham Anglers, Veteran's Field, Chatham. See capecodbaseball.org for schedules. Teams made up of the best NCAA college baseball players play forty-four games from early June through early August, with wooden bats. The Major League Baseball scouts will be there, with speed guns and notebooks. Free admission. Bring your lawn chairs.

Restaurants
Ruggie's: 707 Main St., Harwich; (508) 432-0625. Breakfast and lunch. Try the blueberry pancakes.

Hangar B Eatery, Chatham Municipal Airport: 240 George Ryder Rd., Chatham; (508) 593-3655. Open year-round with an outdoor deck in summer. Great breakfast and lunch. Watch the airplanes take off and land at Chatham Municipal Airport.

Restrooms
There are restrooms at Brooks Park (mile 1.0), the Harwich Community Center (100 Oak St., Harwich), at Chatham Municipal Airport, and at Veteran's Field in Chatham.

West Harwich and West Dennis Beaches

This is a nice easy and scenic loop that rides along Nantucket Sound from the Herring River in West Harwich through Dennis Port to West Dennis, past ocean beaches and marshland for the first half of the ride. It then follows the Bass River, inland through historic Dennis and through rural North Harwich back to West Harwich.

Start: Irish Pub (dirt parking lot by the Herring River) or alternate parking at West Harwich Professional Center, Route 28, West Harwich

Distance: 16.1-mile loop

Approximate riding time: 1 to 2 hours

Best bike: Road

Terrain and surface type: Paved roads

Traffic and hazards: Busy roads and road crossings, CCRT crossings, pedestrian traffic near beaches (especially in summer)

Things to see: Irish Pub, Herring River Estuary, Captain Chase House, site of the Belmont Grand Hotel, Inman Road Beach, Raycroft Beach, Sea Street Beach, Swan River Estuary, Lighthouse Inn and West Dennis Light, West Dennis Beach, Bass River, Kelleys Pond, West Dennis Graded Schoolhouse and playground, 1835 Sea Captain's Church, CCRT, Lothrop Avenue wooden bridge, Holy Trinity Church in West Harwich

Map: *Arrow Street Atlas: Cape Cod including Martha's Vineyard & Nantucket,* p. 57

Getting there: From Route 6 (Mid-Cape Highway), take exit 9A and drive south on Route 134 in South Dennis to Upper County Road. Turn left at the traffic light and take Upper County Road to its end where it merges with Route 28 in Dennis Port. Take Route 28 South (traveling east) to West Harwich, pass North Road on the left and Riverside Drive on the right, then turn left into the Irish Pub parking lot before the Herring River Bridge.

GPS coordinates: N41 40.16' / W70 06.63'

THE RIDE

This ride starts at the parking lot of the Irish Pub, which is only open in summer for a few nights each week, and has a dirt parking lot where people park to fish or rent kayaks. The parking lot is almost always empty during the day, unless it's a Saturday in August during the Irish Pub Road Race. On a Friday or Saturday night, there is always live music, sometimes traditional Irish music that can be heard along the river in this neighborhood with an Irish feel. Parking is also available at the West Harwich Professional Center next door (120 Route 28 on North Road). Route 28 is a busy road so use caution crossing Route 28 onto Riverside Drive past the historic summer home (now an antiques shop) of Chase & Sanborn Coffee Company co-founder Caleb Chase.

Riverside Drive is a long, straight stretch of residential homes built on the old Chase property, far removed in time from when ships were built along the shores of the Herring River in the 18th and 19th centuries. It was a busy port here, with catboats and other fishing boats lining its shores. Up the road on the left, a small vineyard occupies the front yard of a Riverside Drive family, where grapes are harvested each year to make wine for its residents, who invite neighbors to help pick in exchange for a taste of the family vintage. Ride past the small vineyard down this long, straight stretch of road.

Turn right on Lower County Road and then left on Belmont Road, the former entrance to one of the Cape's grand hotels, the Belmont, built in 1894 on twenty-two acres by the sea in West Harwich. Old postcards remember this hotel as the "Summer Wall Street,"

Bike Shops

Barbara's Bike & Sport Equipment, 430 Route 134, South Dennis, (508) 760-4723, barbsbikeshop.com
Dennis Cycle Center, 249 Great Western Rd., South Dennis, (508) 398-0011, denniscyclecenter.com

with Cape Cod's first stock-market ticker-tape machine in the lobby. Now a private condominium complex, the four-story, 225-room Belmont Hotel was one of only a few grand resort hotels built on Cape Cod in the 19th century. The tennis courts on the left are a reminder of a time when the well-to-do played and relaxed here before the "Aristocrat of the Cape" Belmont finally closed its doors in 1974. Turn right on Chase Avenue along the sand-blown paved road that follows the shoreline and many access points to the beach, including Inman Road Beach on the left. The landscape is highly developed here, with hotels, inns, restaurants, and small cottages. Look left through the buildings for views of Nantucket Sound and watch out for families and children crossing the road to head for the water.

Turn right on Depot Road by the highly rated Ocean House Restaurant on the left, and make a quick left onto Old Wharf Road in Dennis. Pass many small cottages and beach access paths on the left including Raycroft Beach, and make a quick detour left on Sea Street, to its beach with the same name. Return back to Old Wharf Road past Sea Street Beach via Shad Hole Road. This is the Dennis Port beach community that's been around for a long time, with many small cottages and smaller hotels and resorts lining the shores. Old Wharf Road bends to the right, away from the water, and ends at Lower County Road. Turn left on Lower County and cross the bridge over the Swan River, which twists out to sea to the left and snakes into South Dennis on the right. The view of the Swan River Marsh and ocean beyond is expansive, with wildlife flourishing here, away from the busy beaches and people off in the distance. Kayaking is popular all along the Swan River, and kayakers can paddle past swans, gulls, cormorants, great blue herons, ducks, and ospreys hovering over the nearly 3 miles of river from Swan Pond to Nantucket Sound.

Ride the rest of Lower County Road and turn left at mile 4.0 onto Lighthouse Road toward West Dennis Beach. Opt to ride all the way out to the mouth of the Bass River at the end of West Dennis Beach, or check out the Lighthouse Inn by turning left on the road with the same name. The inn was the site of a lighthouse that operated off and on from 1885 to 1914. The property was bought and sold and finally became the family inn it is today. In 1989, the lighthouse was relit after seventy-five years of dormancy as the West Dennis Light, although privately owned and maintained. Turn right at the rotary onto Loring Avenue, then left on Surfside Road, where the driveways are slips with boats parked next to the houses, much like so many Florida neighborhoods that look more like marinas than Cape Cod neighborhoods.

The ride heads out of this neighborhood and along the Bass River on Uncle Barney's Road, then veers back away from the river past Kelleys Pond on Pond Street. With the Bass River Bridge to the left, turn right on Ferry, right on Loring, and left on Pond Street, with the big kettle pond on the right. Turn right on School Street past the West Dennis Graded Schoolhouse built in 1867, now used as a public playground and community center. Bear left and merge onto Lower County Road, then turn left on Trotting Park Road, a 1-mile straight ride away from the coast that crosses busy Route 28 and merges with Main Street in Dennis.

Herring River Estuary, looking north, West Harwich

This is a nice stretch of road through historic South Dennis, but with not much of a shoulder, passing many historic homes and buildings. The 1835 Sea Captain's Church, today the South Dennis Congregational Church on the right, houses the nation's oldest working organ. On the left farther up the road is the Village Library, which was once a modest home, a cobbler shop, and the home of a poet. Turn right on Highbank Road, cross Route 134 and four lanes at the traffic light, then turn left on Great Western Road. At mile 10.5 there is the option to turn onto the Cape Cod Rail Trail (CCRT) to connect to other towns and rides, or to ride it instead of Great Western Road to Lothrop Avenue. At mile 11.2, turn left on Depot Street, then right on Main Street in North Harwich. This is a rural and hilly stretch of road through oak and pine forest, with horse farms, grazing sheep, farm animals, and quiet cranberry bogs. Harwich was once devoid of farms, a mostly seafaring and fishing town. All that changed when cranberries started being cultivated in the early 19th century. The unofficial color of Harwich is cranberry red, and that color seems to be everywhere here, from the Cranberry Valley Golf Course (Oak Street, Harwich Center) to Cape Farm Cranberry Bog Tours (1601 Factory Rd., Harwich), both highly recommended. If it's October, the bogs almost glow red as the fruit gets harvested, and it makes for a great ride along this route or the CCRT option along Great Western Road to Lothrop Avenue.

Turn right on Lothrop Avenue, cross the CCRT and Great Western Road, round the left-hand corner, and descend the hill into a sharp right turn over a wooden bridge. The view from the bridge of the Herring River to the right is vast, and the ride through the tall marsh grass on either side of the road is like nowhere else on Cape Cod. At dusk or dawn the light is truly spectacular through this stretch of road. There are plenty of hiking trails through Bell's Neck and the Herring River, and also the Lee Baldwin Memorial Woodlands, up the road on the left. Near the end of Lothrop Avenue, crane your neck right to see the lovely chapel in the woods behind the Holy Trinity Church parking lot.

Turn right on Route 28 and then left on Grey Neck Road through residential wooded and shade-covered neighborhoods. Turn right on Lower County Road and ride past several roads on the left that lead to the beach, some private, some public (Grey Neck Beach and Pleasant Road Beach are public). It's a flat stretch here with a sidewalk on the right and narrow lanes. The road dips, then crosses over the Herring River. Enjoy the view on the left of the mouth of the river to Nantucket Sound, and to the right, the start and finish of this ride off in the distance. This end of the river was once filled with fishing shacks and boats, and the old Doble windmill on the left has been there for eighty years, looking very much like the old postcards from the early 20th century. The windmill could be viewed spinning with full sails from the Belmont Hotel across the river. Turn right on Riverside Drive, smell the grapes if it's fall, and return to the Irish Pub parking lot for the ride finish. There are kayak rentals here in summer if you want to explore the Herring River Estuary further, or you can ride North Road to a footbridge and hike into the Bell's Neck Conservation Area. Bell's Neck also makes for excellent mountain bike and cyclocross riding.

MILES AND DIRECTIONS

0.0 Start this ride at the Irish Pub parking lot (dirt lot on the Herring River).

0.0 Turn right on Route 28.

0.1 Turn left immediately on Riverside Drive.

0.6 Turn right on Lower County Road.

0.8 Turn left on Belmont Road.

1.1 Turn right on Chase Avenue.

1.2 Pass Inman Road Beach on the left opposite Inman Road.

1.4 Turn right on Depot Road and immediately turn left on Old Wharf Road at the Ocean House Restaurant on the left.

1.5 Pass Raycroft Parkway and Raycroft Beach on the left.

1.9 Turn left on Sea Street for Sea Street beach, and then turn immediately right on Shad Hole Road.

2.0 Turn left on Old Wharf Road.

3.1 Turn left on Lower County Road.

3.3 View the Swan River.

4.0 Turn left on Lighthouse Road.

4.3 Enter the West Dennis Beach Rotary.

4.6 Turn left on Surfside Road.

5.0 Turn right on Merchant Avenue.

5.1 Turn left on Loring Avenue.

5.4 Turn right on Uncle Barney's Road.

5.8 Turn right on Ferry Street.

5.9 Turn right on Loring Avenue.

6.0 Turn left on Pond Street.

6.5 Turn right on School Street.

6.9 Bear left and continue on Lower County Road.

West Harwich and West Dennis Beaches

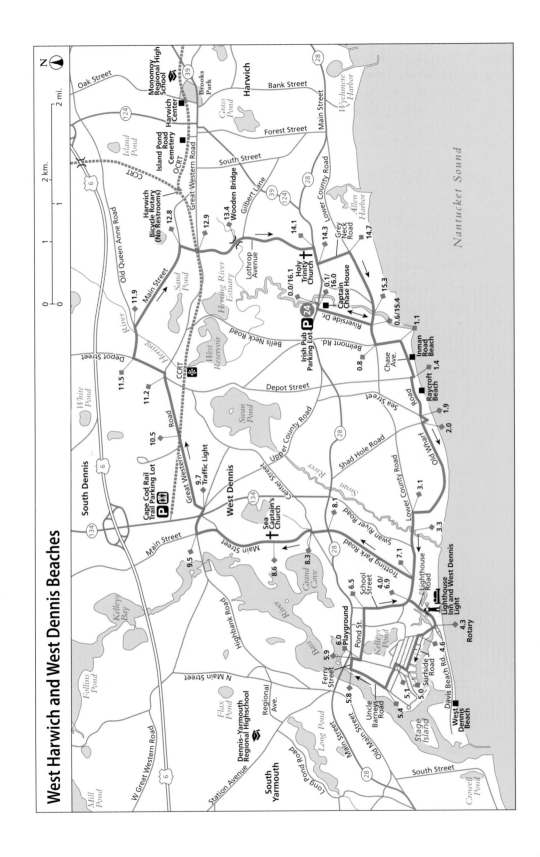

7.1 Turn left on Trotting Park Road.

8.1 Cross Route 28.

8.3 Continue straight ahead on Main Street.

8.6 Pass the 1835 Sea Captain's Church on the right.

9.5 Turn right on Highbank Road (turns into Upper County Road).

9.7 Cross Route 134 at traffic light (heavy traffic and four lanes to cross) and continue on Upper County Road.

9.7 Turn left immediately on Great Western Road.

10.5 Cross the CCRT and continue on Great Western Road.

11.2 Turn left on Depot Street.

11.5 Turn right on Main Street.

11.9 Bear right and continue on Main Street.

12.8 Turn right on Lothrop Avenue.

12.9 Cross the CCRT and Great Western Road. Continue on Lothrop Avenue.

13.4 Cross a wooden bridge in the Herring River Estuary (Bell's Neck).

14.1 Turn right on Route 28.

14.3 Turn left on Grey Neck Road.

14.7 Turn right on Lower County Road.

15.3 Cross over the Herring River.

15.4 Turn right on Riverside Drive.

16.0 Turn right on Route 28.

16.1 Turn left into the Irish Pub parking lot to finish this ride.

RIDE INFORMATION

Local Events and Attractions
Grey Neck Beach: At the end of Grey Neck Road, off Lower County Road.
Pleasant Road Beach: At the end of Pleasant Road, off Lower County Road.
Harwich Junior Theater: 105 Division St., West Harwich; (508) 432-2002. The "Junior" in Junior Theater means they train young actors, but training and performances are for all ages. There are no bad seats in this intimate theater, and many little Cape Codders have their first experience watching theater here. Great for kids and families.

Cape Cod Bumper Boats: 322 Route 28, Harwich Port; (508) 430-1155. Bumper boats in front and batting cages in back for a lot of fun with kids (of all ages). You will get wet.

Wright Chiropractic & Sports Care: 120 Route 28, West Harwich Professional Center, West Harwich; (508) 432-7002. In practice for more than twenty years, Dr. Gregory Wright specializes in sports injuries, with special interest in cycling, triathlon, and running injuries and conditions. He is team physician for a professional cycling team and treats several local and professional athletes of all ages.

Restaurants

Organic Market: 640 Main St. (Route 28) Dennis Port; (508) 760-3043. Darby Ziruk has been in business for more than thirty years with the largest selection of organic produce on Cape Cod, and her daughter Rory Eames now runs this great little store with a juice and smoothie bar, fresh produce, and all sorts of treats. They also have stores in Chatham and Mashpee Commons.

Viera: 11 Route 28, West Harwich; (774) 408-7492. On the West Harwich–Dennis Port town line, locals Ben and Angela Porter make their own bread and pasta and use local farms and fishermen for their great dishes. Gathering excellent reviews in a hurry. Dinner, closed Sunday and Monday.

Ocean House Restaurant: 425 Old Wharf Rd., Dennis Port; (508) 394-0700. The views of Nantucket Sound are gorgeous and the water so close, you almost feel like you're *on* the water. Great seafood in a lively room.

Restrooms

Restrooms are available at the West Dennis Beach (seasonal).

Harwich Port and South Chatham Tour

This ride takes cyclists to two great beaches in Harwich and Chatham, with great views of Nantucket Sound, Monomoy Island, and Stage Harbor Lighthouse off in the distance. On the way, the ride goes through bustling Harwich Port, a summer vacation area with lots going on, and the start/finish at Brooks Park connects to the Old Colony Rail Trail for more riding options.

Start: Brooks Park parking lot, Oak Street, Harwich

Distance: 13.7-mile loop

Approximate riding time: 1 to 2 hours, depending on stops

Best bike: Road or hybrid

Terrain and surface type: Smooth paved main roads and back roads

Traffic and hazards: Busy main roads, especially Route 28 in Harwich Port and along Saquatucket Harbor (worse in summer), and Route 39 in East Harwich (rotary), busy beach parking lots at Red River and Forest Beaches, pedestrians, other bicyclists and vehicles

Things to see: Brooks Park tennis courts and playground, Monomoy Regional High School, Harwich Community Center, Whitehouse Field (NCAA Harwich Mariners Cape Cod Baseball League), Harwich Center, Harwich Port Golf Club, Harwich Port, Saquatucket Harbor, Red River Beach, Forest Street Beach, Forest Beach Overlook, Old Colony Rail Trail

Map: *Arrow Street Atlas: Cape Cod including Martha's Vineyard & Nantucket,* p. 57

Getting there: From Route 6 (Mid-Cape Highway), take exit 10 toward Harwich Center on Route 124 South (Pleasant Lake Avenue), turn left on Old Colony Road, and drive to the end on Oak Street. Cross Oak Street into the Brooks Park parking lot directly in front of you.

GPS coordinates: N41 41.27' / W70 04.20'

THE RIDE

Brooks Park on Oak Street in Harwich is the beginning of this ride, and it's also on the Old Colony Rail Trail (OCRT) for the option of making this 13.7-mile jaunt a bit longer by connecting many other rides in this book. There are restrooms at the Harwich Community Center on Oak Street by turning right out of the start at Brooks Park, but this ride turns left and winds through Harwich Center. Pass Harwich Town Hall and Brooks Free Library on Main Street and then pass the Harwich Historical Society housed in the Brooks Academy Museum, on the corner of Parallel Street and Sisson Road. Descend the hill on Forest Street past a large pond, Grassy Pond Bird Sanctuary, on the left. Farther down Forest Street is the Harwich Port Golf Club, a favorite of former Speaker of the US House of Representatives Thomas P. "Tip" O'Neill, who had a summer home here and whose grave is at adjacent Mount Pleasant Cemetery. Watch for golf carts crossing the road here, and be glad for bicycle helmets.

Turn left onto Route 28 into Harwich Port. The rural road you just took from downtown Harwich ends with busy shops, restaurants, easy access to the beach, and long stretches of sidewalk for strolling. Local artists display in the summer here, and musicians provide entertainment along this stretch as part of Music Stroll in the Port, sponsored by the Harwich Port Merchants Association on Wednesday nights in summer. Stop at Bonatt's for breakfast and get a melt-a-way, or Perk's Coffee Shop for all kinds of coffees, or if it's lunchtime head to George's Pizza for pizza and *spanakopita* or *baklava*. George's

Bike Shop

Dennis Cycle Center, 249 Great Western Rd., South Dennis, (508) 398-0011, denniscyclecenter.com

has been family-owned for more than forty years and is voted Best Pizza on Cape Cod year after year. Opt to turn down any road on the right, such as Sea Street, to get to the beach. Turn left at George's Pizza on Cross Street and then right on Pleasant Street, and wind through the neighborhoods of Harwich Port on back roads that locals use to avoid Route 28 in summer. Take Hoyt Road around a retired bog and turn right on Gorham to access Route 28. As an option, turn right to tour Saquatucket Harbor, where the Freedom Cruise Line high-speed ferry takes passengers and bicycles to Nantucket daily. Brax Landing Restaurant has great views of the harbor and marina and is a local favorite for lunch or dinner. You can backtrack up Route 28 from the harbor to continue this ride.

Ride busy Route 28 to Julien Road and then Old Wharf Road to Red River Beach, a long stretch of beach and a long, narrow parking lot alongside with

Busy Main Street (Route 28) in Harwich Port

bathrooms and a concession stand in summer. Ride to the end for views of Monomoy off the southern tip of Chatham, now an island after a storm broke through and separated the peninsula from the rest of the town. The Red River estuary and marsh offer beautiful views and a lot of beach walking. Walk across the "river" and you're in Chatham, or straddle it and be in two places at once. Even though it's a crowded beach in summer, there is still plenty of room to stretch out.

Before the end of the 250-car parking lot, turn left on Uncle Venies Road, and then right on South Chatham Road, which climbs over a bump and has great views of the huge Red River Marsh on the right. Cross over the intertidal river and enter Chatham, where the road is called Deep Hole Road, which climbs sharply up to Pleasant Street in South Chatham. The ride descends now on back roads with views of Nantucket Sound, turning left on Wadsworth Road, then right and right again to Forest Beach, another gorgeous beach alongside an estuary, the Taylors Pond and Mill Creek marshes. Like Red River Beach, Forest Beach is where kayakers, kite boarders, windsurfers, and others set off for Monomoy Island Wildlife Refuge, a short run from either beach. The view of Monomoy is now closer still, and the Stage Harbor Lighthouse is visible off in the distance. The huge Mill Creek marsh to the east of Forest Beach Road was once the location of a Marconi wireless transmitting station, and the posts from the original towers (it looks a little like Stonehenge) were left behind to provide nesting for ospreys.

Turn around and ride Forest Street, then turn right on Bayview Road for a déjà vu experience with the large marsh on the right. Turn right onto a driveway at mile 6.0 to the Forest Beach Overlook, where the view gets even better. Turn around after soaking in the views, turn right back onto Bayview, and take the side street Kitty's Lane, which dips down then climbs back to Forest Street. Turn right on Forest Street, and at the end of the brief climb, cross over Route 28 onto Morton Road, a 1-mile stretch that rolls gently over the OCRT, merges with Route 137 (Meetinghouse Road), and meets Old Queen Anne Road (not to be confused with Queen Anne Road, a separate road west of here).

Turn left on Old Queen Anne Road and stop by the Corner Store for breakfast, coffee, a burrito, panini, or baked goods. This place is busy but keeps it moving, and it's worth not taking the OCRT shortcut back to the start of this ride, just to eat here. Take Old Queen Anne Road to the East Harwich Rotary, then continue on Route 39 west to Depot Road. There's a second chance to cut this ride short as it crosses the OCRT again, but ride the long and uneventful road to the end and turn right onto Route 28. New England Gardens is to the left and Buca's Tuscan Roadside to the right as it rounds the corner. Turn right off Route 28 on Old Chatham Road and ride a gentle uphill to Long Road. Make a quick left onto Oliver Snow Road, then turn right on Gorham, a lovely road that bends left and rolls out to Bank Street. Turn right and the road climbs up to Main Street, where you pass the library again, and make a quick left on Oak Street back to the start. Check out a Cape Cod Baseball League game at Whitehouse Field if it's summer, behind the Monomoy Regional High School. There might be a band or other event near the bandstand if you time it right. Or just sit under the trees by the OCRT and watch the other cyclists enjoy their adventure.

MILES AND DIRECTIONS

0.0 Start this ride in Brooks Park, Harwich.

0.1 Turn left on Oak Street.

0.2 Turn right on Main Street and make an immediate left on Bank Street.

0.3 Turn right on Parallel Street.

0.5 Turn left on Forest Street.

0.6 Cross Sisson Road past the Brooks Academy Museum (Harwich Historical Society).

1.8 Turn left onto Route 28 into Harwich Port.

2.0 Turn left on Cross Street past George's Pizza on the left.

2.1 Turn right on Pleasant Street.

2.4 Turn left on Freeman Street.

2.5 Turn right on Hoyt Road.

3.1 Turn right on Gorham Road.

3.2 Turn left on Route 28.

3.3 Turn right on Julien Road.

3.7 Turn left on Old Wharf Road.

4.1 Ride past Red River Beach on the right and turn left on Uncle Venies Road.

4.3 Turn right on South Chatham Road.

4.6 Continue on Deep Hole Road and enter Chatham.

5.0 Turn right on Pleasant Street.

5.3 Turn left on Wadsworth Road.

5.4 Turn left on Forest Beach Road Extension.

5.6 Turn right on Woodland Road and turn right immediately on Forest Beach Road.

5.8 Turn around at the end of Forest Beach Road.

6.0 Turn right onto Bayview Road and immediately turn right up the driveway to the Forest Beach Overlook.

6.1 Turn around at the Forest Beach Overlook parking lot and descend the driveway.

6.2 Turn right, back onto Bayview Road.

6.4 Turn left on Kitty's Lane.

6.5 Turn right on Forest Beach Road.

Harwich Port and South Chatham Tour

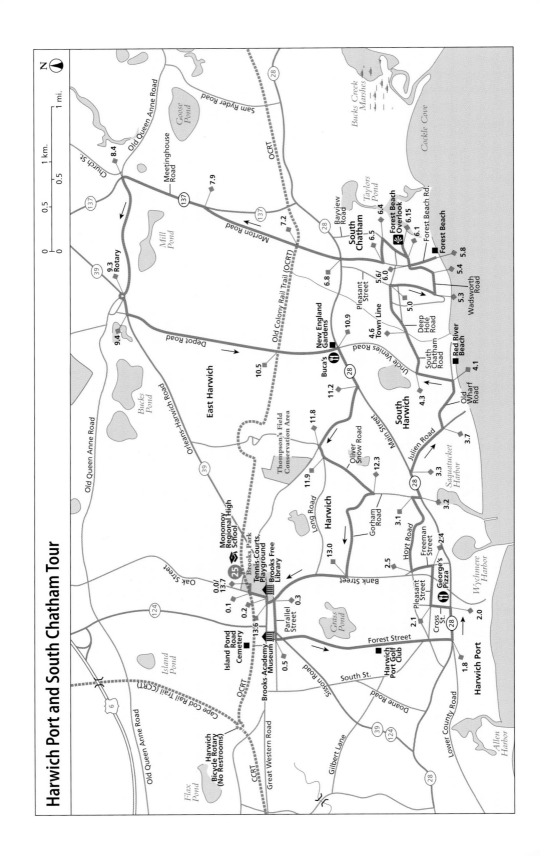

6.8	Cross Route 28 onto Morton Road.
7.2	Cross the OCRT.
7.9	Turn left on Route 137 (Meetinghouse Road).
8.4	Turn left on Old Queen Anne Road.
9.3	Enter rotary at Old Queen Anne Road and Route 39.
9.3	Exit rotary onto Route 39 heading west.
9.4	Turn left onto Depot Road.
10.5	Cross the OCRT.
10.9	Turn right on Route 28.
11.2	Turn right onto Chatham Road.
11.8	Turn left on Long Road.
11.9	Turn left on Oliver Snow Road.
12.3	Turn right on Gorham Road.
13.0	Turn right on Bank Street.
13.6	Turn right on Main Street (Route 39) and immediately turn left on Oak Street (Brooks Free Library on the right).
13.7	Turn right into Brooks Park parking lot to finish this ride.

RIDE INFORMATION

Local Events and Attractions

Music Stroll in the Port: Musicians play along Route 28 in Harwich Port during evenings in July and August. Many of the artists are nationally known with long resumes. Walk the streets in summer and listen (even dance) to your favorite musicians and bands. Free.

Cranberry Valley Golf Course: 183 Oak St., Harwich; (508) 430-5234. This course is one of the best public courses in the United States with many awards.

Harwich Cranberry Festival: Every September in Brooks Park. Music, crafts, art, and cranberries.

Restaurants

George's Pizza: 564 Main St. (Route 28), Harwich Port; (508) 432-3144. George's sons carry on this family-run restaurant and win Cape Cod's awards for best pizza every year for a reason. Excellent pizza and sandwiches. Eat-in or take-out.

Buckie's Biscotti: 554 Main St. (Route 28), Harwich Port; (877) 247-2688. Not as big as its sister in Dennis Port, with fresh baked biscotti, cookies, pastries, cakes, specialty breakfast and lunch items, and prepared foods to go.

Buca's Tuscan Roadhouse: 4 Depot Rd., Harwich; (508) 432-6900. Across from Jay Potter's New England Gardens, Buca's is on a hill in Harwich far from the hills in Tuscany, bringing Tuscan dining to Cape Cod in a cozy restaurant.
The Corner Store: 1403 Old Queen Anne Rd., Chatham; (508) 432-1077. Breakfast, lunch. Rave reviews for sandwiches, burritos, paninis, wraps, and whoopee pies. Great pit stop for bicyclists.

Restrooms
There are restrooms in Brooks Park and at Red River Beach (seasonal).

Chatham Harbors Tour

An easy, short ride from a railroad museum across town to the harbors, beaches, and lighthouses of Chatham. Opt for a side trip through busy downtown Chatham, a side trip to the Monomoy National Wildlife Refuge, or connect to the rest of the Outer Cape via the Old Colony Rail Trail (Ride 23).

Start: Chatham Elementary School (or Chatham Railroad Museum) parking lot

Distance: 5.2-mile loop

Approximate riding time: 1 hour or more, depending on stops

Best bike: Road

Terrain and surface type: Paved road

Traffic and hazards: Busy summer traffic on main roads, rotary (traffic circle), sand in road, busy parking area at Chatham Lighthouse and Beach

Things to see: Chatham Railroad Museum, Oyster Pond, Stage Harbor and Lighthouse, Morris Island, Monomoy National Wildlife Refuge, Stage Island, Chatham Lighthouse and Beach, Main Street Chatham, the Outer Beach (and Chatham "break"), Chatham Bars Inn and Restaurant, Chatham Fish Pier

Map: *Arrow Street Atlas: Cape Cod including Martha's Vineyard & Nantucket*, p. 35

Getting there: From Route 6 (Mid-Cape Highway), take exit 11 and turn onto Route 137 headed south. Continue on Route 137 and cross Route 39 in East Harwich to Old Queen Anne Road. Turn left on Old Queen Anne Road and follow it to its end at Route 28. Turn left on Route 28 (Main Street), then left on Depot Road at the intersection with Crowell Road and Old Queen Anne Road. Crowell Road is a hard left; Depot

Road is between Crowell Road and Route 28 (Main Street). Turn left on Hitching Post Road. The Chatham Elementary School parking lot start is immediately on the right.

GPS coordinates: N41 41.21' / W69 57.76'

THE RIDE

Chatham is the outer elbow of Cape Cod, facing the Atlantic, Africa, and Europe to the east and Nantucket to the south. This ride gets to the water's edge and rides past two lighthouses, beautiful harbors, a grand resort, and beautiful expensive homes. This is one of my favorite places to ride in summer, with a lot going on, and connects to the Old Colony Rail Trail (OCRT; Ride 23). Start out at the Chatham Elementary School parking lot (Chatham Railroad Museum) on Hitching Post Road and ride past Veteran's Field and a big playground on Depot Road. Turn right on Old Harbor Road to the Main Street Rotary, and avoid town by heading straight on Stage Harbor Road. Tranquil Oyster Pond is on the right, with swimming, boating, and restrooms available. Oyster Pond has a direct route to Nantucket Sound via the Oyster River, so some pretty big boats will be sitting out there. Turn right on Cedar Street and ride the rolling hills upward to the end. Turn left on Battlefield Road for this ride. (Opt to turn right for an out-and-back down Stage Neck Road to Eldridge Point to view the Oyster River.)

Turn left again on Champlain Road, and take your time here, one of the best short stretches of road on Cape Cod. Turn the corner right to see breathtaking views of Stage Harbor, Morris Island, and Stage Island, with the 1880 Stage Harbor Lighthouse off in the distance to the right. Descend the hill and bear left on Champlain Road, over a hill past the Stage Harbor Yacht Club and down to the fishing docks on Stage Harbor Road. Turn left at the bottom of this hill past the Harbormaster's Office and then right on Bridge Street, where splintering wood on the old Mitchell River Bridge could cause cyclists some tire problems. The bridge is due for a rebuild with completion scheduled for 2016, so use caution when crossing. It is the last wooden drawbridge in Massachusetts. It's also a popular spot for fishing, with the Mitchell River flowing underneath and Mill Pond to the left. Continue on Bridge Street over rolling hills through a very nice residential section lined with privet and white picket fences. At the end of Bridge Street, turn left onto Main Street in front of the Chatham Lighthouse, an active lighthouse and Coast Guard station, originally established in 1808 under the Jefferson presidency and visible for more than 20 miles out to sea.

There is the option here to turn right and descend the hill to Morris Island Road and do an out-and-back ride to Stage Island and Morris Island. These are not actual islands, but might be one day, if erosion continues on this storm-battered peninsula. At Morris Island, the US Fish & Wildlife Service operates the Monomoy National Wildlife Refuge from its headquarters on Wiki's Way, off Morris Island Road on the left (after passing Stage Island Road on the right). The refuge is a great place to learn about and see the seal population that has attracted sharks to these waters of late, including great white sharks, and is well worth the visit. The refuge offers a self-guided trail map of Morris Island, with a 0.75-mile trail among the many shorebirds and occasional seal. Most of the seals hang out on Monomoy Island, accessible only by boat after a storm in April 1958 separated the spit from the mainland. Monomoy itself was split into two islands after a strong nor'easter blasted this area, still referred to by locals as the Blizzard of 1978 (February 6 and 7, 1978). The inactive Monomoy Point Lighthouse still stands on South Monomoy, a 40-foot cylinder of cast iron built in 1849 and maintained by the refuge. You can get a tour of Monomoy from local guides who will ferry you out to the islands.

The Chatham Lighthouse and Chatham South Beach across the street are major draws to the town, especially in summer, so watch for cars pulling in and out of the narrow and crowded parking lot on the right. Chatham Lighthouse is an active Coast Guard station and not open to the public except for a limited number of tours, mostly in summer (usually one weekly). Like Truro's Highland Light before it, the Jefferson Administration commissioned Chatham Light just nine years

Bike Shop

Monomoy Sail & Cycle, 275 Orleans Rd. (Route 28), North Chatham, (508) 945-0811, chathambikeshop.com

later, in 1806. The two lighthouses were side by side, each with a fixed light. The Chatham twin lighthouses were rebuilt several times over the span of the next hundred years, and in 1879–80, both fell off the bluff into the sand. Look out from the parking lot at the beach to see where these twins used to stand; the edge of the cliff was out there in the 19th century. In 1923, one of the rebuilt lighthouses was moved to Eastham and is now Nauset Light opposite Nauset Light Beach.

The beach across from Chatham Light is called South Beach today, but it might not be after the next major storm. Before 1987, South Beach was called the Outer Beach, and extended to Nauset Beach in Orleans. This long strip of sand is known as a "barrier beach," an ever-changing coastal dune that has formed and reformed along this coast from long shore currents that deposit huge amounts of sand along the harbor. The best way to describe a barrier beach is dynamic and unstable, and in 1987 a huge storm ripped through the Outer Beach, creating a South Island and North Beach. The 1987 breach, known locally as "the break," created new shipping lanes and treacherous currents for mariners here. By 1993, South Island eventually rejoined the mainland creating the beach you see today, which grew and connected to North Monomoy by 2006. In 2007 another breach separated North Beach in two at Pleasant Bay, and then in 2013 Monomoy broke off from South Beach again. South Beach is worth coming back to again and again, year after year, just to

Stage Harbor Lighthouse, Chatham

see the migration of the sand and dune from never-ending wind and wave energy.

Continue this ride past the Chatham Lighthouse down Main Street, descending past a line of old Cape homes on the right and old neighborhoods to the left. Continue straight on Shore Road (Main Street takes a 90-degree left turn and is an option to explore downtown, not to be missed) and ride the hills to one of the crests at mile 4.1, with a great view of the Outer Beach, where the cottages are gradually being removed due to erosion and storms. The Outer Beach can be accessed via Nauset Beach in Orleans (Ride 27) by motor vehicle (permit required) or fat tire bike (no permit required), so gaze across the water at your next ride. Continue on Shore Road past the elegant Chatham Bars Inn, with the main inn and restaurant up the hill on the left, and the Beach House with beachfront dining down to the right along the beach. The Chatham Bars Inn recently acquired farmland on Route 6A in East Brewster to grow its own ingredients and raise its own chickens, and can be seen on Ride 17 just before Millstone Road (listen for the rooster and chickens).

Turn left away from the water on Seaview Street with the option to continue along Shore Road to visit the Chatham Fish Pier and Market just ahead on the right, to see the commercial boats unloading today's catch. There are often seals here, too (they always know where the fresh fish are), and the fish-and-chips or lobster rolls are the freshest. Otherwise turn left on Seaview Street past the Chatham Bars Inn golf course, and then right on Highland Avenue. Turn left on Old Harbor Road and make a quick right on Depot to return to the start. The Chatham Railroad Museum is a great place to stop for a history of the Chatham Branch of the Old Colony Railroad, now the Old Colony Rail Trail (mostly), which connects to this ride (see Ride 23). If this little 5-mile loop isn't enough for those legs, use the OCRT to connect to every Cape Cod town from Dennis to Wellfleet.

And if you turned left at mile 3.7 onto Main Street instead of going straight on Shore Road, be sure to visit the Chatham Candy Manor across from the Chatham Squire (a fisherman's bar with attached restaurant), an unofficial center of this "quaint drinking village with a fishing problem." Main Street in Chatham is great for walking as a side trip for this ride, with its many small shops, restaurants, and the newly renovated Chatham Orpheum Theater, an old-fashioned movie theater with comfy seats and a great restaurant. There are too many great little shops to mention. Like the Candy Manor. Or Artful Hand. Or the Mayflower. If it's a Friday night in summer, don't miss the weekly band concert, where kids and adults can dance around the bandstand in an area roped off from the crowd on blankets with picnic baskets and balloons all around.

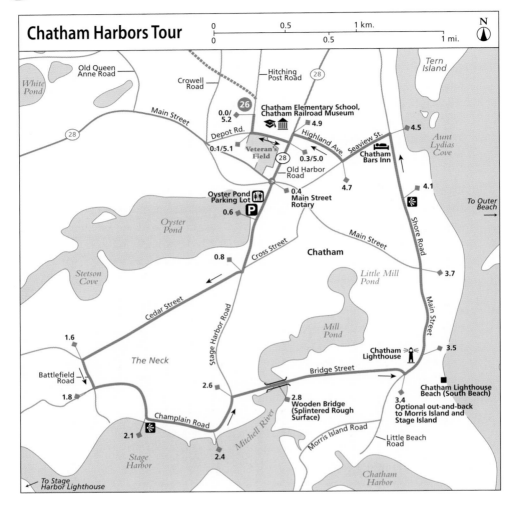

MILES AND DIRECTIONS

0.0 Start this ride at the Chatham Elementary School parking lot (adjacent to the Chatham Railroad Museum) on Hitching Post Road.

0.0 Turn left on Hitching Post Road.

0.1 Turn left on Depot Road.

0.2 Turn right on Old Harbor Road.

0.4 Enter the rotary on Main Street and continue on Stage Harbor Road.

0.6   Pass Oyster Pond parking lot on the right (beach, swimming, restrooms).

0.8   Turn right on Cedar Street.

1.6   Turn left on Battlefield Road.

1.8   Turn left on Champlain Road.

2.1   Bear left with views of Stage Harbor and the Stage Harbor Lighthouse on the right.

2.4   Turn left on Stage Harbor Road.

2.6   Turn right on Bridge Street.

2.8   Cross the wooden drawbridge (splintered rough surface).

3.4   Turn left onto Main Street (or turn right for optional out-and-back on Little Beach Road to Morris Island Road, Morris Island and Stage Island, and the Monomoy National Wildlife Refuge Headquarters).

3.5   View Chatham Lighthouse on the left and Chatham Lighthouse Beach on the right.

3.7   Continue straight on Shore Road (or turn left to continue on Main Street for an out-and-back through the center of town).

4.1   View the Outer Beach and the Atlantic Ocean on the right.

4.5   Turn left on Seaview Street.

4.7   Turn right on Highland Avenue.

4.9   Turn left on Old Harbor Road.

5.0   Turn right on Depot Road.

5.1   Turn right on Hitching Post Road.

5.2   Turn right into the parking lot at Chatham Elementary School to finish this ride.

RIDE INFORMATION

Local Events and Attractions

Chatham Orpheum Theater: 637 Main St., Chatham; (508) 945-4900. First opened in 1913, Chatham's downtown movie theater closed in 1987. It reopened to the public as a nonprofit cinema in 2013. Movies are back on Main Street in a state-of-the-art movie theater. Really comfy seats, and excellent restaurant called Vers (508-945-4300).

Chatham Candy Manor: 484 Main St., Chatham; (508) 945-0825. Homemade chocolate and penny candy, since 1955. Hand-dipped creams, caramels, and truffles. Your sweet tooth needs this.

Chatham Band, Inc: Kate Gould Park (behind the Wayside Inn), 512 Main St., Chatham; chathamband.com. Band concerts every Friday night at 8 p.m. from early July through early September (canceled in inclement weather). Bring a picnic dinner and get there early. Dance with your children around the bandstand. Not to be missed.

Restaurants

Vers Restaurant and Patisserie: 637 Main St., Chatham; (508) 945-4300. At the Chatham Orpheum Theater. All-day dining and treats for theatergoers. Excellent dinner.

Chatham Squire: 487 Main St., Chatham; (508) 945-0945. A bar for the locals, a fun and crowded place, with attached restaurant. The last time I had a beer in the tavern, there was a crowd watching a fishing show on the big-screen TV.

Chatham Wayside Inn: 512 Main St., Chatham; (508) 945-5590. An institution and elegant place to stay. The Wild Goose Tavern is the restaurant. Pricey dinner. Great lunch, good place to people watch on Main Street. Beautiful bar for cocktails.

Restrooms

There are restrooms at Veteran's Field, at Oyster Pond Beach, and at the many restaurants on Main Street in Chatham.

Orleans Center to Nauset Beach Loop

Explore downtown Orleans, ride out to East Orleans and Nauset Beach, and enjoy this expansive barrier beach. Return through the old neighborhoods in Tonset, along the bays by Nauset Inlet and Orleans Town Cove.

Start: Depot Square public parking lot, Orleans

Distance: 10.0-mile loop

Approximate riding time: 1 hour

Best bike: Road

Terrain and surface type: Pavement, rough in some spots, with a sandy paved parking lot at Nauset Beach

Traffic and hazards: Busy traffic on main roads through Orleans Center, East Orleans, and on the Beach Road to Nauset Beach; vehicles and pedestrians in the Nauset Beach parking lot; sand in the road

Things to see: Orleans Center, Cape Cod Rail Trail, Nauset Beach (with vehicle or fat tire bike access to the Outer Beach), historic neighborhood of Tonset, Town Cove and Nauset Harbor, Eldredge Park (home of Orleans Firebirds, Cape Cod Baseball League)

Map: *Arrow Street Atlas: Cape Cod including Martha's Vineyard & Nantucket*, p. 66

Getting there: From Route 6 (Mid-Cape Highway), take exit 12 and drive east on Route 6A toward Orleans Center. Turn left on Main Street at the traffic light, then turn left again on Old Colony Way. Depot Square parking lot is on the right, across from the Hot Chocolate Sparrow.

GPS coordinates: N41 47.27' / W69 59.62'

THE RIDE

This ride heads east to Nauset Beach down Main Street in Orleans Center, starting at a major lower Cape hub of cycling adjacent to the Cape Cod Rail Trail (CCRT). It returns along the Orleans Town Cove in a loop pattern, having made two out-and-back trips to the Atlantic Ocean. Start this ride at the Depot Square dirt parking lot across from the Hot Chocolate Sparrow, a meeting place for cyclists from all over Cape Cod as well as a place for coffee, Internet access, homemade chocolate, and ice cream. A Sunday group ride stops at the Sparrow year-round at 9 a.m. on its way to Wellfleet and points north from Dennis. There are two bike shops just a short walk from the start, and this ride passes many shops on Main Street in Orleans, which can be explored before or after the ride.

Turn left out of the Depot Square lot on Old Colony Way, then turn right on Main Street across from Orleans Cycle. Main Street crosses busy Route 6A, then descends and crosses busy Route 28, and finally crosses Tonset Road into East Orleans. Ride Main Street past the Academy of Performing Arts playhouse, the Orleans Cemetery, and a white church, all on the left, then ride the flat stretch through the village of East Orleans. There is the option to stop at any one of the shops here before turning onto Beach Road, which rambles over rolling hills and descends to the beach. Turn left on Beach Road at the fork with Pochet Road, past Joe's and the Barley Neck Inn on the right. This is a nice stretch through residential neighborhood with a few inns near the beach, with good pavement and a decent-sized shoulder. After Nauset Heights Road on the left, the road dips quickly down to the beach.

Nauset Beach in Orleans, not to be confused with Nauset Light Beach in Eastham, is the main attraction for tourists visiting this town, perhaps because its Outer Beach can be driven and extends 9 miles from Orleans to Chatham. And that's good news because the off-road vehicle beach also allows fat tire bikes, at least for now. The Nauset Beach parking lot is closed to bicyclists during the summer season. Park your bike at the bike racks near the gatehouse and walk to the beach.

Despite the restrictions on bicycles in the parking lot, fat tire bikes are allowed on Nauset Beach, on the ORV beach that extends toward Chatham, with the entrance at the right rear of the parking lot. But how do you get to the ORV beach if you can't walk or ride your bike across the parking lot to the entrance at the far end of the lot? For now, the Nauset Beach cycling experience in summer ends at the guardhouse. In the off-season, which is most of the year (with some pretty good weather in the shoulder season), you can ride through the quiet parking lot. And you can ride the Outer Beach toward Chatham on a fat bike in the off-season, too.

Hot Chocolate Sparrow bicycle parking, Orleans

For now, continue this ride on Beach Road, ride the rolling hills, and turn right on Brick Hill Road near the bottom of the descent at mile 4.7. The historic houses on meandering Brick Hill Road seem to get older the farther down you go, with some very old homes near the end. Pass a frog pond on the right, an overgrown cranberry bog, and stands of cedar, and make a sharp right turn at a steep downhill onto Tonset Road. Tonset Road is an out-and-back to Weeset Point, where there is a stairway down to the beach. There are great views of Town Cove and the very productive habitat of Nauset Marsh. The Outer Beach is off in the distance here, its dunes stretching across the horizon. Turn around and climb back up Tonset Road, passing Brick Hill Road on the left, then descending back to Main Street along some easy rollers. Cross Main Street at the traffic lights and turn right on busy Route 28 past Eldredge Park on the left, next to Nauset Regional Middle School. Ride past the field over the hill past the middle school, and turn left on Main Street.

Bike Shops

Orleans Cycle, 26 Main St., Orleans, (508) 255-9115, orleanscycle.com
Idle Times Bike Shop, 29 Main St., Orleans, (508) 240-1122, idletimesbikes.com

If you haven't done so, check out some of the shops here. The Orleans Whole Food Store always seems to have bicycles parked out front and people enjoying lunch on the old wood porch above street level. Main Street Wine & Gourmet has all-day wine-tasting next door. Get a bicycle tune-up or rent bikes for your next adventure at Orleans Cycle, or Idle Times Bike Shop, where Main Street intersects with the CCRT. The Rock Harbor Grill, right next to the Depot Square parking lot finish of this ride, is a great place to have dinner and drinks, or a brick oven pizza with the kids. And of course, there's the Hot Chocolate Sparrow, where there always seems to be cyclists hanging around for conversation, even in winter.

MILES AND DIRECTIONS

0.0 Start this ride at the Depot Square parking lot (next to the CCRT) by turning left on Old Colony Way.

0.1 Turn right on Main Street.

0.2 Cross Route 6A at the traffic light.

0.4 Cross Route 28 (traffic light) and continue on Main Street.

0.7 Cross Tonset Road at the traffic light.

1.7 Turn left at the fork onto Beach Road.

Orleans Center to Nauset Beach Loop

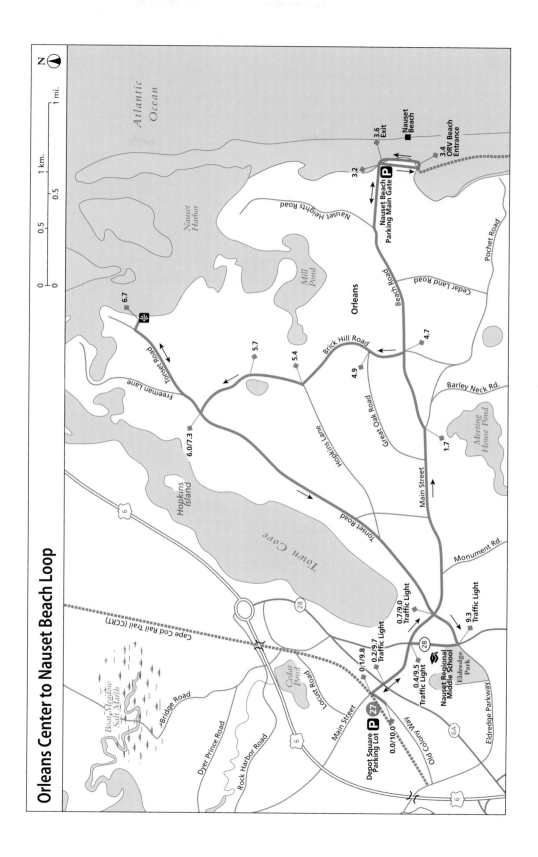

N

Atlantic Ocean

Nauset Harbor

Mill Pond

Nauset Beach

3.6 Exit

3.4 ORV Beach Entrance

3.2

Nauset Beach Parking Main Gate P

Nauset Heights Road

Beach Road

Cedar Land Road

Pochet Road

Orleans

6.7

Freeman Lane

Tonset Road

5.7

5.4

Brick Hill Road

4.9

4.7

6.0/7.3

Hopkins Lane

Great Oak Road

Barley Neck Rd.

1.7

Meeting House Pond

Main Street

Hopkins Island

Town Cove

Tonset Road

Monument Rd.

Cape Cod Rail Trail (CCRT)

28

Boat Meadow Salt Marsh

Bridge Road

Cedar Pond

Locust Road

Dyer Prince Road

Rock Harbor Road

6

0.1/9.8

0.2/9.7 Traffic Light

0.7/9.0 Traffic Light

9.3 Traffic Light

0.4/9.5 Traffic Light

Nauset Regional Middle School

Eldredge Park

28

Old Colony Way

Main Street

Depot Square Parking Lot P 27

0.0/10.0

6A

Eldredge Parkway

6

0 0.5 1 km.
0 0.5 1 mi.

3.2   Turn right into the Nauset Beach parking lot past the main gate.

3.4   Note the Outer Beach vehicle and fat tire bike access point at the far end of the parking lot for future reference as you loop around the parking lot.

3.6   Turn left back out of the parking lot onto Beach Road.

4.7   Turn right onto Brick Hill Road.

4.9   Bear right.

5.4   Bear right.

5.7   Bear left.

6.0   Turn right on Tonset Road.

6.7   Turn around at the end of Tonset Road. Enjoy the view of Town Cove and Nauset Harbor.

7.3   Continue straight on Tonset Road.

9.0   Cross Main Street at the traffic light and continue on Tonset Road.

9.3   Turn right on Route 28 at the traffic light. Pass Eldredge Park and Nauset Regional Middle School on the left.

9.5   Turn left on Main Street at traffic light.

9.7   Cross Route 6A at the traffic light.

9.8   Turn left on Old Colony Way.

10.0   Arrive at the ride finish at Depot Square parking lot.

RIDE INFORMATION

Local Events and Attractions

Cape Cod Baseball League Orleans Firebirds: Games at Eldredge Park, Nauset Regional Middle School, 70 Route 28, Orleans. The NCAA's best baseball players play in the Cape League from early June through early August. Watch the Firebirds play under the lights. Free. The Cape Cod Symphony Orchestra also performs summer Pops concerts here. Not free.

Academy Playhouse: 120 Main St., East Orleans; (508) 255-1963 (box office). It's a 160-seat theater built inside the historic 19th-century Old Town Hall, with popular productions by a resident theater company. The Academy School, located around the corner at 5 Giddiah Hill Rd., Orleans, (508) 255-5510, has early childhood classes and instruction in music, ballet, and many other types of dance, including tap and jazz.

Restaurants

Hot Chocolate Sparrow: 5 Old Colony Way, Orleans; (508) 240-2230; hot chocolatesparrow.com. See the listing under Ride 18.

Orleans Whole Food Store: 46 Main St., Orleans; (508) 255-6540. Organic products and healthier choices. Coffee, sandwiches, snacks for the ride, with bikes always parked out front.

Hole-in-One: 98 Cranberry Hwy. (Route 6A), Orleans; (508) 255-3740. The best fresh, hand-cut donuts on the lower Cape; bakery, cafe, diner.

Abba: 89 Old Colony Way, Orleans; (508) 255-8144. Chef Erez Pinhas creates fine Mediterranean dishes with Israeli and Thai influence and flavors.

Rock Harbor Grill: 18 Old Colony Way, Orleans; (508) 255-3350. See the listing under Ride 18.

Joe's Beach Road Bar & Grille (Barley Neck Inn): Beach Road, East Orleans; (508) 255-0212. The two sides of this restaurant complement one another: on one, a fine dining experience that is quiet, and on the other, a lively bar with music and large stone fireplace.

Restrooms

There's a port-o-potty at Depot Square (on the CCRT) and restrooms at Nauset Beach (seasonal).

Orleans and Eastham Bayside Beaches

Ride away from Orleans Center toward Cape Cod Bay and hug the beautiful bay-side coastline to visit several beaches, with your choice of salt- or fresh-water swimming and viewing. The sunsets can be spectacular here, as most of these beaches face west. Return to Orleans through the back roads of Eastham and a stretch of the Cape Cod Rail Trail.

Start: Depot Square public parking lot, Orleans

Distance: 18.1-mile loop and lollipop

Approximate riding time: 1-2 hours or more depending on stops at beaches

Best bike: Road

Terrain and surface type: Paved back roads

Traffic and hazards: Sand in the road, especially near the beaches

Things to see: Depot Square parking lot (restrooms), Hot Chocolate Sparrow, Orleans Center, Cape Cod Rail Trail, Salty Ridge Road (connection to points west on CCRT), Skaket Beach, Rock Harbor, Rock Harbor Beach, Boat Meadow Marsh, Samoset Road (First Encounter Beach), Wiley Park and Beach, Thumpertown Beach, Campground Beach, Cook's Brook Beach, Great Pond Beach, Bridge Road Cemetery, Cape Cod Rail Trail Bridge over Route 6 and Rock Harbor Road

Map: *Arrow Street Atlas: Cape Cod including Martha's Vineyard & Nantucket*, p. 66

Getting there: From Route 6 (Mid-Cape Highway), take exit 12 and drive east on Route 6A toward Orleans Center. Turn left on Main Street at the traffic light, then turn left again on Old Colony Way. Depot Square parking lot is on the right, across from the Hot Chocolate Sparrow.

GPS coordinates: N41 47.29' / W69 59.66'

THE RIDE

This ride explores five lesser-known saltwater beaches along Cape Cod Bay in Orleans and Eastham, including two fresh-water pond beaches that are off the beaten track. If you're looking for a beach with the potential for beautiful sunsets, or a lot of room to stretch out even in the busy months of July and August, especially at low tide, all the Cape Cod Bay beaches listed on this ride are for you. This ride is also good for road riders who want a longer ride with beach views at every turn, and it can be combined with other rides to double or triple the distance using downtown Orleans on Ride 27 or the Cape Cod Rail Trail (CCRT) on Ride 18 connecting to Ride 32. Many other combinations are possible.

Start out at the Depot Square parking lot across from Hot Chocolate Sparrow, adjacent to the CCRT on Old Colony Way in Orleans. Turn right on Old Colony Way, spin down a very gentle decline behind a strip mall, and turn right on West Road. Watch for merging CCRT traffic on the right and crosswalk traffic on the left, then go up and over the highway on the bridge. Riders following the CCRT to points west (Brewster, Harwich, and South Dennis) will turn left on Salty Ridge Road, which connects to the paved trail. Continue on and turn left on Skaket Beach Road to the end. Skaket Beach is a big beach that gets exponentially bigger at low tide, with tidal flats extending for miles around the inner hook of Cape Cod Bay. All the bayside beaches are subject to the tides, so timing this ride is important if you plan on a swim (high tide) or a tidal flat walk (low tide). Turn around in the parking lot at Skaket and ride back on Skaket Beach Road, bearing left at the intersection with West Road.

Continue parallel to the highway on the right, then turn left on Rock Harbor Road. Descend the smooth pavement here to Rock Harbor Marina and turn left on Bayview Drive with the marina and the Community of Jesus to the right. The beach at Rock Harbor is the inner elbow of Cape Cod, and the pine tree channel markers make it a very unique-looking harbor. This is a great place to watch fireworks on the Fourth of July. Turn around and continue on Rock Harbor Road past the cash-only BYOB Capt' Cass Rock Harbor Seafood on the left.

Bike Shops

Orleans Cycle, 26 Main St., Orleans, (508) 255-9115, orleanscycle.com
Idle Times Bike Shop, 29 Main St., Orleans, (508) 240-1122, idletimesbikes.com
Idle Times Bike Shop, 4550 Route 6, Eastham, (508) 255-8281, idletimesbikes.com
Little Capistrano Bike Shop, 30 Salt Pond Rd., Eastham, (508) 255-6515, littlecapistrano bikeshop.com

The next turn is left onto Bridge Road, which makes a sharp right and then left over a bridge, through the Boat Meadow estuary on both sides of the

Watching the sunset at Skaket Beach, Orleans

road. Cape Cod Bay is visible off in the distance to the left. Turn left onto Herring Brook Road after a slight incline and follow it to Samoset Road, with views of the Herring River Estuary on the left. Cross Samoset Road, where there is an optional out-and-back ride to First Encounter Beach by turning left. Herring Brook Road passes the entrance to Wiley Park on the right, a half-mile from Samoset Road. Opt to hike the trails or swim at the beach at fresh-water Great Pond. Turn left on Thumpertown Road and ride a straight shot down to the beach. Thumpertown Beach is a small beach that becomes a huge beach, like the rest of Cape Cod Bay, at low tide. It rests higher than other beaches along Eastham's Cape Cod Bay shoreline, on cliffs requiring a descent down a steep stairway to the beach. Turn right on Shurtleff Road, which winds quietly to another smaller beach, Campground Beach. This one tends to be more crowded in summer. Shurtleff Road is one of my favorites even though it's so short, because it sees so little traffic, connects to these gorgeous beaches, and is like a reward for taking the time to ride to the outer reaches of the Cape. Turn right on Campground Road, then left on Higgins Road, ride up and over a hill, then turn left on Steele Road, which dead-ends at Cook's Brook Beach. The views of Wellfleet Harbor and Great Island in Wellfleet are beautiful at Cook's Brook Beach, and the parking lot is bigger than the last two on this ride.

Turn away from the beach and ride Steele Road to its end (or beginning) and turn right on Massasoit Road, which climbs and then levels off around a bend to the right. Turn right on Herring Brook Road and backtrack a little, then turn left on Weir Road. Ride through this quiet residential neighborhood to its end, and turn left on Kingsbury Beach Road. Pass Locust Road on the left and ride down a short steep hill under the canopy of oak that opens to Great Pond Beach on the right, across from the beach in Wiley Park, from earlier in the ride. This is a nice, sandy beach with great sunsets, swimming, sailing, and fishing that gets crowded despite limited parking. Turn left past the beach on Samoset Road, cross the CCRT, and turn right on Bridge Road.

This quiet stretch of Bridge Road goes past the historic Bridge Road Cemetery (on the right) where many of Cape Cod's earliest settlers are buried. The surnames from Eastham's early 18th-century settlers—Atwood, Cole, Doane, Freeman, Higgins, Knowles, Myrick, and Snow, among others—speak to the early history of the East Ham, an early settlement of the Pilgrims east of Plymouth. The graves of the 1700s, crumbling or disappearing at so many cemeteries across Cape Cod, are in relatively good shape here, and the oldest gravestone here, from 1754, is still legible. The road bends a little to the right after the cemetery, and this ride turns left onto the CCRT to return to Orleans Center. Cross Governor Prence Road, go over the bridge, and ride the slight incline back to Main Street. Cross Main and turn left into the Depot parking lot. Explore the many shops, great restaurants, and stores in Orleans.

MILES AND DIRECTIONS

0.0 Start this ride at the Depot Square parking lot, Orleans.

0.6 Turn right on West Road.

0.7 Pass Salty Ridge Road (connect to the CCRT) on the left.

Orleans and Eastham Bayside Beaches

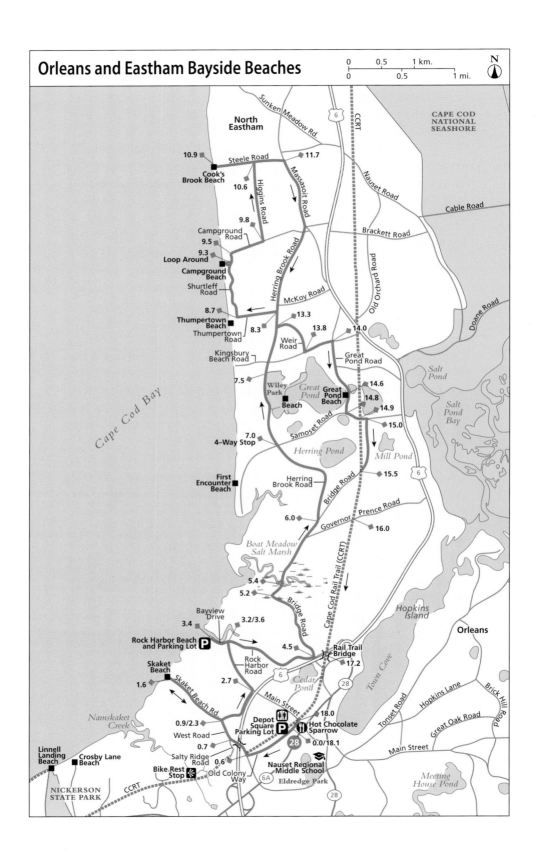

N

0   0.5   1 km.
0   0.5   1 mi.

North Eastham

CAPE COD NATIONAL SEASHORE

Sunken Meadow Rd

6

CCRT

Nauset Road

Cable Road

10.9

Steele Road

11.7

Cook's Brook Beach

10.6

Higgins Road

Massasoit Road

Brackett Road

9.8

Campground Road

9.5

9.3

Loop Around

Campground Beach

Shurtleff Road

Herring Brook Road

McKoy Road

Old Orchard Road

Doane Road

8.7

Thumpertown Beach

8.3

Thumpertown Road

13.3

13.8

14.0

Weir Road

Great Pond Road

Salt Pond

Kingsbury Beach Road

Great Pond Road

7.5

Wiley Park

Great Pond

Great Pond Beach

14.6

14.8

Salt Pond Bay

Beach

14.9

Cape Cod Bay

Samoset Road

15.0

7.0

4–Way Stop

Herring Pond

Mill Pond

6

First Encounter Beach

Herring Brook Road

Bridge Road

15.5

6.0

Governor Prence Road

16.0

Boat Meadow Salt Marsh

Cape Cod Rail Trail (CCRT)

Hopkins Island

Orleans

5.4

5.2

Bridge Road

Bayview Drive

3.2/3.6

3.4

Rock Harbor Beach and Parking Lot

4.5

Rail Trail Bridge

17.2

Skaket Beach

Rock Harbor Road

6

1.6

Skaket Beach Rd

2.7

Cedar Pond

28

Town Cove

Main Street

Hopkins Lane

Brick Hill Road

Namskaket Creek

0.9/2.3

West Road

Depot Square Parking Lot

18.0

Hot Chocolate Sparrow

Tonset Road

Great Oak Road

0.7

Salty Ridge Road

28

0.0/18.1

Main Street

Linnell Landing Beach

Crosby Lane Beach

0.6

Bike Rest Stop

Old Colony Way

Nauset Regional Middle School

6A

Eldredge Park

Meeting House Pond

NICKERSON STATE PARK

CCRT

28

0.9 Turn left on Skaket Beach Road.

1.6 Visit Skaket Beach and then turn around.

2.3 Bear left and continue on Skaket Beach Road.

2.7 Turn left on Rock Harbor Road.

3.2 Turn left on Bayview Drive.

3.4 Turn around at Rock Harbor Beach, at the end of the parking lot.

3.6 Continue straight on Rock Harbor Road.

4.5 Turn left on Bridge Road.

5.2 Bear right and continue on Bridge Road.

5.4 Pass the wide expanse of Boat Meadow Marsh.

6.0 Turn left onto Herring Brook Road.

7.0 Cross Samoset Road at the four-way stop. Option to turn left for an out-and-back to First Encounter Beach.

7.5 Visit Wiley Park (and its beach on Great Pond) via this entrance.

8.3 Turn left on Thumpertown Road.

8.7 Turn right on Shurtleff Road or stop at Thumpertown Beach.

9.3 Visit Campground Beach and travel the perimeter of the parking lot.

9.5 Turn right on Campground Road.

9.8 Turn left on Higgins Road.

10.6 Turn left on Steele Road.

10.9 Visit Cook's Brook Beach at the end of Steele Road and turn around in the parking lot.

11.4 Continue on Steele Road.

11.7 Turn right on Massasoit Road.

12.3 Turn right on Herring Brook Road.

13.3 Turn left on Weir Road.

13.8 Turn left on Kingsbury Beach Road.

14.0 Turn right on Great Pond Road.

14.6 Pass Great Pond Beach (fresh water) on the right.

14.8 Turn left on Samoset Road.

14.9 Cross the CCRT.

15.0 Turn right on Bridge Road.

15.5 Turn left onto the CCRT.

16.0 Cross Governor Prence Road.

17.2 Cross over Rock Harbor Road and Route 6 on the Rail Trail Bridge.

18.0 Cross Main Street.

18.1 Turn left at the Depot Square parking lot to finish the ride.

RIDE INFORMATION

Local Events and Attractions

Main Street Wine & Gourmet: 42 Main St., Orleans; (508) 255-1112. This is probably the best wine shop on Cape Cod, with a great selection, wine tastings, beer, and a relaxed loft where you can sit, read, drink, and people watch. Very friendly and knowledgeable staff. Gourmet foods.

First Encounter Coffee House: 220 Samoset Rd., Eastham; (508) 255-5438. In its fortieth year of acoustic music performances by notable performers including Wellfleet native Patty Larkin, Vineyard resident Livingston Taylor, and folk singer David Roth, who now lives on Cape Cod.

Restaurants

See the listings under Ride 27 for restaurants in Orleans.

Restrooms

There are porta-potties at Depot Square (on the CCRT), and porta-potties at most of the beaches on this ride.

Grand Tour of the Outer Cape

This is the long road ride on the Outer Cape that road cyclists want, with a rich history, a tour of both Cape Cod Bay and the "backside" of Cape Cod, facing the Atlantic Ocean. This is an unforgettable ride that can be extended easily to Provincetown if you've got the legs.

Start: Hot Chocolate Sparrow parking lot (or Depot Square parking lot across the street on Old Colony Way)

Distance: 53.7-mile double-lollipop

Approximate riding time: 3.5 hours

Best bike: Road

Terrain and surface type: Paved roads with some sandy stretches, paved rail trail, hilly sections with some steep climbs and fast descents

Traffic and hazards: Busy traffic on main roads, winding roads with blind corners, sand in roads, main highway (Route 6) crossings in Wellfleet and Truro, travel in shoulder of Route 6 with no marked bike lane (although it is technically a popular "bike route")

Things to see: Orleans Center, Boat Meadow Marsh, Herring River Marsh, Wellfleet Drive-In, Mass Audubon Sanctuary at Wellfleet Bay, Cape Cod National Seashore, Marconi Beach, Lecount Hollow Beach, White Crest Beach, Gull Pond, Truro Center, Highland Museum & Cape Cod Lighthouse (Highland Light), Jenny Lind Tower, Shore Road (easy access to Provincetown Center), Cape Cod Bay, Truro Vineyards, Edward Hopper House, Cape Cod Bay, Wellfleet Center, Miles Tibbetts ghost bike memorial

Map: *Arrow Street Atlas: Cape Cod including Martha's Vineyard & Nantucket, p. 66*

Getting there: From Route 6 (Mid-Cape Highway), take exit 12, drive east on Route 6A toward Orleans Center. Turn left on Main Street at the traffic light, then turn left again on Old Colony Way. The Hot Chocolate Sparrow parking lot is on the left, across from Depot Square.

GPS coordinates: N41 47.31' / W69 59.59'

THE RIDE

This ride combines two classic Cape road cycling routes connecting Wellfleet and Truro in a double-lollipop shape, riding along Cape Cod Bay through Orleans and Eastham, then crossing over to the east coast of Wellfleet and Truro headed north, and returning along Cape Cod Bay riding south. At nearly 55 miles, this ride will challenge most riders, and the many climbs on this ride through Wellfleet and Truro will eliminate the thought of Cape Cod as a flat place. This ride offers spectacular bay and ocean views, and tours of Highland Light and Truro Vineyards, places you'll want to come back to again and again.

Heading north on Main Street, the road descends and turns into Rock Harbor Road, which bends right at Rock Harbor and continues past the marsh and Rock Harbor Creek on the left, visible through the old Capes that line this road. A left onto Bridge Road travels through the larger Boat Meadow Marsh, where sunsets and sunrises are often colorful, or where the fog rolls in and there is nothing to see but gray. After a slight incline on a longer straightaway, turn left on Herring Brook Road, which descends, then climbs, and then descends again around a left-hand bend. Cross the Herring River and head north with views across the marsh of Cape Cod Bay all the way to Brewster and Dennis on the left. After the road dips down and crosses Samoset Road, Herring Brook Road bends to the right, passes Wiley Park, and ascends around the park on a bumpy section into a longer straightaway. Descending again, Herring Brook ends at a stop sign at the three-way intersection of Massasoit Road and Oak Road. The thrift shop on the corner was an old general store and later a mitten factory. The Idle Time Bike Shop is just down the street in case of emergency repairs by heading down Oak Road and crossing Route 6.

Turn left on Massasoit and ride through a residential area with a deserted church parking lot on the right. The road here is smooth, and after a nice downhill, the road climbs up again, bearing right into a rougher section of road. At the end of this stretch, past the Sunken Meadow Roads that both lead to bayside beaches on the left, there is a steep, fast descent. At the bottom of the descent is a small creek, but you won't notice it. The bottom of this descent is the Wellfleet town line, and the road is now called West Road. On the right, speed past the backside of the Wellfleet Drive-In Theater screen and then climb past, descending again through the Wellfleet Bay Audubon

Sanctuary. There are bad potholes on this descent through the trees, and an entrance to the sanctuary that crosses the road is dangerous, as cars crossing from either the right or left don't always stop for cyclists on West Road.

Cross Route 6 at the end of West Road and turn left and ride in the breakdown lane on a long straightaway through South Wellfleet. The highway is two lanes here, having lost a lane farther south at the entrance to the drive-in theater. This is a dangerous stretch of road, with a history of fatal accidents among vehicles, pedestrians, and cyclists. Unfortunately, there is no avoiding it for sections of this ride. The wind is often strong here, out of the north in the morning and then shifting to the south in the afternoon. The shoulder is wide for most of this segment of Route 6, but the fog line shifts near a couple of intersections and riders have to pay attention or else end up in the sand off-road. So the combination of vehicle traffic, wind, varying widths of breakdown lane (to the right of the fog line), and impatient drivers makes for a dangerous stretch of riding. But that's road riding on the Outer Cape from Eastham to Truro; you have to deal with Route 6. It's best to wear bright clothing, use flashing red taillights, and keep your wits about you.

The highway is mostly straight here, with slight inclines and declines, and then it bends left slightly up more of an incline to Marconi Beach Road on the right. You can turn right here and then make a quick left turn over the rumble strips onto the Cape Cod Rail Trail (CCRT) to Lecount Hollow Road or continue on Route 6 and turn right to get there. The intersection of Lecount Hollow and Route 6 is the home of the P.B. Boulangerie, another hub of cycling, with lines out the bakery door, lots of bicycles in the bike racks, and cyclists in full aerodynamic kits. Close your eyes, listen to the French music, and it's Paris in the middle of Wellfleet. Owner and world-class chef Philippe Rispoli loves cyclists and cycling, and it shows. The restaurant's proximity to the CCRT (the parking lot is a short walk around the corner on Lecount Hollow Road) and the natural fit between road cycling and anything French is as good a match as a baguette and a jersey pocket. The recent addition of a log-burning, cylindrical stone-encased fire pit next to the lengthy bike rack is a welcome sight in the winter and shoulder seasons.

Ride to the end of Lecount Hollow Road past the rail trail through Cape Cod National Seashore property. Turn left at Maguire's Landing (Lecount Hollow Beach) and challenge yourself on the hill up Ocean View Drive. Once at the top, the road flattens out and the ride passes spectacular views of the Atlantic. This is a plateau, and the beaches and homes to the right lie precariously on cliffs that are constantly eroding. The parking lot at Maguire's Landing falls into the ocean every few years and has to be rebuilt, and the private homes on the edge of the cliffs on the right here will soon disappear. Ocean

View Drive will also eventually disappear, so ride it while you can! Gaze right on occasion to see spouting whales and ships off in the distance.

Descend the road slightly on this plateau, and pass the "surfer's beach," White Crest Beach, on the right. The road now climbs more steeply to a crest, then descends again past Cahoon Hollow Beach, down the road to the Beach-comber of Wellfleet, a former life-saving station (before there was a Coast Guard) turned beach bar, nightclub, and restaurant (in that order), with a nice outdoor deck. They're closed in the off-season. Pass Long Pond Drive on the left, then ride the rolling hills and make a sharp left onto Gross Hill Road. There is the option to descend the rest of the road here, a short out-and-back to Newcomb Hollow Beach. In January 2008, a mysterious shipwreck washed ashore here, and archaeologists found that the remains of the hull date to a mid- to late-19th-century schooner. The National Park Service decided that the best policy for the wreck was to leave it in place. It reappeared in 2009 with the shifting sands, and rested about a half-mile south of the parking lot. There were more than 3,500 known shipwrecks off Cape Cod between 1850 and 1980, so feel free to comb the beautiful cliff beaches here or at any of the cliff beaches along Ocean View Drive. You might get lucky. Thoreau stayed nearby during one of his trips to Cape Cod, at the home of the "old Wellfleet oysterman" John Young Newcomb.

Gross Hill Road takes riders away from the coast and rides through a heavily oak- and pine-forested region of the National Seashore, past kettle ponds, sandy fire roads, and private homes that predate the 1961 national park. Gross Hill continues left when riders turn right at the fork onto Gull Pond Road, winding past Gull Pond on a roller coaster of a ride out to Route 6. The ride then turns right onto Route 6 again, crosses into Truro, and turns right onto a hidden crescent of a road, Rose Road, that allows access onto Collins Road, a little-known secret route that follows the "Old King's Highway" past two ponds on the left and forested fire roads through the National Seashore. The road surface is fairly rough here, but smooths out as it ascends slightly past the ponds. After it crests, the road descends sharply through the woods past a few houses and ends on South Pamet Road. Making a sharp left, riders pass through quiet residential neighborhood, under the highway, and turn right onto Truro Center Road.

This is a good place to rest and refuel at Jam's Gourmet Grocery (seasonal), because the road turns upward here, and the hills are pretty steady for the rest of this part of the ride. Bear right past Jam's at the fork and continue on Truro Center Road past Blackfish Restaurant on the right, up and over the hill, into a descent. Make a very hard left on Bridge Road and climb one of the steepest climbs on Cape Cod. Bear right on Meetinghouse Road at the top and hit a long, steep, and fast descent all the way to Castle Road. With views

Highland Lighthouse, Truro

of the Pamet Marsh on the left, you're climbing again. The next descent is also steep and fast but with a sharp right turn. Don't make the mistake of bearing left onto Corn Hill Road here, although if you do, you'll find a beautiful beach. Hug the curve and bear right, continuing on Castle Road, which climbs up one last time before descending around a right bend to Route 6. Cross Route 6 with caution and ride the climb to South Highland Road, turning right and continuing a climb.

The road is smooth pavement and descends before climbing again toward Highland Lighthouse (previously known as Cape Cod Lighthouse), the oldest and tallest lighthouse on Cape Cod, established in 1797 (present structure built in 1857) as the twentieth lighthouse in the United States. It was moved 450 feet over eight days in 1996 to its present location away from the cliffs. Don't miss the tour up the spiral staircase to the top, with 360-degree views of the Outer Cape, or just pause and admire the views here. If you do decide to climb up, you'll be able to view this entire route. Turn around, ride back down the road, and turn right onto South Highland Road. Then turn left on Highland Road past some campgrounds.

Going under the highway here, use caution near the exit and entrance ramps. Turn right on Shore Road, past the old Dutra's Market, now known as the Salty Market with new owners, one of whom grew up across the street.

The old general store, with a 160-year history, has been redone, a lot cleaner and brighter, with a full deli and liquor store inside the market, but with the same exterior. Take the right past Salty Market into a steep climb known to local cyclists as the Last Gasp hill, the last steep climb before the finish of the popular fundraiser that goes from Sandwich to Provincetown. Shore Road actually has several smaller and less-steep rollers along this stretch, before cresting into a downhill in North Truro. Before the last descent, the view of Provincetown Harbor and the Pilgrim Monument is striking. You can see the end of the "hook" here, with Land's End and its lighthouse off in the distance to the left.

Descend the hill and continue along Shore Road, which is often windy, but with great views of Provincetown Harbor at sea level, between the row houses on the left. This ride ends before Provincetown, here in North Truro by simply turning around on Shore Road. Turn around at a short side street called Stott's Crossing (mile 27.5), where there is the option to cross Route 6 and connect to Ride 33 on High Head Road, just a few yards north of Stott's Crossing on the other side of Route 6. If you want more mileage, you can get to downtown Provincetown by simply continuing straight, or head to the Province Lands dunes (Ride 34) from Shore Road by riding straight on Bradford Street, turning right on Conwell Street, crossing Route 6, and continuing on Race Point Road to the Province Lands Visitor Center.

Turn around at Stott's Crossing and backtrack along Shore Road. Pass the Salty Market on the left, and cross Highland Road, being careful of vehicular traffic crossing from either side. The tendency is to speed up quite a bit on the descent here, and even though Highland Road on the left and Pond Road on the right both have stop signs, cars don't always look for speeding cyclists descending the hill. Continue on Shore Road, wind around a church, and arrive at Truro Vineyards on the left. If it's a nice day, this is the perfect place to stop for lunch or a snack. Blackfish chef Eric Jenson has opened a food truck called Crush Pad that is parked at the Vineyard, and is well worth checking out. It is a nice complement to wine-tasting and a vineyard tour. Don't miss the Chinese mulberry tree and the spiced rum.

Bike Shops

Orleans Cycle, 26 Main St., Orleans, (508) 255-9115, orleanscycle.com
Idle Times Bike Shop, 29 Main St., Orleans, (508) 240-1122, idletimesbikes.com
Idle Times Bike Shop, 4550 Route 6, Eastham, (508) 255-8281, idletimesbikes.com
Little Capistrano Bike Shop, 30 Salt Pond Rd., Eastham, (508) 255-6515, littlecapistrano bikeshop.com
Little Capistrano Bike Shop, 1446 Route 6, Wellfleet, (508) 349-2363, littlecapistrano bikeshop.com

Continue on Shore Road past the vineyard up a longer climb to Route 6. Descend quickly past Truro's finest, and turn right onto Castle Road, backtracking a ways. This time ride the entire stretch of Castle Road rolling and winding past the Pamet Marsh on the right, and merge with Truro Center Road at the bottom of the hill. Pass Jam's Gourmet Grocery again, this time on your right, and turn right on Depot Road, which climbs and then levels off to a fork in the road. Turning right and continuing on Depot takes you to Pamet Harbor, and you can return to this ride via Mill Pond Road, a scenic option. Instead bear left on Old County Road, start climbing and look to the right for a last view of Provincetown. Pass Perry's Hill Way on the right and descend a steep hill that bears left with magnificent views of another branch of the Pamet River Marsh to the right. If you look closely, you can see the old railway trestle that ends at the edge of the water, where a bridge used to connect the land for railroad travel from Boston to Provincetown.

After climbing to the top of Old County Road here, start a long descent to Pamet Point Road and turn right on Bound Brook Island Road, winding around Duck Harbor, which cannot be seen from the road. Turn right on Pole Dike Road and wind some more, then go up and over a hill that descends rapidly into a left-hand turn on West Main Street past the Wellfleet Library on the right. Take a break in Wellfleet Center on Main Street at the many places to shop or eat. One of my favorite places is Hatch's Fish Market at the end of the public parking lot behind the Winslow Tavern, or the Wicked Oyster up the road on the left, just before Route 6. The supermarket across the street, Wellfleet Market, is always available, too. Stay on Main Street past the market and bear left up the hill. There is the option to turn left on Long Pond Road at the bottom of the hill opposite East Commercial Street and return to South Wellfleet via Ocean View Drive and Lecount Hollow Road.

But this ride takes Route 6 from Main Street all the way back to West Road, returning the way it started. It's a riskier way to go, but it's quicker, and there are things to see that are well worth seeing. The first site is the ghost bike on the right past Cahoon Hollow Road, a memorial to 16-year old Miles Tibbetts, a Nauset Regional High School student who was killed by a motorist when he was crossing Route 6 on his bicycle in 2013. The Ghost Bikes organization, based in Boston, promotes cycling and cycling-friendly environments, and ghost bike memorials can be seen all around the world. Continue on Route 6 past the Wellfleet Harbor Actors Theater on the right, up and down the rolling hills, past Lecount Hollow Road, Marconi Beach Road, and finally to West Road.

If the wind is from the north, you'll fly down Route 6 from Wellfleet Center. There are usually some sandy patches along this long hilly stretch, so use caution, or escape the highway altogether by using the CCRT all the way back to Orleans Center. There are two escape hatches to the CCRT, by turning left at either Lecount Hollow Road or left at Marconi Beach Road off Route 6. When you've finished riding back through Eastham and Orleans via Massasoit, Herring Brook, Bridge, and Rock Harbor Roads, reward yourself at the Hot Chocolate Sparrow, where you can meet other cyclists and share stories of your adventures.

MILES AND DIRECTIONS

0.0 Start at the Hot Chocolate Sparrow parking lot, and turn right on Old Colony Way.

0.1 Turn left on Main Street and continue straight on Rock Harbor Road.

1.1 Bear right and continue on Rock Harbor Road.

2.1 Turn left on Bridge Road.

2.9 Bear right and continue on Bridge Road.

3.6 Turn left on Herring Brook Road.

4.7 Cross Samoset Road (four-way stop signs).

6.8 Turn left on Massasoit Road.

8.1 Pass the Wellfleet Drive-In on the right.

8.6 Turn left onto Route 6 (use caution when crossing).

9.0 Turn right on Lecount Hollow Road. Pass the P.B. Boulangerie on the left and the CCRT parking lot on the right.

9.8 Turn left on Ocean View Drive.

10.8 Pass White Crest Beach on the right.

11.5 Pass Cahoon Hollow Beach (Beachcomber Bar) on the right.

12.6 Turn left on Gross Hill Road.

13.3 Turn right on Gull Pond Road.

14.7 Turn right on Route 6 (use caution).

16.0 Turn right on Rose Road.

16.2 Turn right on Collins Road.

18.3 Turn left on South Pamet Road.

19.0 Turn right on Truro Center Road.

19.8 Turn left on Bridge Road into a steep climb.

19.9 Bear right on Meetinghouse Road (steep, fast descent).

20.4 Turn right on Castle Road.

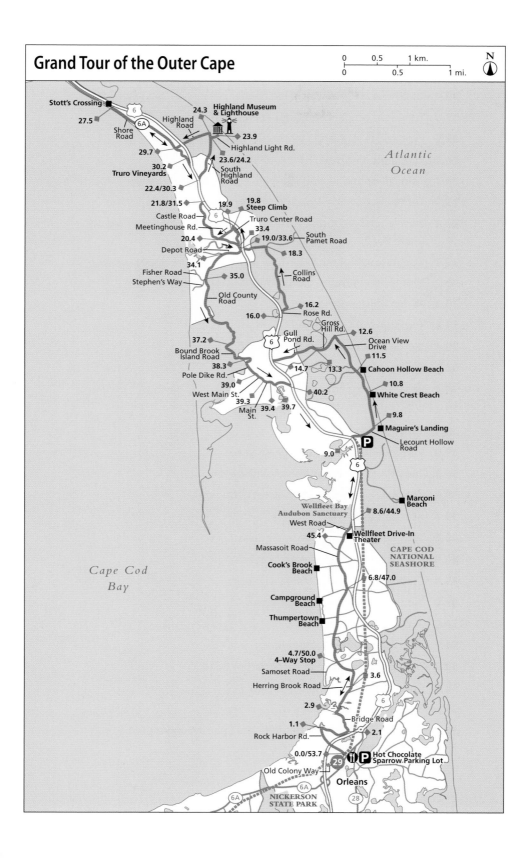

Grand Tour of the Outer Cape

0   0.5   1 km.
0   0.5   1 mi.

N

Atlantic Ocean

Stott's Crossing
27.5
6
6A
Shore Road
24.3
Highland Road
Highland Museum & Lighthouse
23.9
Highland Light Rd.
29.7
23.6/24.2
South Highland Road
30.2
Truro Vineyards
22.4/30.3
21.8/31.5
Castle Road
Meetinghouse Rd.
19.9
6
19.8
Steep Climb
Truro Center Road
33.4
20.4
Depot Road
19.0/33.6
South Pamet Road
34.1
Fisher Road
Stephen's Way
35.0
18.3
Collins Road
Old County Road
16.2
Rose Rd.
16.0
Gross Hill Rd.
12.6
Gull Pond Rd.
6
Ocean View Drive
37.2
Bound Brook Island Road
11.5
38.3
Pole Dike Rd.
14.7
13.3
Cahoon Hollow Beach
39.0
West Main St.
40.2
10.8
White Crest Beach
39.3
Main St.
39.4
39.7
9.8
Maguire's Landing
Lecount Hollow Road
P
9.0
6
Marconi Beach
Wellfleet Bay
Audubon Sanctuary
8.6/44.9
CAPE COD
NATIONAL
SEASHORE
West Road
Wellfleet Drive-In Theater
45.4
Massasoit Road
Cook's Brook Beach
6.8/47.0
Cape Cod Bay
Campground Beach
Thumpertown Beach
4.7/50.0
4–Way Stop
Samoset Road
3.6
Herring Brook Road
2.9
6
1.1
Bridge Road
Rock Harbor Rd.
2.1
0.0/53.7
Hot Chocolate Sparrow Parking Lot
P
29
Old Colony Way
Orleans
6A
NICKERSON
STATE PARK
28

21.8 Turn left on Route 6 (use caution).

22.4 Turn right on South Highland Road.

23.6 Turn right on Highland Light Road.

23.9 Explore the Highland Lighthouse, then turn around.

24.2 Turn right onto South Highland Road.

24.3 Turn left on Highland Road.

25.3 Turn right on Shore Road (Route 6A) into a short, steep climb.

27.5 Turn around at Stott's Crossing (or continue to Provincetown on Shore Road).

29.7 Continue straight through intersection on Shore Road (caution).

30.2 Visit Truro Vineyards, then continue on Shore Road.

30.3 Merge right onto Route 6.

31.5 Turn right on Castle Road.

33.4 Merge right onto Truro Center Road.

33.6 Turn right on Depot Road.

34.1 Bear left onto Old County Road.

37.2 Turn right on Bound Brook Island Road.

38.3 Turn right on Pole Dike Road.

39.0 Continue straight on West Main Street.

39.3 Turn left to remain on West Main Street.

39.4 Continue straight on Main Street (stop sign).

39.7 Bear left up the hill.

40.2 Turn right on Route 6 at traffic light.

44.9 Turn right onto West Road.

45.4 Continue straight on Massasoit Road.

47.0 Turn right on Herring Brook Road.

50.0 Turn right on Bridge Road.

51.7 Turn right on Rock Harbor Road.

52.7 Turn left to continue on Rock Harbor Road.

53.5 Continue straight on Main Street.

53.6 Turn right on Old Colony Way.

53.7 Finish this ride at the Hot Chocolate Sparrow parking lot.

Local Events and Attractions

Main Street Wine & Gourmet: 42 Main St., Orleans; (508) 255-1112. See the listing under Ride 28.

First Encounter Coffee House: 220 Samoset Rd., Eastham; (508) 255-5438. See the listing under Ride 28.

Truro Vineyards: 11 Route 6A, North Truro; (508) 487-6200. Wine tastings, rum tastings, gift shop, and the Crush Pad food truck by Chef Eric Jansen. Great spot for lunch and wine.

Highland Light and Museum: 27 Highland Rd., North Truro. Thoreau visited here, stayed in the lighthouse keeper's home, and wrote about it in *Cape Cod*. This lighthouse is the brightest one on the Cape Cod coast. Lighthouse tours for those over 48 inches tall. Great views, especially at dusk and dawn.

Wellfleet Oyster Festival: Downtown Wellfleet is closed to vehicle traffic every year in October for the two days of OysterFest. There are more than 86 artisans, 21 food vendors, 12 raw bars, 15 community organizations, and crowds of people clogging Main Street. Don't miss the annual Oyster Shuck-Off competition. Family activities, lots of oysters prepared multiple ways.

Jam's Gourmet Grocery: 12 Truro Center Rd., Truro; (508) 349-1616. Great pit stop in the Pamet section of Truro.

The Salty Market: 2 Highland Rd., North Truro; (508) 487-0711. Another great pit stop. Deli and lots of treats. Great place to refuel.

Restaurants

Also see the listings under Ride 27 for restaurants in Orleans.

Wicked Oyster: 50 Main St., Wellfleet; (508) 349-3455. Great food in the living room of a home that was floated across Wellfleet Harbor from Billingsgate Island, which washed away to sea over a hundred years ago.

Blackfish: 17 Truro Center Rd., Truro; (508) 349-3399. Dinner in a house tucked in a hollow on a hill. Excellent food and service, romantic little spot with candlelight and a cozy bar.

Restrooms

There's a porta-potty across the street at Depot Square (on the CCRT) and at the Wellfleet end of the CCRT (both at mile 9.0 of this ride). There are restrooms at Highland Light.

An easy ride from the Cape Cod Rail Trail (CCRT) or the Salt Pond Visitor Center at Cape Cod National Seashore in Eastham. Great for kids and families or anyone else, with great views of Nauset Marsh, Nauset Inlet, and Coast Guard Beach. Lots to do at the Cape Cod National Seashore, with helpful rangers at the Visitor Center, a great place to get orientation to the region.

Start: CCRT at Locust Road, Eastham (optional start at Salt Pond Visitor Center parking lot, Eastham)

Distance: 5.0 miles, out-and-back.

Approximate riding time: 30 to 45 minutes

Best bike: Road, hybrid

Terrain and surface type: Smooth pavement, with some sand, a wooden bridge boardwalk, hilly terrain through forest, and flat stretches past marsh

Traffic and hazards: Vehicle traffic and bicycles on CCRT intersection with Locust Road, highway crossing, busy parking lot, other cyclists and pedestrians on the Nauset Trail

Things to see: CCRT, Salt Pond Visitor Center at Cape Cod National Seashore, Doane Rock picnic area (parking, restrooms), Nauset Bay and marsh, hiking trails, wildlife, Coast Guard Beach, surfers, sunbathers, whales, seals, and ships at sea

Map: *Arrow Street Atlas: Cape Cod including Martha's Vineyard & Nantucket,* p. 44

Getting there: Take Route 6 to the Orleans-Eastham Rotary and continue on Route 6 to the Salt Pond Visitor Center at 50 Nauset Rd. in Eastham. Look for the big Cape Cod National Seashore sign on the right, after passing the Eastham Police Department.

GPS coordinates: N41 50.19' / W69 58.91'

THE RIDE

This is an out-and-back ride and also a connector route from the Cape Cod Rail Trail (CCRT) to the Nauset Trail at the Salt Pond Visitor Center in Eastham. The Nauset Trail is a paved bike path maintained by the National Park Service, and was freshly repaved in 2014. The Nauset Trail begins at the Salt Pond Visitor Center in the Cape Cod National Seashore in Eastham. If you are connecting by bicycle from the CCRT, start this ride at the intersection with Locust Road in Eastham. Turn onto Locust Road and ride downhill, headed east. If you go uphill on Locust Road, you are going the wrong way. From Orleans, turn right, and from Wellfleet, turn left onto Locust Road. People get lost here all the time, for some reason. Ride down the hill on Locust Road, climb a short incline, and turn left on Salt Pond Road. Pass the Little Capistrano bike shop on the right, and dismount to walk your bicycle across Route 6 at the traffic light (there is a walk button). Remount and follow the paved path past the Salt Pond Visitor Center on the right.

If arriving by car, start the ride here at the parking lot (the 0.5 mile mark of this ride). Continue to the end of the parking lot on the paved path, and enter a woods at a sign marked Nauset Trail. The Nauset Trail bends right up a short hill and then levels off in the woods, traveling through cedar, oak, and pine forest on a meandering and roller-coaster path. It's a great short ride for kids, and challenging but fun, with the many ups and downs. It's away from vehicle traffic, and very safe despite a few road crossings that are well marked with stop signs and warnings. But then it rounds a bend and dramatically opens up to a panoramic view of Nauset Bay and marsh, over a boardwalk that is part of the trail. It's beautiful on both sides of the boardwalk, with the bay to the right and marsh to the left.

As you gaze out across Nauset Bay here, look off in the distance where Henry Beston wrote *The Outermost House*, the naturalist classic published

Bike Shops
Idle Times Bike Shop, 4550 Route 6, Eastham, (508) 255-8281, idletimesbikes.com
Little Capistrano Bike Shop, 30 Salt Pond Rd., Eastham, (508) 255-6515, littlecapistrano bikeshop.com

in 1928, 2 miles south of this spot on the Outer Beach. Beston spent a year at a small house on a raised section of dune, just 30 feet from the beach, with a wood stove and no electricity. Some believe that his praise for the natural world helped inspire and create the Cape Cod National Seashore, and people still hike to the spot where his house, once designated a National Literary Landmark, washed away during the powerful nor'easter of 1978. For *The Outermost House*, Beston won the American Academy of Arts and Sciences

Walkway to Coast Guard Beach, Eastham

Medal in 1959, just two years before the Cape Cod National Seashore became a reality.

Ride across the boardwalk bridge, up the hill to the left to Coast Guard Beach. Bike racks are just past the gazebo, with a short walk down to the beach. Opt to turn right, up to the parking lot next to the Coast Guard station for a better view of Nauset Marsh. Or walk on the short paved footpath just to the left of the station house, down to a sitting area with benches and historical placards. Down the hill from the station on the left are restrooms and outdoor showers, and a wooden plank boardwalk to the beach. Look out at the barrier beach from any elevated lookout point here and see harbor seals, whales (if you're lucky), and the coastline that has wrecked 3,000 ships since the wreck of the *Sparrowhawk* in 1626. In Massachusetts, the many shipwrecks led to the formation of the Massachusetts Humane Society in 1786, which established shelter huts for shipwrecked mariners who made it to shore. By the late 1800s, Congress organized a Life-Saving Service along the nation's coastline, and that evolved over the years to become the United States Coast Guard. The Coast Guard station here was decommissioned in 1958. The building now houses the Cape Cod National Seashore National Environmental Educational Development program for schools.

To finish this ride, turn around and return to the start, or connect here to Ride 31 to add the loop to Nauset Light Beach and back. Don't miss a visit to the Salt Pond Visitors Center, with frequent film presentations of the natural history of Cape Cod, hikes around Salt Pond and Nauset Marsh, and a National

Nauset Trail at Salt Pond Visitor Center

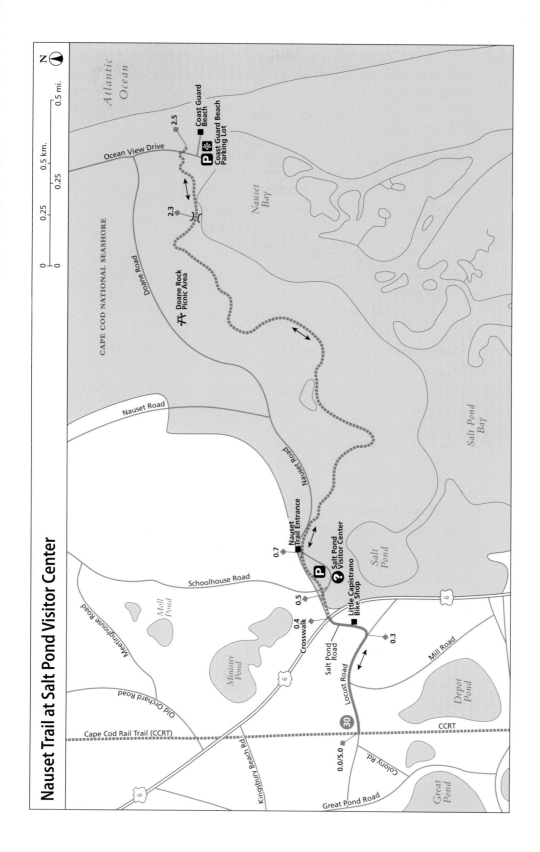

Park gift and bookstore, museum, and restrooms. The park rangers here are very friendly and helpful, and will get you where you want to go. If you connected here from the CCRT, cross Route 6 and turn right on Locust Road to get back to the trail.

MILES AND DIRECTIONS

0.0 Start this ride on the CCRT at Locust Road if arriving by bicycle.

0.3 Turn left on Salt Pond Road.

0.4 Cross Route 6 at the crosswalk (with walk button).

0.4 Follow the bike path at the end of crosswalk.

0.5 Start the ride here at the Salt Pond Visitor Center parking lot if arriving by car.

0.7 Continue to the Nauset Trail entrance at the far end of the parking lot.

2.3 Ride on the wooden bridge with views of Nauset Marsh and Bay on the right.

2.5 Cross Ocean View Drive at the crosswalk and park your bicycle at the bike racks at Coast Guard Beach. Turn around to return the way you came.

5.0 Finish the ride at start at Locust Road.

RIDE INFORMATION

Local Events and Attractions

Cape Cod National Seashore: 99 Marconi Site Rd., Wellfleet; (508) 771-2144. Forty miles of pristine sandy beach, marshes, ponds, and uplands supporting diverse species on more than 43,000 acres. Lighthouses, historic homes, natural and cultural landscapes all offer a glimpse of Cape Cod's past and present. Swimming beaches and walking and biking trails await you. A must-see. Use the Salt Pond Visitor Center to orient yourself to the vast Cape Cod National Seashore.

Restaurants

Karoo: 3 Main St., Unit 32B (Route 6), Eastham; (508) 255-8288. A little Cape Town on Cape Cod. Authentic South African fare from Chef Sanette Groenewald, who brings the African, Indian, and European flavors from her southern hemisphere homeland to, of all places, Eastham. Open year-round (except January).

Arnold's Lobster & Clam Bar: 3580 State Hwy. (Route 6), Eastham; (508) 255-2575. A Cape Cod clam shack, a very good one. Mini-golf, ice cream, lots of parking, right on the CCRT with bike racks. Seasonal.

Restrooms

There are restrooms at the Salt Pond Visitor Center year-round and at Coast Guard Beach.

This is an easy loop with a lot to see. Lighthouses, beaches, and the choice to make a longer trip via the Cape Cod Rail Trail (CCRT).

Start: Salt Pond Visitor Center main parking lot, Cape Cod National Seashore, 50 Nauset Rd., Eastham

Distance: 7.6-mile loop

Approximate riding time: 1 hour

Best bike: Road, hybrid

Terrain and surface type: Paved main roads and back roads, hilly sections, paved bike path on the CCRT

Traffic and hazards: Busy traffic on main roads in summer, school traffic in and out of Nauset Regional High School on Cable Road, other cyclists, pedestrians, dogs and other animals on the CCRT, traffic and cars in main parking lot of Visitor Center

Things to see: Salt Pond Visitor Center at Cape Cod National Seashore, Doane Rock picnic area (parking, restrooms), Nauset Bay and marsh, hiking trails, wildlife, Coast Guard Beach, surfers, sunbathers, whales, seals, ships at sea, Nauset Lighthouse, Nauset Light Beach, Three Sisters Lighthouses, Nauset Regional High School, CCRT

Map: *Arrow Street Atlas: Cape Cod including Martha's Vineyard & Nantucket*, p. 45

Getting there: Take Route 6 to the Orleans-Eastham Rotary and continue on Route 6 to the Salt Pond Visitor Center at 50 Nauset Rd. in Eastham. Look for the big Cape Cod National Seashore sign on the right, after passing the Eastham Police Department.

GPS coordinates: N41 50.29' / W69 58.41'

THE RIDE

This ride is a loop, so it can start anywhere along its course, with parking at Doane Rock Picnic Area (mile 0.9), the Nauset Light Beach parking lot (fee required in season), along Cable Road by the Three Sisters lighthouses (a few spaces), Nauset Regional High School (not during school hours), or at the start of this ride, the Salt Pond Visitor Center (free parking), just off Route 6 in Eastham on Nauset Road. Starting at the visitor center, this ride parallels the Nauset Trail for 1.5 miles on Nauset Road, and then Doane Road at mile 0.5. There is the option to ride the Nauset Trail, but riding the roads avoids pedestrians and other users of the multi-use trail, where speeds have to be slower. At mile 0.9, pass Doane Rock Picnic Area on the right. Doane Rock is the largest exposed glacial boulder on Cape Cod, carried here by glacial ice sheets 18,000 years ago. It is accessible from the parking lot on the right, with picnic tables, restrooms, hiking trails, and a memorial to Deacon John Doane, an original founder of Eastham and the oldest of its first seven settlers. This area was originally known as the East Ham, or hamlet, of Plymouth Colony.

Descend past Doane Rock as Doane Road bends right and downhill to Ocean View Drive. Riding this stretch gives a great view of the Atlantic off in the distance, disappearing behind the dunes during the descent. This is the section of land first sighted by Captain Christopher Jones of the *Mayflower*, and Coast Guard Beach is where the *Mayflower* first made landfall on November 9, 1620. The ship was supposed to sail to the mouth of the Hudson River (then Northern Virginia), but this hazardous Cape Cod coastline turned them around toward Provincetown and Plymouth. Since the Pilgrims arrived, more than 3,000 ships have been wrecked in these waters. Ride a bicycle here any time from December through February if you want to see the harsh winter environment the Pilgrims first faced. And remember that almost half the passengers did not survive that first winter. Fortunately, you will.

Turn right, ride over the bridge past the park ranger's guardhouse, and up around a rotary (traffic circle) into the Coast Guard Beach parking lot. There is a scenic viewing area at the far left end of the parking lot, with a bench. From here there are panoramic views of Nauset Bay, where Henry Beston lived a year of his life in a small house 2 miles south of this spot and wrote *The Outermost House*, a literary classic. This is also the start of Henry David Thoreau's Great Beach, and it can be walked from Eastham northward all the way to Provincetown from here. Headed south along the barrier beach from the other side of Nauset Bay past Nauset Inlet, you can still walk to Chatham, although not as far as before an April 2007 storm that breached Pleasant Bay in North Chatham.

Circle around the parking lot and ride past the old Coast Guard Station, decommissioned in 1958 and now an environmental learning center run by

Ocean View Drive and Coast Guard Beach Station, Eastham

the National Park Service for school programs. Down the hill, a bathhouse with outdoor showers is on the right with a main walkway to the beach. The bike racks are behind that, next to a gazebo. Coast Guard Beach is a wide expanse of beach with the cliffs getting taller farther north. Closer to the inlet into Nauset Bay, the currents whip up some pretty good waves with the help of some shoals offshore, and surfers ride the waves here frequently. Don't expect anything like Hawaii, of course, but the storm-chasing surfers will travel the northeast coastline to get a good wave, and they often end up here.

Head back over the bridge with Nauset Marsh on the left, then climb Ocean View Drive to a plateau overlooking the Atlantic Ocean. The road then descends past private homes set well back from the road, through scrub pine. At the bottom of the hill, through the pines, the Nauset Lighthouse comes to view. Pass Nauset Light Beach on the right as you approach the lighthouse, and take an optional tour of either or both. Nauset Light was moved from its old location in the nick of time (only 43 feet from the edge of the cliffs), 336 feet to the present site in 1996. The top half was painted red in the 1940s, and the structure itself was moved from Chatham to replace three 1838 light-houses known as the Three Sisters in 1923. Turn left on Cable Road and the Three Sisters still stand in a park maintained by

Bike Shops

Idle Times Bike Shop, 4550 Route 6, Eastham, (508) 255-8281, idletimesbikes.com
Little Capistrano Bike Shop, 30 Salt Pond Rd., Eastham, (508) 255-6515, littlecapistrano bikeshop.com

the National Park Service, in their original configuration, about 150 feet apart. Originally, the Three Sisters were constructed to distinguish them from the single light at Highland in Truro and the twin lights at Chatham, to help guide ships along the treacherous coastline of the "backside" of Cape Cod. With the advent of electricity and rotating lights, more than one lighthouse at any geographic point was no longer needed.

Ride a couple of gentle rollers on Cable Road from Nauset Light Beach past the Three Sisters, and pass Nauset Regional High School on the right. It is the only public high school built in a national park, a testament to the cooperation that was required to form the Cape Cod National Seashore in 1961. Turn right on Nauset Road through a residential neighborhood and come to a five-way stop sign where the CCRT crosses Nauset Road and intersects with Railroad Avenue. Turn left on the CCRT and ride a 1.5-mile straight, flat stretch to Old Orchard Road. Stop at Arnold's on the right for a game of mini-golf, some fried seafood, or ice cream, or just turn left on Old Orchard Road and ride a winding, hilly route through quiet residential streets back to the Salt Pond Visitor Center. This ride can be connected to longer rides, of course, by riding the CCRT in either direction from this ride. After the ride, be sure to check out the Salt Pond Visitor Center, with gift shop and bookstore, museum, indoor theater, restrooms, view of Salt Pond from large glass windows, outdoor amphitheater, and hiking trails to Nauset Marsh and Salt Pond out back. The indoor theater presents several short films daily, and the museum exhibits salt-marsh plants and animals, beach dynamics, upland plant communities, and prominent residential and migratory birds. It also features works by local artists. If it's raining, this is a great place to dry off, grab a book from the bookstore, and relax.

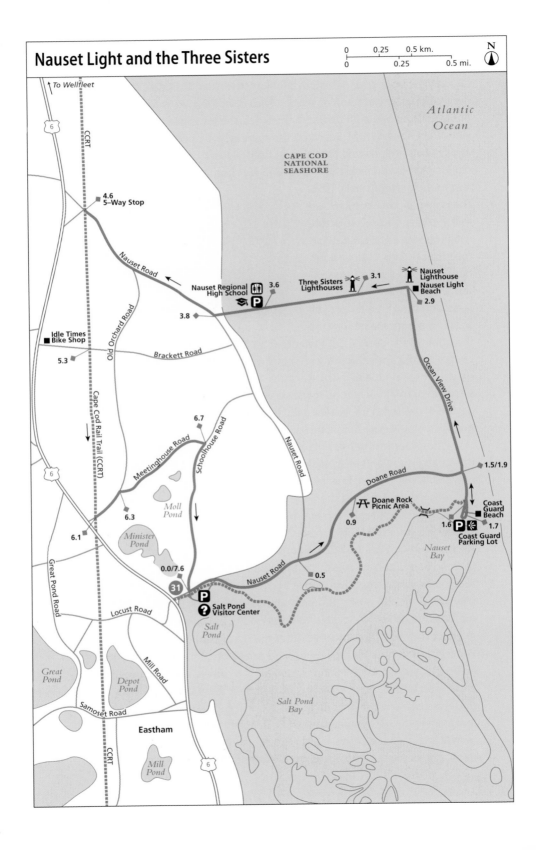

Nauset Light and the Three Sisters

0   0.25   0.5 km.
0   0.25   0.5 mi.

N

↑ To Wellfleet

6

CRT

Atlantic Ocean

CAPE COD NATIONAL SEASHORE

4.6
5–Way Stop

Nauset Road

Nauset Regional High School   3.6

3.8

Three Sisters Lighthouses   3.1

Nauset Lighthouse
Nauset Light Beach
2.9

Old Orchard Road

Idle Times Bike Shop

5.3

Brackett Road

Ocean View Drive

6.7

Meetinghouse Road

Schoolhouse Road

Nauset Road

6.3

6.1

Moll Pond

Minister Pond

0.0/7.6

31

Doane Road

1.5/1.9

Doane Rock Picnic Area

0.9

1.6

Coast Guard Beach
Coast Guard Parking Lot
1.7

Nauset Bay

Cape Cod Rail Trail (CCRT)

6

Great Pond Road

Locust Road

Salt Pond Visitor Center

Salt Pond

Nauset Road

0.5

Mill Road

Great Pond

Depot Pond

Samoset Road

Salt Pond Bay

Eastham

CCRT

6

Mill Pond

0.0 Start this ride at the Salt Pond Visitor Center, Cape Cod National Seashore, 50 Nauset Rd., Eastham.

0.5 Continue straight on Doane Road.

0.9 Pass Doane Rock Picnic Area on the right (restrooms, picnic tables).

1.5 Turn right onto Ocean View Drive and ride up to the parking lot to explore Nauset Bay.

1.6 Circle the Coast Guard Beach Station parking lot.

1.7 View Nauset Bay.

1.9 Bear right up Ocean View Drive.

2.9 Explore Nauset Lighthouse and Nauset Light Beach.

3.1 Explore the Three Sisters Lighthouses on the right.

3.6 Pass Nauset Regional High School on the right (optional parking, restrooms).

3.8 Turn right on Nauset Road.

4.6 Turn left onto the CCRT at the five-way stop.

5.3 Cross Brackett Road.

6.1 Turn left onto Old Orchard Road.

6.3 Turn right on Meetinghouse Road.

6.7 Turn right onto Schoolhouse Road.

7.6 Finish the ride at the Salt Pond Visitor Center.

RIDE INFORMATION

Local Events and Attractions
Cape Cod National Seashore: 99 Marconi Site Rd., Wellfleet; (508) 771-2144. See the listing under Ride 30.

Restaurants
See the listings under Ride 30 for restaurants in Eastham.

Restrooms
There are restrooms at the Salt Pond Visitor Center year-round and at Coast Guard Beach, Nauset Light Beach (seasonal).

32

Wellfleet Ocean-to-Bay Tour

An east-west ride that explores the Atlantic Ocean beaches, the Cape Cod National Seashore forests, Cape Cod Bay, the lost island of Billingsgate, shipwrecks, real pirates, and real pirate treasure recovered by a National Geographic explorer.

Start: Cape Cod Rail Trail parking lot on Lecount Hollow Road in Wellfleet

Distance: 18.0 miles, out-and-back with two lollipops

Approximate riding time: 1.5 to 2 hours

Best bike: Road

Terrain and surface type: Paved main roads and back roads, with many rolling hills, some steep

Traffic and hazards: Busy beach traffic to beaches on Lecount Hollow Road and Ocean View Drive, heavy traffic in Wellfleet Center on Main Street, heavy traffic on East Commercial Street, Commercial Street, and Kendrick Avenue along Wellfleet Harbor and Mayo Beach

Things to see: Lecount Hollow Beach and Maguire's Landing, White Crest Beach, Cahoon Hollow Beach (Beachcomber Bar and former life-saving station), Long Pond, Duck Creek, Uncle Tim's Bridge (hiking), Wellfleet Harbor, Mayo Beach, Wellfleet Harbor, Chequessett Neck, Chequessett Neck Road Bridge and Dike, Herring River Estuary, Griffin Island, Great Island, Wellfleet Center, Gull Pond, Newcomb Hollow Beach, Barry Clifford searching for treasure from the *Whydah* off the coast of South Wellfleet

Map: *Arrow Street Atlas: Cape Cod including Martha's Vineyard & Nantucket*, p. 89

Getting there: Take Route 6 to Wellfleet and exit at Lecount Hollow Road. Pass the P.B. Boulangerie on the left and immediately turn right into the parking lot for the Cape Cod Rail Trail (CCRT; maintained by Nickerson State Park).

GPS coordinates: N41 54.96' / W69 59.26'

Save a perfect sunny day for this ride, because the views are breathtaking when visibility is good. Start early to see the sun rise over the Atlantic Ocean, and beat the beach traffic along this route. This 18-mile ride is very hilly, with some very steep but short climbs in Wellfleet, from the steep cliffs overlooking the Atlantic Ocean to the bronze cliffs of Great Island reflecting the sunlight on Cape Cod Bay. This ride avoids dealing with the heavy traffic on Route 6 by taking the only bridge over it in Wellfleet on Long Pond Road. And instead of heading north-south like so many rides on the Outer Cape's forearm, this one cuts east-west across the National Seashore through pine, oak forest, and kettle ponds, along Wellfleet Harbor and Mayo Beach (the only beach in Wellfleet where a parking permit is not required) to the summit of Griffin Island overlooking Great Island in Cape Cod Bay. It's not quite an out-and-back, with the return trip riding through town and then turning left up the steep climb on Lawrence Road, so familiar to riders in the annual Pan Mass Challenge. The Gross Hill Road return takes you all the way back to Newcomb Hollow Beach before returning along Ocean View Drive to where the ride starts.

Start in the parking lot at the entrance to the CCRT on Lecount Hollow Road in Wellfleet. There is additional parking in the lot for the South Wellfleet General Store, the backside of which is visible through this parking lot, and it can be accessed off Route 6 (it has its own exit ramp) or from Lecount Hollow Road across from the P.B. Boulangerie. This excellent French restaurant (dinner), with lines out the door for its bakery every weekend, also has limited parking for patrons. At the end of the parking lot on Lecount Hollow Road, stop before turning right, and look across the street at the dirt road with the sign labeled Railroad Avenue. This is the path that the Old Colony Railroad used to take to Provincetown, and this dirt road continues along the old railroad bed to Route 6.

Turn right on Lecount Hollow Road and head down the flat, smooth pavement toward Maguire's Landing through the Cape Cod National Seashore. There won't be an Entering the National Seashore sign in most places you go on Cape Cod, and there isn't one here. Maguire's Landing is spelled wrong about three different ways if you try to find out more information online. The Town of Wellfleet website spells it like I do, but locals mostly call it Lecount Hollow Beach. The town's official name for it is Maguire's Landing at Lecount Hollow. Just don't let us locals confuse you.

You can opt to take a short side trip into the Maguire's Landing parking, and I literally mean short, because this parking lot is shrinking. The cliffs at the end of the lot provide a beautiful view of the Atlantic, with the beach down below. But erosion took a big chunk out of the end of the parking lot in the winter of 2013, and the lot was closed because the pavement had broken off and was hanging off the vertical cliff face. It was too dangerous to walk, ride, or drive near the edge. The storms that winter took more than 20 feet of shoreline in some areas of the Cape Cod National Seashore. Wellfleet did a quick and beautiful repair job in plenty of time for the summer season, though, and you'd never know anything happened by looking at the parking lot now. Enjoy the view at Maguire's Landing, but the next time you visit, the trip down Lecount Hollow Road will likely be even shorter.

Turn left up the short, fairly steep climb on Ocean View Drive. At the top, the road flattens out and the ride takes you over the plateau overlooking the Atlantic Ocean on the right. This may be the most beautiful view of the Atlantic Ocean anywhere on Cape Cod, elevated above the dune cliffs with one of the longest stretches of water view at this height. White Crest Beach, or the "surfer's beach," on the right at mile 1.8 has an even more dramatic cliff edge than Maguire's Landing. Of course, this ride just gained about 60 feet in elevation climbing from there. The road then dips a little past White Crest, and then climbs to an elevation of about 260 feet above sea level, the highest point along Ocean View Drive in Wellfleet. This is where I usually get dropped on the club Sunday ride, and you're going to need a good power-to-weight ratio for this deceptively difficult climb. If there's a headwind (and there often is), that just adds to the pleasure of this climb on a hot day. The expansive view more than makes up for any difficulty, and the descent is a breeze.

Bike Shop

Little Capistrano Bike Shop, 1446 Route 6, Wellfleet, (508) 349-2363, littlecapistrano bikeshop.com

Pass Cahoon Hollow Beach on the right, at the end of Cahoon Hollow Road, which technically crosses Ocean View Drive here at mile 2.5 of this ride, although it looks more like a driveway on the right where it descends to the Beachcomber Bar and Restaurant. The Beachcomber shares the edge of the bluff with the beach, and beach parking is behind the restaurant. This is a great place to stop in summer for a drink, fresh seafood, music, and a view of the Atlantic. It's often very crowded and loud when there's a live band, but that's why it's so popular, especially with college students, who gather from all parts of the country to get here in summer. The Beachcomber is housed in a building that was once the Cahoon Hollow Life-Saving Station. See it before it falls into the ocean! Turn left on Long Pond Road away from the ocean, descending and rolling through the pine and oak forest around curves and then climbing and descending a big hill to Long Pond Beach on the left. Long Pond Road is a little hairy since there is no fog line and the road bends past many blind driveways. But since cyclists use this road so often, most cars will expect you (but not all). Pass the beach on the left at the bottom of this descent and then start climbing again, past the scrub pine and the sandy dunes of the Old King's Highway, now a fire road under the power lines. The old railroad used to pass through here from Railroad Avenue across from the ride start, and it is still possible to ride a bicycle along the old railroad bed from this spot all the way to Wellfleet Harbor.

After another summit on Long Pond Road, cross over the highway and descend around a sharp left bend in the road, through a shaded oak stand to a stop sign on Main Street. Don't overshoot this stop sign by taking the descent too fast, as Main Street in Wellfleet is often busy, and cars go a bit faster descending to this spot from downtown. Turn right on Main, then make an immediate left on East Commercial Street and head past Mac's Shack on the left. If you look left across Duck Creek, past Uncle Tim's Bridge, you can see the old train trestle spanning the inner basin of Wellfleet Harbor. Pass Railroad Avenue on the right, where the train went through a tunnel under the hill in years gone by, and ascend to a straightaway to Wellfleet Town Pier on the left. The road bends 90 degrees right, around a newer restaurant called the Pearl, which has upstairs outdoor seating on a deck overlooking the harbor and Cape Cod Bay. Turn right onto Kendrick Avenue, and ride this long stretch past Mayo Beach and Wellfleet Harbor on the left. There is a ball field and playground on the right, past the Bookstore Restaurant, with a skate park, tennis courts, and public restrooms.

On the left, the view opens up across the harbor to Great Island, the turnaround point of this ride. The cliffs in the distance often glow bronze or red in the light reflecting off the harbor, and if it's hot, the breeze here is refreshing. At the far left end of Great Island there is a long spit of land leading to Jeremy Point, exposed only at low tide. Missing from the horizon is the lost island of Billingsgate, an island just south of Jeremy Point that washed away to sea in 1942. In the 19th century when Thoreau visited Cape Cod, Billingsgate had around thirty homes, a school, a lighthouse built in 1822, and its own baseball team. Thoreau wrote about a Wellfleet oysterman who recounted old stories about Billingsgate, and Thoreau's map of Cape Cod shows Billingsgate Island and its lighthouse, now gone from any map of Cape Cod. Billingsgate Island started to wash away to sea in the years just after Thoreau's visit, and one smart sea captain decided to float his Billingsgate house across Wellfleet Harbor into town to safety. The resting place of that house, built in 1750, is now the main dining room of the Wicked Oyster Restaurant on Main Street. Billingsgate Island today is just a small circle of sand visible only at low tide, with blocks from the old lighthouse foundation scattered on the sand. As you admire the view of Great Island, the lost island of Billingsgate is a reminder of how fragile Cape Cod truly is.

Continue on Kendrick Avenue, which bends right, away from the water, then left, and merges with Chequessett Neck Road. It's beautiful here, with panoramic views off to the left, as the road rolls upward over three or four hills, past Powers Landing on the left, then the Chequessett Yacht and Country Club golf course on the right. The road finally climbs to the top of the neck before descending to a long bridge and dike over the Herring River, the Chequessett Neck Road Bridge.

Looking left from the Chequessett Bridge, you can see the narrow strip of land connecting Wellfleet to Great Island called the "Gut," which encloses another arm of Wellfleet Harbor. Ships used to anchor in this secluded little harbor and come ashore to Samuel Smith's Tavern, which provided ale and hospitality to whalers and other seafarers for a few decades after it was built in 1690 on Great Island. Cross the bridge and climb up the hill to the top of Griffin Island, where there is a fork in the road. Bear right for an optional out-and-back side trip to Duck Harbor via Griffin Island Road. For this ride, bear left and turn around at the entrance of the parking lot to Great Island, which is maintained by the National Park Service. If you continue on Chequessett Neck Road to the left, it descends to a dead-end at the Gut. Up here at the parking lot, there are restrooms and a picnic area, with lots of shade from the pine forest growing on top of this hill. Hiking trails leaving from the parking lot cross the Gut to Great Island and trail maps are available. I first hiked here twenty years ago, and happily not much has changed. The 1690 tavern site is marked and there is a memorial for a Wampanoag woman at the trailhead. The beauty of this place is unsurpassed.

Turn around and head back across the bridge on Chequessett Neck Road, this time bearing left at mile 9.7, staying left on Chequessett Neck Road as Kendrick Avenue bears right. The road goes through a quiet, wooded residential neighborhood, descending into town. Make a left on Holbrook Avenue then a quick right on Main, and you're in the center of town. You can stop by Hatch's Fish Market at the back of the parking lot behind Winslow's Tavern on the left, or stop at the Wellfleet Marketplace on the right at the corner of Main and Bank Streets. Ride right through town, up the hill past Bank Street, and turn left on Long Pond Road. You're backtracking here, so déjà vu is possible as you climb the hill, bend right around the corner, and cross over Route 6. Hopefully you're very fit as you turn left on Lawrence Road, a short but steep climb past the Wellfleet Elementary School, and descend sharply past the Wellfleet Fire Department on the left. Watch out for merging traffic and make a hard right onto Gross Hill Road, which climbs quickly and starts rolling up and down as you re-enter the National Seashore. Gross Hill Road is covered by

Bike racks overlooking White Crest Beach, Ocean View Drive, Wellfleet

oak and pine forest and is a fun stretch of road with a fast descent and a long climb near the intersection with Ocean View Drive at mile 13.4. Turn left and descend the hill to Newcomb Hollow Beach.

A 19th-century schooner was found washed ashore at Newcomb Hollow Beach in 2008, and the remains of the hull disappear then reappear with the shifting sands. Explore the beach or turn around and ride up the hill a short way to a dirt road on the right called Thoreau Way, which travels north past Higgins Pond and Williams Pond. The "old Wellfleet oysterman" in Thoreau's *Cape Cod* had a house just east of Williams Pond where Thoreau stayed during one of his visits here. The oysterman's name was John Newcomb, and his grave in the Duck Creek Cemetery on Route 6 in Wellfleet states that he lived to be 94 years old (he is descended from the Wellfleet Newcomb family, as am I). Continue up the hill and turn left on Ocean View Drive on the roller coaster ride back to Cahoon Hollow. The view of the ocean on the left for the return of this ride is even better, especially at the crest of the hill just past Cahoon Hollow Road and the Beachcomber.

As you gaze out at the Atlantic looking southward, east of South Wellfleet along the horizon (just north of Marconi Beach), look for a gathering of ships belonging to an underwater archaeological research team. Buried beneath the ocean floor where you are gazing is what remains of the slave ship turned pirate ship *Whydah*, discovered in 1984 by underwater explorer and treasure hunter Barry Clifford. The *Whydah* carried stolen treasure from more than fifty other ships when it sank off the coast of Wellfleet on April 26, 1717, with four tons of gold and silver on board. Captained by Samuel "Black Sam" Bellamy, the *Whydah* is the first pirate ship ever discovered in North America, with the only pirate treasure ever recovered. Old stories told by his uncle inspired Clifford as a boy growing up in Brewster, and tales speak of Black Sam Bellamy having a mistress named Maria Hallett of Wellfleet. No one knows for sure if Black Sam was headed to Cape Cod for a rendezvous with her when his ship wrecked in a vicious nor'easter that April (I imagine he was headed for Samuel Smith's tavern on the eastern tip of Great Island). Only 2 of the 146 crewmembers survived the wreck, and the rest disappeared or washed ashore on the Outer Beach in Wellfleet. One pirate escaped and was never found, and the other was brought to trial, where court records tell much of the story of the *Whydah* and Black Sam Bellamy's exploits.

Descend Ocean View Drive and see if you can see Clifford and his team along the horizon, diving and dredging for the rest of the treasure. Clifford returned to the wreck site in 2013, believing there was a lot more treasure after discovering a colonial-era document that said Bellamy had robbed two more ships of 400,000 pieces of gold. In September 2013 one of Clifford's divers brought up what looked like a large clump of rock, but x-rays showed that inside were coins and gold. There is, by several accounts, much more treasure out there from the *Whydah*. Most of the treasure already unearthed is on a traveling exhibition with *National Geographic*, with more than 200 artifacts recovered from the shipwreck on tour. Clifford currently has a few artifacts on display at the *Whydah* Museum in Provincetown at MacMillan Pier (the main wharf), and is looking to find a bigger space for his museum. If Clifford's dives off the Wellfleet coast continue to yield more treasure, he'll need it.

Descend the crest of the hill and pass White Crest Beach with more views of this treacherous but beautiful coastline, climb up the gradual incline, and then descend the hill on Ocean View Drive to Maguire's Landing. Turn right 90 degrees onto Lecount Hollow Road, and be careful not to swing too far to the left around the corner, as approaching vehicles turning left sometimes cut the blind corner here. Finish the ride at the CCRT parking lot where you started, or pass by the lot and continue to the P.B. Boulangerie on the right, just before the road ends at Route 6. Park your bike by the fire pit and follow the scent of fresh baked bread and croissants. The line to the bakery may be out the door here, but you can talk about your ride with the many other cyclists who park their bikes in the racks out front. Or just close your eyes, smell the bakery, listen to the French music, and pretend you're in Provence. Sample a *bombe au chocolat* or a *croque monsieur*. You earned it.

MILES AND DIRECTIONS

0.0 Start this ride at the CCRT parking lot in Wellfleet.

0.1 Turn right on Lecount Hollow Road.

0.7 Turn left on Ocean View Drive.

2.5 Turn left on Long Pond Road.

3.8 Pass by the Long Pond swimming area.

4.7 Turn right on Main Street.

4.8 Turn left on East Commercial Street. Pass Uncle Tim's Bridge on the left.

5.0 Continue on Commercial Street, passing Bank Street on the right.

5.5 Turn right on Kendrick Avenue past Wellfleet Town Pier on the left, then pass Mayo Beach and parking lot on the left.

6.3 Bear left on Chequessett Neck Road; pass the Chequessett Yacht and Country Club on the right.

7.5 Cross the bridge at Chequessett Neck over the Herring River onto Griffin Island.

Wellfleet Ocean-to-Bay Tour

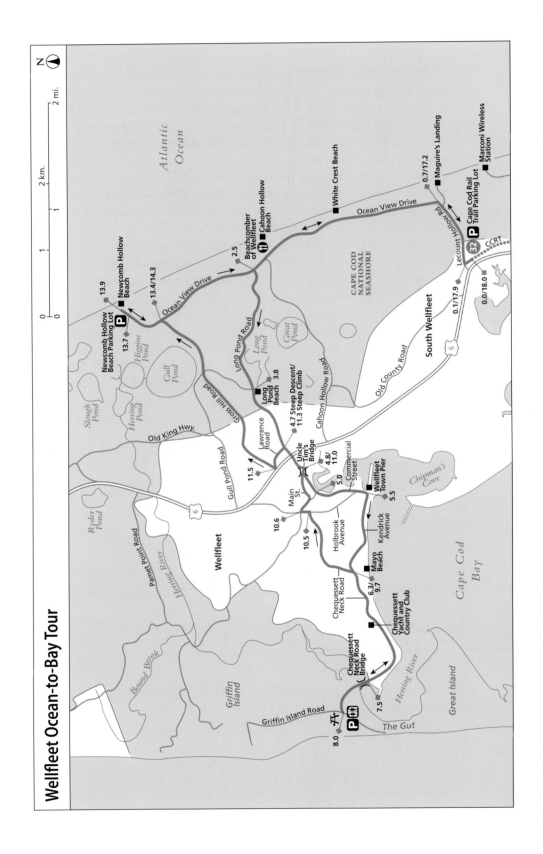

N

2 mi.

2 km.

Atlantic Ocean

Newcomb Hollow Beach Parking Lot 13.7

Newcomb Hollow Beach 13.9

13.4/14.3

Ocean View Drive 2.5

Beachcomber of Wellfleet

Cahoon Hollow Beach

White Crest Beach

Ocean View Drive

0.7/17.2

Maguire's Landing

Marconi Wireless Station

Cape Cod Rail Trail Parking Lot

32 CCRT

Lecount Hollow Rd.

0.1/17.9

0.0/18.0

CAPE COD NATIONAL SEASHORE

South Wellfleet

Higgins Pond

Gull Pond

Slough Pond

Herring Pond

Old King Hwy.

Gross Hill Road

Long Pond Road

Long Pond

Great Pond

Long Pond Beach 3.8

4.7 Steep Descent/ 11.3 Steep Climb

Cahoon Hollow Road

Old County Road

Ryder Pond

Gull Pond Road

Lawrence Road

11.5

Pamet Point Road

Herring River

Bound Brook

Griffin Island

Griffin Island Road

8.0

Chequessett Neck Road Bridge

7.5

The Gut

Great Island

Chequessett Neck Road

Chequessett Yacht and Country Club

6.3/ 9.7

Mayo Beach

Cape Cod Bay

Kendrick Avenue

Wellfleet Town Pier 5.5

Chipman's Cove

Holbrook Avenue

10.5

10.6

Commercial Street

5.0

4.8/ 11.0

Uncle Tim's Bridge

Main St.

6

6

Wellfleet

8.0   Arrive at the summit of Griffin Island, explore the Gut and Great Island, and then turn around (restrooms and parking lot with picnic area and hiking trails). Continue on Chequessett Neck Road back toward town.

9.7   Bear left and continue on Chequessett Neck Road.

10.5   Turn left on Holbrook Avenue.

10.6   Turn right on Main Street in Wellfleet Center.

11.0   Turn left on Long Pond Road.

11.3   Turn left on Lawrence Road (steep climb).

11.5   Turn right (hard right) onto Gross Hill Road.

13.4   Turn left at the intersection with Ocean View Drive and descend the hill to Newcomb Hollow Beach.

13.7   Arrive at Newcomb Hollow Beach parking lot.

13.9   Turn around at the end of the Newcomb Hollow Beach parking lot.

14.3   Turn left on Ocean View Drive.

17.2   Turn right on Lecount Hollow Road.

17.9   Turn left into the CCRT parking lot.

18.0   End the ride in the parking lot.

RIDE INFORMATION

Local Events and Attractions

Marconi Wireless Station and Beach: See the listing under Ride 18.

Maguire's Landing Beach: Great beach at the end of Lecount Hollow Road.

White Crest Beach: Also known as the "surfer's beach," a beautiful cliffside beach on this ride.

Cahoon Hollow Beach: Home of the Beachcomber, formerly the site of a Life-Saving Station for shipwrecked sailors, now a beach bar and restaurant with live music.

Newcomb Hollow Beach: Yet another gorgeous beach easily accessed from this ride.

Great Island Trail: Great hiking trails and site of Samuel Smith's Tavern. View what's left of Billingsgate Island at low tide from the bluffs.

Wellfleet Drive-In Theater: Route 6, Wellfleet; (508) 349-7176. One of the last ones left. First-run movies, a playground, a throwback to earlier days. Use the speakers or tune in to the exclusive radio station. Concessions.

Restaurants

The Beachcomber: 1220 Old Cahoon Hollow Rd., Wellfleet; (508) 349-6055. An institution, and favorite college summer hang out. Serving surfers, families, beach-goers, and music lovers for more than fifty years at Cahoon Hollow Beach. Restaurant, bar, nightclub. Closed in winter. Reason? Freezin'!

Ceraldi: 15 Kendrick Ave., Wellfleet (next to the pier); (508) 237-9811. Seven-course dinner for $70. More than dining, it is more of an event. Expensive but worth it. Formerly in Provincetown.

P.B. Boulangerie and Bistro: 15 Lecount Hollow Rd., Wellfleet; (508) 349-1600. See the listing under Ride 18.

Wicked Oyster: 50 Main Street, Wellfleet; (508) 349-3455. See the listing under Ride 29.

Van Rensselaer's Restaurant and Raw Bar: 1019 Route 6, Wellfleet; (508) 349-2127. See the listing under Ride 18.

Pearl: 250 Commercial St., Wellfleet; (508) 349-2999. Dining on the deck on the second floor gives a great view of Wellfleet Harbor and Great Island. Fun atmosphere and good food.

South Wellfleet General Store: 1446 State Hwy. (Route 6), Wellfleet; (508) 349-1100. Deli, groceries. Less expensive option for snacks, sandwiches, and coffee.

Restrooms

Restrooms are available at the many restaurants along this ride, and there are porta-potties at the ride start in Wellfleet and at Great Island.

Head of the Meadow Trail

An easy, flat trail to the beach, great for families with kids. Gives the sense of truly being away from civilization. Beautiful beaches and wildlife with a chance to find the Pilgrim Spring.

Start: The small dirt parking lot on a dirt road that branches left off High Head Road at the intersection with Cliff Road, North Truro

Distance: 4.8 miles out-and-back

Approximate riding time: 1 hour

Best bike: Hybrid, mountain bike, cyclocross bike, fat tire bike

Terrain and surface type: Rough pavement on the trail with some dirt single track, also smooth pavement on roads and parking lots

Traffic and hazards: Sand in the road and trail, rough trail in spots, vehicle traffic entering and exiting the two Head of the Meadow beaches, other bicyclists, pedestrians on trail

Things to see: High Head, Pilgrim Heights, Pilgrim Spring, Head of the Meadow National Park Service Beach, Head of the Meadow Town of Truro Beach, Atlantic Ocean

Map: *Arrow Street Atlas: Cape Cod including Martha's Vineyard & Nantucket*, p. 82

Getting there: Take Route 6 to North Truro, turn right on High Head Road (after the Pilgrim Heights exit). Bear left onto a dirt road where Cliff Road rises uphill, and park in the dirt parking lot. The entrance to the trailhead is opposite the small parking lot.

GPS coordinates: N42 03.54' / W70 06.87'

THE RIDE

This is a short ride, but it's bumpy, with stretches of rough pavement and places where there is no pavement, just a dirt path. In the rain, this would be a miserable trip for roadies or children through several muddy sections. All that said, this ride is one of the best on Cape Cod, especially for those who don't want to ride far, and those with small children wanting a bit of an adventure. The trail is tucked behind a long stretch of dunes and a salt meadow to the left, and old farmland with hidden kettle ponds to the right. Just make sure you have good shock-absorption, internal or external.

The Head of the Meadow Trail runs from High Head Road to Head of the Meadow Beach in North Truro, ending at the Head of the Meadow Beach parking lot that is maintained by the National Park Service (NPS). Head of the Meadow Beach has two vehicle entrances and two parking lots, one reached from Route 6 (in your car) by turning left on Holden Street to the NPS beach, and the other by bearing right at the fork and entering the Town of Truro beach. Both parking lots require a fee, and you can start this out-and-back ride from either end of the trail. Since I never want to pay for parking, ever, this ride starts at the small, but free, dirt lot at the end of High Head Road. Just turn left off the paved road before Cliff Road, which ascends steeply to the right. The bike trail starts off the dirt road turnaround on the other side of the parking lot.

If there is one overwhelming feature of this ride, it's the sound of birds. And that's the great beauty of this trail. It feels like you're away from everything, with just the sun, sand, sky, and the birds. An abandoned 19th-century farm next to this trail, tucked away in the woods to the right, was owned by Thomas Small, who arrived at this lush spot in Truro in the 1860s. He planted grape, lilac, plum, apple, and soapwort, whose roots produce a lather when mixed with water. Soapwort was also used for cleaning, adding a foamy head to beer, or just having a fragrant smell around the house, its blossoms sweetly scented. The farm is now a bird's paradise, overgrown with those plants, fruits, and flowers planted by Small, which intertwine and grow with the native swamp azalea, bearberry,

Bike Shops

Little Capistrano Bike Shop, 1446 Route 6, Wellfleet, (508) 349-2363, littlecapistranobikeshop.com

Arnold's Bike Shop, 329 Commercial St., Provincetown, (508) 487-0844, provincetownbikes.com

Ptown Bikes, 42 Bradford St., Provincetown, (508) 487-8735, ptownbikes.com

Gale Force Bikes, 144 Bradford St. Extension, Provincetown, (508) 487-4849, galeforce.com

Riders at Head of the Meadow National Park Service Beach

blueberry, and other flora. The Small family must have chosen this spot for its proximity to the ocean while still protected by the salt meadow to the east (left of the trail) and the pine forest (on the right) that climbs up to High Head cliffs to the west, overlooking Cape Cod Bay and Provincetown.

    Pilgrim Spring is located at mile 0.8 of this ride, where a bridge goes over a small stream. Pilgrim Spring is where the Pilgrims first searched for and found fresh water to drink on Cape Cod. A stone marker was placed at the location of the spring and is located just off the bike trail. I'll leave it to you to find it. You can opt to park the bike and climb up to the cliffs overlooking the Atlantic Ocean atop High Head. If you choose to hike here, the trail to the right takes you up to the top of the cliffs, and the trail to the left through forest.

At the end of the trail (mile 2.0), this ride takes a tour through two parking lots. That may not at first sound appealing, but the first lot, on the left, is the National Park Service beach. The helpful park rangers at the booth will point you to a nice walking trail through the dunes at the end of the lot, at mile 2.2 of this ride. Circle around the lot and exit via Holden Street, where you make a sharp left onto Head of the Meadow Road. That takes riders to the second beach and parking lot, managed by the Town of Truro. Both beaches are called Head of the Meadow, which can be a bit confusing. The Truro side has a great view of the beach and ocean, while the National Park beach has dunes blocking the view from the lot, so you have to climb over on foot to see the water. So, I decided to make the Truro town beach the final turnaround point of this ride so you would never have to dismount your bicycle to see a water view.

Of course, this ride is also a beach destination, so getting off the saddle and parking at the bike racks at either beach may be your goal. They are both gorgeous beaches that are easily accessible from one another, and if you go before 9 a.m. or after 6 p.m., you won't need a beach sticker to park at the town beach. The NPS beach has changing rooms and outdoor showers, and a food truck often appears in summer. Turn around at the town beach and return to the trail entrance at the NPS beach. The beaches are home to a large seal population, and you can walk the beach from here all the way to Provincetown or Eastham like Thoreau did. Or just ride the last 2 miles on the bike trail back to the High Head Road parking lot.

MILES AND DIRECTIONS

0.0 Start this ride in the High Head Road parking lot (dirt/sand).

0.1 Enter the Head of the Meadow Trail.

0.8 Find Pilgrim Spring, where the Pilgrims first found fresh water, located near here.

2.0 Arrive at the end of the trail and turn left into the National Park Service beach.

2.2 Ride to the end of the lot for hiking trails in the dunes, then turn around.

2.3 Exit the NPS lot onto Holden Street.

Head of the Meadow Trail

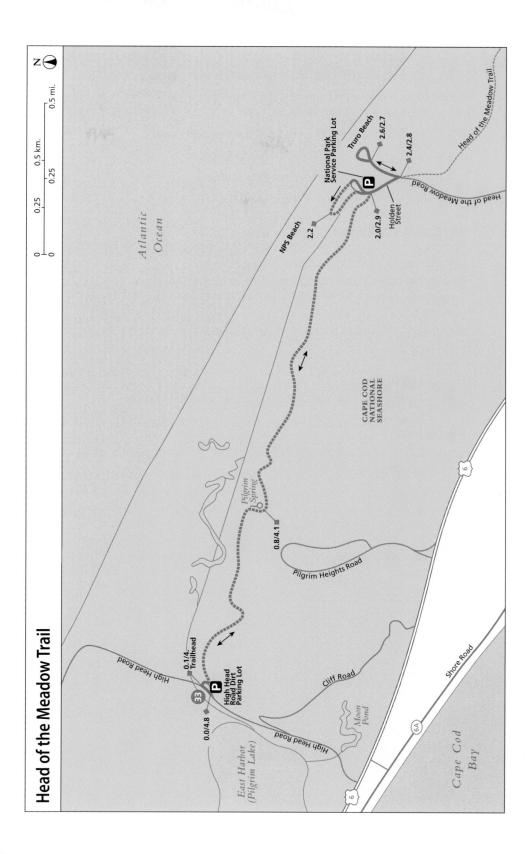

2.4 Make a sharp left turn on Head of the Meadow Road.

2.6 Enter the Town of Truro beach and turn around at the bike racks on the far right of the parking lot.

2.7 Exit the parking lot onto Head of the Meadow Road.

2.8 Make a sharp right turn onto Holden Street.

2.9 Turn left onto the Head of the Meadow Trail.

4.8 End this ride in the High Head Road parking lot.

RIDE INFORMATION

Local Events and Attractions
Pilgrim Heights: Nearby hiking trails with no bicycle trail access.

Truro Vineyards: 11 Route 6A, North Truro; (508) 487-6200. See the listing under Ride 29.

Highland Light and Museum: 27 Highland Rd., North Truro. See the listing under Ride 29.

Restaurants
See the listings under Ride 29 for restaurants and markets in Truro.

Restrooms
There are restrooms at both the NPS beach and the town beach at Head of the Meadow Beach.

34

Province Lands Trail

Almost like being in the desert, but also through beautiful forest and then along the beach. This ride is fun, like a mountain bike trail but on a paved path. Opt to take a short trip into Provincetown from the end of Herring Cove Beach. Great views, lots of hills, lots of history.

Start: Province Lands Visitor Center, Race Point Road, off Route 6, Provincetown

Distance: 10.9 miles, a loop with three out-and-back segments

Approximate riding time: 1 hour

Best bike: Road, hybrid

Terrain and surface type: Smooth paved bike path over winding, hilly terrain

Traffic and hazards: Other cyclists, pedestrians, in-line skaters, out-of-control riders, steep hills, sharp curves, sand on the trail, wet areas of trail in wetlands, congested parking lots, especially at Herring Cove Beach, potential high winds

Things to see: Province Lands Visitor Center, downtown Provincetown (via Herring Cove Beach), Race Point Lighthouse, Race Point Ranger Station, Old Harbor Life-Saving Station Museum, Pilgrim Monument, dunes, beech and oak forest, beaches, and panoramic views of Provincetown

Map: *Arrow Street Atlas: Cape Cod including Martha's Vineyard & Nantucket*, p. 72

Getting there: Take Route 6 to Provincetown. Turn right on Race Point Road. Follow it to the Province Lands Visitor Center, following signs that are clearly marked.

GPS coordinates: N42 04.43' / W70 12.35'

THE RIDE

The Province Lands Trail was opened in September 1967 as the first bike trail ever built by the National Park Service in the United States, and was dedicated by President Eisenhower's personal physician, Dr. Paul Dudley White. Dr. White was a cardiologist and cofounder of the American Heart Association, an avid cyclist whose name also appears along the Charles River in Boston as the bike path named after him (see *Best Bike Rides Boston* by Shawn Musgrave). More challenging than other paved multi-use trails in this book (exception perhaps Nickerson State Park), caution is recommended. This trail has been described by some as a "paved mountain bike trail" because of its fast descents, steep climbs, and dangerous curves. Other dangers are two narrow, low tunnels and wet areas due to seasonal flooding. It's not a trail for small children, inexperienced bikers, or those with poor bike-handling skills.

All that said, there are ways to ride flatter parts of the trail with smaller children and still have a memorable adventure, without the steeper hills and sharp curves (see below). And the more experienced members of the cycling population will absolutely *love* this trail. Riding the entire trail is a unique experience, almost surreal at times, since much of the path is surrounded by massive parabolic sand dunes that at times make it impossible to see anything but dune and sky. You feel like you're in the desert, especially if it's a dry, sunny day in July or August. And that's the main attraction of this ride for people who don't actually want to ride *over* the sand dunes, but want to ride *through* them, on a smooth, paved path. But no fat tire bikes are needed here; a road bike or hybrid is the best bike for this ride, repaved in 2011. And fortunately, the National Park Service also took cyclists' concerns to heart and made major improvements to 4.5 miles of the trail, which were completed recently. The reconstruction widened and resurfaced the bike trail to a width of ten feet in most areas. Wood retaining walls were rebuilt, new signage installed, and a center line was painted, along with other safety improvements. Beach grass and other vegetation native to the dune habitat was planted in places where sand blows across the trail to try to reduce the drifts.

This trail has more to offer than just the spectacular massive dunes, which would be enough to make it a unique ride. There are also large forested areas with hiking trails, kettle ponds, panoramic views of the ocean and bay, and side trips to huge, beautiful beaches on both the Cape Cod Bay and the Atlantic Ocean shores, with a lighthouse, the Old Harbor Museum, and a 19th-century Cape Cod Life-Saving Station. And there is easy access to downtown Provincetown and Commercial Street, the only street in Massachusetts (possibly the United States) where it is legal to ride your bike the wrong way down a one-way street (if you want to take your life into your own hands).

Breakwater Walk to Wood End Lighthouse, Provincetown

Commercial Street is not to be missed, however, with its vibrant nightlife and many shops, galleries, and restaurants. Just don't break any cycling laws, like riding down any *other* one-way streets, or failing to stop at stop signs and crosswalks. Enforcement of bicycle laws in the town has stepped up recently. No need to worry about all that on the Province Lands Trail, however, away from the crowded streets downtown.

Start this ride at the Province Lands Visitor Center parking lot, where the views of the park are impressive and expansive, and the Pilgrim Monument stands tall above the dunes to the south. There is an immediate steep downhill onto the main loop of this trail, past an outdoor amphitheater on the left. Proceed slowly on this descent, or walk your bike down the hill, then turn right at the trail map in front of you. The trail descends quickly through forest for 0.25 mile and then immediately climbs another 0.1 mile through dune. After a second descent, it levels off for the next 0.5 mile before a smaller hill as the trail parallels Race Point Road. At 1.4 miles, cross Race Point Road and the parking lot to enter Beech Forest, a dense beech, oak, and pine forest with ponds scattered in the woods. If you're looking for shade on a hot summer day, this is the place.

At mile 2.8, bear left and head off the main loop to one of the kettle ponds that was formed by glacial retreat at Bennett Pond thousands of years ago. There is an easy 1-mile hike around the pond here, with ducks, frogs, and an occasional turtle, a fun side trip for kids. If you want to ride this trail from the parking lot and combine this hike with children, the part of the trail between the parking lot and Bennett Pond is flat enough for smaller children and makes for a good out-and-back short ride. Continuing on, turn left back onto the main loop and be prepared for some challenging climbing and a steep descent into a sharp left-hand turn at mile 4.1. Use caution through the tunnel as it is almost too narrow for two bicyclists, and approaching cyclists from the other side are also descending a steep hill. Follow the trail toward Herring Cove Beach over a couple more short but challenging climbs and then enter the Herring Cove Beach parking lot, a long, narrow parking lot with cars pulling in and out of spaces on the right. Find two-way bike lane with sharrows (share-the-road bike arrows) pointing in both directions on the other side of the lot, on the left of the road heading away from you. Use caution. You'll be riding on the wrong side of the road in a lane that is often covered with sand from the dunes on the left. To make matters worse, there are speed bumps here. The bike lane then changes sides to the right at mile 5.6, just before the main entrance to Herring Cove Beach. It then continues to the end of the second parking lot on the right, following the right border of the lot by making a sharp right followed by a sharp left turn to its end.

Bike Shops

Arnold's Bike Shop, 329 Commercial St., Provincetown, (508) 487-0844, provincetownbikes.com
Ptown Bikes, 42 Bradford St., Provincetown, (508) 487-8735, ptownbikes.com
Gale Force Bikes, 144 Bradford St. Extension, Provincetown, (508) 487-4849, galeforce.com

You can turn around after your fill of beach here at the end of the second parking lot, with stunning sunsets and views of Race Point Light to the north (behind you). But I've mapped a little beyond the second parking lot here, because there is another short section of paved bike path that connects to a crosswalk on Province Lands Road. You can continue to Provincetown Center by turning right here as an option, using the bike lane on Province Lands Road. This is one of the few places on Cape Cod with bicycle lanes on both sides of a main road. Otherwise, turn around and ride the Herring Cove Beach parking lot bike lane to return to the entrance to the paved Province Lands Trail at mile 6.9 of this ride.

Enter the Province Lands Trail at the far left of the parking lot to retrace your ride. Head back through the dunes, and descend around the right bend into the tunnel carefully, turning left onto the main trail loop. Head north for Race Point Beach, the Race Point Ranger Station, and the Old Harbor Life-Saving Station. Use caution and brake on the downhill before a second tunnel under Province Lands Road at mile 9.0, then continue past the airport on the left to the parking lot at the end of this branch of the trail. There are bike racks there and it's a short walk to the ranger station and museum, which is well worth a visit. The Life-Saving Museum was an actual station, moved here from Chatham in 1977, and one of thirteen stations on the Outer Beach on Cape Cod. Read more about the history of the Life-Saving Service under Ride 30.

As another option from the Race Point parking lot, take the long walk (or drive your ORV and check with the Cape Cod National Seashore for information) to the Race Point Lighthouse, which is currently open just two times per month. This is a very long, arduous walk, and not for children, but well worth it. And if you're a star-gazer, a shorter walk to the beach from the parking lot here is not to be missed, especially if the only view of the sky where you live is in a bright city. Turn around and backtrack a short way past the airport, now to the right, and turn left at the crosswalk crossing Race Point Road at mile 10.3 toward the Visitor Center. Ride through the pine forest and at mile 10.8, turn right and climb up the steep hill back to the parking lot. Make sure to visit the Visitor Center, with 360-degree views of the dunes and ocean from the top deck. See whales spouting to the west in Cape Cod Bay or north in the Atlantic when they come to visit. Use the free viewfinders on the decks to locate the dune shacks off to the northeast, first built by the Life-Saving Service for stranded shipwreck survivors, and then taken over in the 1920s by famous artists and writers. Eugene O'Neill, Jackson Pollock, Tennessee Williams, Jack Kerouac, Harry Kemp, Norman Mailer, and E.E. Cummings all lived in the dune shacks, finding peace and quiet away from the city and creating some of their best works of art and books in these small shacks. Without electricity or running water, the dune shacks are still used by writers and artists today, through an arrangement with the National Park Service. They are located in an area of Provincetown and Truro known as the Peaked Hill Bars Historic District (named after the former Life-Saving Station), which is the 1,900 acres of dunes from Race Point to High Head in Truro visible from the upper deck. Inquire at the Visitor Center about the thirteen surviving dune shacks, as the friendly park rangers here are always very knowledgeable and helpful. Best of all, the Visitor Center is free.

MILES AND DIRECTIONS

0.0   Start this ride at the Province Lands Visitor Center parking lot. The path to the trail is just to the left of the stairway of the Visitor Center, next to the bike racks. Descend the steep hill and turn right onto the Province Lands Bike Trail.

1.4   Cross the Race Point Road Crosswalk.

2.8   Bear left into Bennett Pond.

3.0   Visit Bennett Pond and turn around.

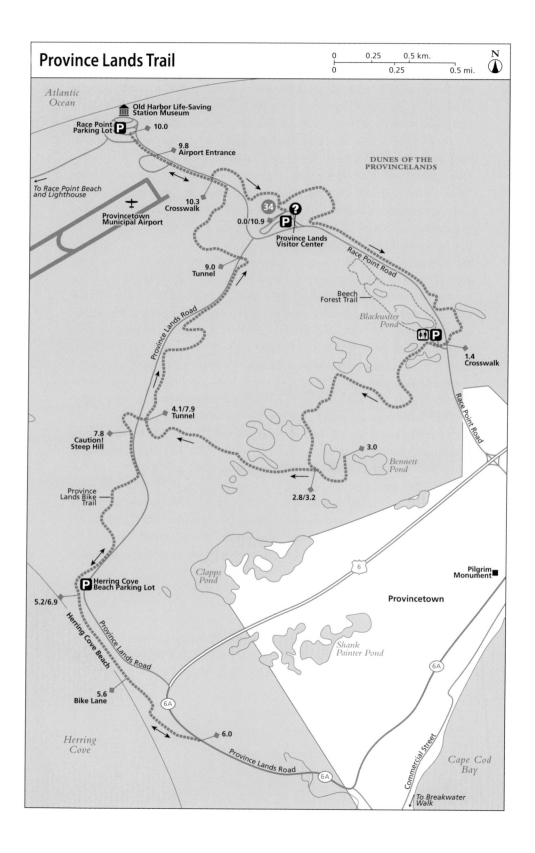

Province Lands Trail

0   0.25   0.5 km.
0   0.25   0.5 mi.

N

Atlantic Ocean

Old Harbor Life-Saving
Station Museum

Race Point
Parking Lot **P**   10.0

9.8
Airport Entrance

*To Race Point Beach
and Lighthouse*

10.3
Crosswalk

Provincetown
Municipal Airport

0.0/10.9

34   **?**

P

Province Lands
Visitor Center

DUNES OF THE
PROVINCELANDS

9.0
Tunnel

Province Lands Road

Race Point Road

Beech
Forest Trail

*Blackwater
Pond*

P

1.4
Crosswalk

4.1/7.9
Tunnel

7.8
Caution!
Steep Hill

Province
Lands Bike
Trail

3.0

*Bennett
Pond*

2.8/3.2

Race Point Road

*Clapps
Pond*

6

Pilgrim
Monument ■

Provincetown

Herring Cove
Beach Parking Lot **P**

5.2/6.9

Province Lands Road

Herring Cove Beach

5.6
Bike Lane

6A

*Shank
Painter Pond*

6A

Commercial Street

*Herring
Cove*

6.0

Province Lands Road

6A

*To Breakwater
Walk*

*Cape Cod
Bay*

3.2 Turn left and continue on the trail.

4.1 Turn left toward Herring Cove Beach and use caution through narrow tunnel.

5.2 Enter the Herring Cove Beach parking lot and find the bike lane on the other side of the lot.

5.6 The bike lane changes sides to the right, just before the main entrance to Herring Cove Beach, then continues to the end of the second parking lot.

6.0 Turn around and retrace the ride back to the Province Lands Trail. Or opt to continue into Provincetown Center on Province Lands Road by turning right.

6.9 Re-enter the Province Lands Bike Trail at the north end of the Herring Cove Beach parking lot.

7.8 Descend the hill and brake for the tunnel around the corner.

7.9 Turn left toward Race Point.

9.0 Use caution through the tunnel under Province Lands Road.

9.8 Cross the Provincetown Municipal Airport entrance crosswalk.

10.0 Turn around at the Race Point parking lot.

10.3 Turn left at the crosswalk and cross Race Point Road toward the Visitor Center.

10.8 Turn right and climb the short steep hill.

10.9 Finish this ride at the Province Lands Visitor Center parking lot.

RIDE INFORMATION

Local Events and Attractions

Race Point Lighthouse: Race Point, Provincetown; (508) 888-9784. Not an easy hike. You can book a stay at the lighthouse buildings that are attached, both restored to accommodate small groups who want to experience the lifestyle of a 20th-century lighthouse keeper. Reserve online at mybnbwebsite.com/racepointlighthouse or call (855) 722-3959.

Old Harbor Life-Saving Station and Museum: Race Point Beach, at the end of Race Point Road, Provincetown; (508) 349-3785. Fascinating history.

Pilgrim Monument and Provincetown Museum: High Pole Hill Road, Provincetown; (508) 487-1310. Climb the stairs all the way to the top and get the best aerial view of Cape Cod not requiring an airplane. The museum is both Provincetown history and Arctic history, as Robert Peary's fellow explorer

Donald B. MacMillan was from Provincetown. Don't miss the annual lighting of the monument if you're here in November. The Shallop Cafe offers concessions.

Expedition *Whydah* Sea Lab & Learning Center: Macmillan Wharf, Provincetown; (508) 487-8899; whydah.com (open May–October). The slave ship turned pirate ship *Whydah* sank in a brutal storm in 1717 with plunder from fifty ships, stolen by infamous pirate Black Sam Bellamy. It was discovered in 1984 in waters off South Wellfleet (see Ride 32) by Barry Clifford. Most of the good stuff is unfortunately on tour with *National Geographic*.

Provincetown Municipal Airport: (508) 487-0241. You could have flown here.

Commercial Street, Provincetown: All the shops, restaurants, art galleries, and nightclubs make for an exciting ride or walk around town. It's the only street in Massachusetts, maybe the United States, where you can ride your bike the wrong way down a one-way street. But why would you want to?

Breakwater Walk, Wood End Lighthouse, and Long Point Lighthouse: Take the long hike across the breakwater jetty on the walkway, or ride the water taxi to Long Point and its lighthouse, at the very tip of Cape Cod. Wood End Light is also an active lighthouse worth seeing, at the western end of Long Point, and easier to get to on foot.

Art's Dune Tours: 4 Standish St., Provincetown; (508) 487-1950. Take a guided tour through the dunes of Provincetown and top it off with a clambake. There is much more out there than you think.

Restaurants

Jimmy's Hideaway: 179 Commercial St., Unit 1, Provincetown; (508) 487-1011. Intimate restaurant and bar with excellent food and service.

Victor's: 175 Bradford St. Extension, West End, Provincetown; (508) 487-1777. Excellent food and service.

The Mews Restaurant and Cafe: 429 Commercial St., Provincetown; (508) 487-1500. One of the best restaurants on Cape Cod.

Far Land Provisions: 150 Bradford St., Provincetown; (508) 487-0045. Great sandwiches, good place to refuel. Open year-round.

Wired Puppy: 379 Commercial St., Provincetown; (508) 487-0017. Great coffee stop.

Provincetown Portuguese Bakery: 299 Commercial St., Provincetown; (508) 487-1803. Great bakery, breakfast, lunch, and dinner. Late night. Many century rides seem to stop here, with bikes parked in the alley. It is a good sign.

Restrooms

There are restrooms at the Province Lands Visitor Center (seasonal) and at Herring Cove Beach (seasonal).

Oak Bluffs to Edgartown Beach Road

This is a great way to start your Martha's Vineyard vacation. This flat out-and-back ride hugs the eastern side of Martha's Vineyard, from Oak Bluffs to Edgartown along Beach Road with beautiful ocean views. This one is easy for kids and families, or can be combined with any other Martha's Vineyard ride (Rides 36 to 39) for a longer ride.

Start: *Island Queen* Ferry parking lot, Oak Bluffs Harbor, Oak Bluffs

Distance: 12.6 miles, out-and-back.

Approximate riding time: 1 to 2 hours, depending on stops

Best bike: Road or hybrid

Terrain and surface type: Smooth pavement on main roads, side streets, and paved bike path; some gentle hills, but no difficult climbs or descents

Traffic and hazards: Busy ferry parking lot at Oak Bluffs Harbor, busy main street (Seaview Avenue), pedestrians, other cyclists, other users of the multi-use bike path on Beach Road, busy street crossings; in Edgartown, poor bike path design with many side streets, exiting and entering vehicle traffic on Upper Main Street, impatient and entitled motorists, very busy vehicle and pedestrian traffic

Things to see: Oak Bluffs shops and restaurants; MVCMA (Martha's Vineyard Camp Meeting Association), aka Wesleyan Grove, with gingerbread houses and tabernacle; beautiful views of the Atlantic Ocean and Martha's Vineyard coast, Vanessa the Sea Serpent (for kids), Sengekontacket Pond, Joseph Sylvia State Beach or "State Beach," *Jaws* Bridge (American Legion Memorial Bridge), Upper Main Street shops, Edgartown Center, Edgartown Lighthouse, Lighthouse Beach, Chappy Ferry (it's always on time)

Map: *Arrow Street Atlas: Cape Cod including Martha's Vineyard & Nantucket,* p. 108

> **Getting there:** The *Island Queen* Ferry in Falmouth takes passengers and bikes to the start of this ride in Oak Bluffs. The Steamship Authority docks are 0.1 mile away.
>
> **GPS coordinates:** N41 27.59' / W70 33.44'

THE RIDE

Start at the parking lot of the *Island Queen* ferry or the Steamship Authority ferry (subtract 0.1 mile from every waypoint on this ride if starting at the Steamship Authority) and head up the hill on Seaview Avenue, being very cautious in the huge amount of traffic in the high season here (July and August). Weekends will still be busy in the shoulder seasons, but not usually as much. There is the immediate option of riding through Oak Bluffs and touring the town, including the Trinity Park and the Martha's Vineyard Camp Meeting Association (Wesleyan Grove), with its colorful gingerbread cottages circling the church Tabernacle, a huge wooden construction built in 1879 for a Methodist summer campground. There really isn't anything like this neighborhood anywhere else, and it's worth the short bike ride from Seaview Avenue (see Ride 39 for directions). Circle around Trinity Park and the Tabernacle, now a Trinity United Methodist Church, listed as a National Historic Landmark. It's an easy optional side trip that you won't want to miss in Oak Bluffs. Just be sure not to get lost on the many one-way side streets, and busy Circuit Avenue does not allow bicycle travel.

Continue past the Steamship Authority docks on the left and pass Ocean Park on the right, with its gazebo and beautiful homes lining Ocean Avenue at the far end of the park. There is a fountain that is lit at night, and this is the place to be for Fourth of July fireworks. There always seem to be a lot of kids playing here in summer, with kites flying and people sun tanning on blankets or having a picnic. It's still a very congested ride just past Ocean Park, with side streets and busy traffic along Seaview Avenue. Ride over a small hill and at mile 0.7, bear right and ride onto the paved bike path that begins just after Vanessa Way on the right. Ride past Farm Pond on the right and be sure to check for Vanessa the Sea Serpent, a floating wooden sculpture that appears frequently in the pond. The path bends a little and then at mile 2.0 crosses over the northern inlet to Sengekontacket Pond, a large pond protected by the beach this bike path rides upon, with expansive views of Nantucket Sound to the left. The Joseph Sylvia State Beach, or "State Beach" as the locals call it, is a nice 2-mile stretch of quiet beach that's great for children, a good place to park your bike and go for a swim, fish, kayak, or watch a variety of shorebirds.

Bike parking, Edgartown

It is open to all visitors and there is no fee, with bike racks at mile 2.8. Cross the southern inlet into Sengekontacket Pond over the American Legion Memorial Bridge, also known as *Jaws* Bridge, at mile 3.2, where both locals and tourists jump off the bridge (where *Jaws* character Chief Brody's son has a close encounter with a great white shark) for fun, even though it is forbidden by law (and never enforced). After the bridge, the beach is called Bend-in-the-Road Beach as the bike path enters Edgartown. The path next passes a large marsh on the right, the Caroline Tuthill Wildlife Preserve, which has a nice 1.4-mile out-and-back trail for hikers called the Garrett Family Trail.

The bike path now bends right and turns away from the ocean toward town, climbing a little at mile 4.5 and then continuing toward Edgartown Center. Just ahead, Beach Road ends and merges with the Edgartown–Vineyard Haven Road to become Upper Main Street. The bike path makes a sharp right turn at mile 5.0 before the merge and immediately turns left on Edgartown–Vineyard Haven Road at the crosswalk. The bike path on Upper Main Street runs parallel to a sidewalk, and with a lot of side streets and vehicular traffic all around, Upper Main Street is a bit confusing and dangerous for pedestrians and cyclists, with confusion about the rules of the road. When I rode here in June, most pedestrians were using the wider bike path (a multi-use path) instead of the narrower sidewalk, and cyclists were using the sidewalk or riding on Upper Main Street to avoid pedestrians, dog-walkers, and other hazards. It's an accident waiting to happen, since this stretch of Upper Main Street sees up to a thousand bicyclists each day in July and August.

Cross Cooke Street at mile 5.5 with caution, then proceed past the intersection with the Edgartown–West Tisbury bike path on the right at mile 5.7, where the bike path ends and this ride continues on the road. It's very congested here in summer, and it's best to proceed with caution, turning left at mile 5.8 on Pease's Point Way North. Turn right at mile 5.9 on Pease's Point Way and pass a long line of bicycles and racks where people ditch their bikes to walk the busy streets of downtown Edgartown. There is the option for you to park your bicycle here, too, with an easy turnaround to return the way you came after you're done exploring Edgartown. This would make for a true out-and-back measuring 12 miles. But I decided to extend this ride to the Chappaquiddick Ferry for the option to connect to Ride 36.

To continue on this ride, turn right past all the bicycles on Simpson's Lane (mile 6.0), make a left on North Water Street, and then an immediate right on Daggett Street to descend down to the Chappaquiddick ("Chappy Ferry") Ferry dock, the official turn-

Bike Shops

Anderson's Bike Rentals, 23 Circuit Avenue Extension, Oak Bluffs, (508) 693-9346, andersonsbikerentals.com

Oak Bluffs Bike Rentals, 7 Circuit Avenue Extension, Oak Bluffs, (508) 696-6255, oakbluffsbikerentals.com

Edgartown Bicycles, 212 Main St., Edgartown, (508) 627-9008, edgartownbicycles.com

Martha's Vineyard Bike Rentals (R.W. Cutler), 1 Main St., Edgartown, (800) 627-2763, marthasvineyardbike.com

Wheel Happy Bicycle Shop, 18 North Summer St., Edgartown, (508) 627-7210, www.wheelhappybicycles.com

around point of this ride. You cannot actually return the way you just came, because it's one-way on North Water Street, and no one wants to break any laws. So here are directions back to Upper Main Street that allow you to follow traffic laws: Bear right past the ferry dock on Dock Street, turn left onto South Water Street, turn right on Cooke Street, and follow it all the way to Upper Main Street.

For lighthouse fans, there is the option to continue on North Water Street past the turn to the Chappy Ferry to the Edgartown Lighthouse and Lighthouse Beach. If your legs need more exercise, combine this ride with Ride 37 for a quick 7.5-mile loop to South Beach and back to Edgartown. South Beach used to extend east all the way to Chappaquiddick, enclosing Katama Bay, until a breach in 2007 broke through the barrier beach. It is expected that the breach, which has been migrating eastward for the past few years, will close in the next few years. So if you're on a fat tire bike, you'll be able to ride from Edgartown to Chappaquiddick without taking the ferry. For now, connect to Chappaquiddick with Ride 36, where the ferry is always on time.

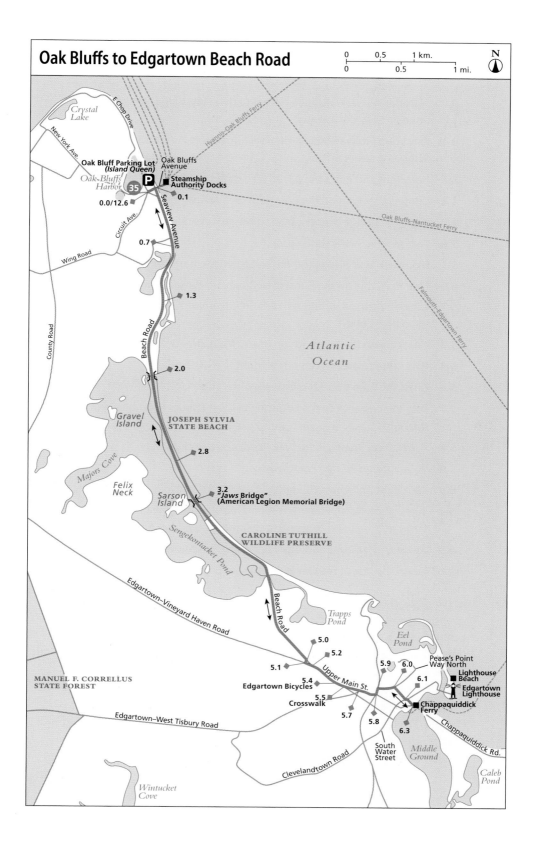

Oak Bluffs to Edgartown Beach Road

| 0 | 0.5 | 1 km. |
| 0 | 0.5 | 1 mi. |

N

Crystal Lake

E Chop Drive

New York Ave.

Oak Bluff Parking Lot
(Island Queen)

Oak Bluffs Avenue

Oak-Bluffs Harbor

35

P

0.0/12.6

0.1

Steamship Authority Docks

Seaview Avenue

Circuit Ave.

Wing Road

0.7

County Road

Beach Road

1.3

2.0

Hyannis-Oak Bluffs Ferry

Oak Bluffs-Nantucket Ferry

Atlantic Ocean

Falmouth-Edgartown Ferry

Gravel Island

JOSEPH SYLVIA STATE BEACH

Majors Cove

Felix Neck

2.8

Sarson Island

3.2
"Jaws Bridge"
(American Legion Memorial Bridge)

CAROLINE TUTHILL WILDLIFE PRESERVE

Sengekontacket Pond

Edgartown-Vineyard Haven Road

Beach Road

Trapps Pond

Eel Pond

Pease's Point Way North

Lighthouse Beach

Edgartown Lighthouse

5.0

5.2

5.9   6.0

6.1

MANUEL F. CORRELLUS STATE FOREST

5.1

Upper Main St.

Edgartown Bicycles

5.4

5.5
Crosswalk

5.7

5.8

6.3

Chappaquiddick Ferry

Chappaquiddick Rd.

Edgartown-West Tisbury Road

Clevelandtown Road

South Water Street

Middle Ground

Caleb Pond

Wintucket Cove

MILES AND DIRECTIONS

0.0 Start this ride at Oak Bluffs Harbor parking lot (*Island Queen*) and continue on Seaview Avenue.

0.1 Cross Oak Bluffs Avenue crosswalk (Steamship Authority terminal across the street).

0.7 Bear right and enter the paved bike path.

1.3 Continue straight on the bike path (Beach Road begins).

2.0 Cross the bridge over the inlet to Sengekontacket Pond.

2.8 Pass Joseph Sylvia State Beach.

3.2 Ride over *Jaws* Bridge (American Legion Memorial Bridge).

5.0 Bear right toward the Edgartown-Vineyard Haven Road.

5.1 Cross the crosswalk and turn left on Edgartown–Vineyard Haven Road bike path.

5.2 Continue on the bike path on Upper Main Street.

5.4 Pass Edgartown Bicycles on the right.

5.5 Cross the Cooke Street crosswalk with caution.

5.7 Pass the entrance to the Edgartown–West Tisbury Road bike path on the right.

5.8 Turn left on Pease's Point Way North and use caution.

5.9 Turn right on Pease's Point Way.

6.0 Turn right on Simpson's Lane.

6.2 Turn left on North Water Street and make an immediate right on Daggett Street and descend to the Chappaquiddick Ferry.

6.3 Arrive at the Chappaquiddick Ferry on Dock Street.

12.6 Finish the ride at the Oak Bluffs Harbor parking lot.

RIDE INFORMATION

Local Events and Attractions

Island Queen **Ferry**: 75 Falmouth Heights Rd., Falmouth. The best bicycle ferry from mainland Cape Cod for this ride is the *Island Queen* in Falmouth. As long as you're not taking a vehicle to Martha's Vineyard, the *Island Queen* is more convenient and faster than the Steamship Authority ferry in Woods Hole or Hyannis. The *Island Queen* sails out of Falmouth Inner Harbor and has parking a short ride down the street from the ferry dock on Falmouth Heights Road, a much less congested place than Woods Hole. Store your bicycle on bike racks toward the stern of the boat, on the lower deck with indoor benches and outdoor seating adjacent to the racks. Unlike the Steamship Authority, you handle your own bike, store it yourself, and keep an eye on it yourself. The ferry costs $20 round-trip for adults, plus $8 round-trip for a bicycle. Cash only, no credit cards.

Restaurants

Back Door Donuts: 5 Post Office Sq. (behind the Oak Bluffs Post Office), Oak Bluffs, Martha's Vineyard; (508) 693-3688. Get here after midnight after a night out, and look for a line out the back door that the locals keep secret. Or just try the donuts, pastries and coffee. Excellent!

20byNine: 16 Kennebec Ave., Oak Bluffs; (508) 338-2065. Everything here is delicious, and it's also a whiskey bar, with forty-five bourbons and whiskeys and sixteen beers on tap. The name references the dimensions of Martha's Vineyard, in miles.

Linda Jean's Restaurant: 25 Circuit Ave., Oak Bluffs; (508) 693-4093. Kid-friendly and friendlier on the wallet.

Among the Flowers Cafe: 17 Mayhew Ln., Edgartown; (508) 627-3233. Affordable, with nice outdoor patio dining. The food is reasonably priced and the friendly staff keeps it moving.

l'Étoile: 22 N. Water St., Edgartown; (508) 627-5187. Fine dining inside what was once an Edgartown home, one of the few places that has a chef's tasting menu on the Vineyard.

Restrooms

There are restrooms at the ferry docks in Oak Bluffs, and at the many restaurants in Edgartown.

36

Chappaquiddick

This is a ride that takes you out there, away from it all, onto the quiet island of Chappaquiddick. The road goes from pavement to dirt, and you'll need a mountain bike or fat tire bike when you get to Wasque Road (mile 3.9). At the end of the road there is nothing but miles and miles of pristine barrier beach. It's wild and beautiful.

Start: Chappaquiddick Road, at the Chappaquiddick Ferry

Distance: 9.2 miles out-and-back

Approximate riding time: 1 hour

Best bike: Mountain bike, fat tire bike (for sandy roads and beach), road bike (for paved road ride only)

Terrain and surface type: Paved roads until mile 3.9 on Wasque Road, where the surface is sand, gentle hills, and mostly flat riding

Traffic and hazards: Very little vehicular traffic, sandy roads will present a challenge for road cyclists, and only experienced bike handlers will be able to ride the sand on Wasque Road. A fat tire bike is ideal for riding the sand, and would offer the option of riding on the barrier beach from Wasque Point north to the Poge Lighthouse at the northern tip of Cape Poge.

Things to see: Mytoi Japanese Gardens, Salt Marsh hiking trail to Poucha Pond, Dike Road Bridge, Wasque Reservation, Wasque Point, Cape Poge Wildlife Refuge, Cape Poge Bay and inlet, Cape Poge Light, Norton Point Beach

Map: *Arrow Street Atlas: Cape Cod including Martha's Vineyard & Nantucket*, p. 105

Getting there: Ride to the Chappy Ferry from anywhere in Edgartown or use Ride 35 from Oak Bluffs for directions.

GPS coordinates: N41 23.32' / W70 30.50'

The island of Chappaquiddick, separated from downtown Edgartown by 527 feet, is accessible by car or bicycle *only* on the Chappy Ferry, which runs every few minutes. While the wait for cars on the Chappy Ferry can be lengthy in the summer, especially in the mornings when heading to Chappy or in the late afternoon when all the beachgoers are heading back to town, there is no such wait for bicyclists. On-time ferries are never late, there's never much of a wait, and there is no schedule, except for opening and closing hours. To get to Chappaquiddick, you simply pay the fee of $6 (bike and rider, round-trip) in cash to a deckhand who collects your money, board the ferry with your bike, and you're off. A few minutes and 527 feet later, you're there.

Start this ride on the only paved road there is, Chappaquiddick Road. It's a straight shot off the ferry, with Edgartown Light and the outer harbor to the left, and the inner harbor on the right. At the start, it's a flat ride, with Caleb Pond on the right, and the private Chappaquiddick Beach Club with its red, white, and blue striped tents on the left. Pass Litchfield Lane on the right and the road starts to climb, reaches a peak at the Chappaquiddick Community Center, and then descends past the Chappy Store and Service Station on the left at mile 2.0 (219 Chappaquiddick Rd.). It looks like a

Bike Shops

Edgartown Bicycles, 212 Main St., Edgartown, (508) 627-9008, edgartownbicycles.com
Martha's Vineyard Bike Rentals (R.W. Cutler), 1 Main St., Edgartown, (800) 627-2763, marthasvineyardbike.com
Wheel Happy Bicycle Shop, 18 North Summer St., Edgartown, (508) 627-7210, www.wheelhappybicycles.com

shack in the middle of a car junkyard. Continue riding to mile 2.4, where the road flattens out and then bends sharply to the right at the intersection with Dike Road and School Road.

It would be difficult to mention Chappaquiddick without taking note of the events that happened at this L-shaped intersection at mile 2.4 of this ride one late July night in 1969. Driving from a late-night party, US Senator Edward M. Kennedy and a former campaign worker for Robert F. Kennedy, Mary Jo Kopechne, were traveling down Chappaquiddick Road in the other direction (they would be facing you here), and turned right onto Dike Road. In sworn testimony, Kennedy claimed he was heading for the Chappaquiddick Ferry and made a wrong turn. As he approached the narrow, wooden Dike Road Bridge, the road was dark, with the angle of the bridge not in line with the road. He lost control of his Oldsmobile, went over the side of the narrow bridge, and plummeted into the strong currents of the Cape Poge Bay inlet

Riding the sand at Wasque Point, Chappaquiddick

below, resulting in Kopechne's drowning. The rest is history, water under the bridge, and unfortunately all most people will ever know about this beautiful, almost untouched island.

Take the optional side trip down Dike Road to the bridge, rebuilt in 1996, with beautiful views of the barrier beach, inlet, and Nantucket Sound. About halfway down Dike Road be sure to visit Mytoi, a Japanese-styled fourteen-acre garden set within a grove of pines, with a lovely, winding half-mile hiking trail to Poucha Pond through forest and salt marsh. If you made the trip with children, this is a great place to see turtles, frogs, and goldfish in the garden pond, or to relax at a shelter overlooking the garden and its many types of flowers and plants. Another must-see is the Poge Lighthouse at the very northern tip of the barrier beach, and tours guided by the Trustees of Reservations, leaving from Mytoi, will take you there. Another option is to explore the beach with an over-sand vehicle, and if you want to rent one or drive here yourself, you can. This would also be a great place to ride a fat tire bike, on my personal bucket list.

Turn right on School Road at the Dike Road intersection and ride past wide-open farmland on both sides of the road. Pass the Chappaquiddick Fire Station on the right and continue down this flat stretch to mile 3.2, then make a hard left on Wasque Road, which is paved for part of the way. Continue on Wasque Road up a hill, where the pavement ends at mile 3.9. If you are riding a road bike, you will need good bike-handling skills on the sandy dirt road. A fat tire bike, mountain bike, or cyclocross bike would be much easier, especially on the return trip over this hill. Continue on Wasque Road to the Wasque (pronounced "way-squee") Reservation entrance at mile 4.4, a heavily wooded and shady area. This ride continues down the sandy path out of the woods to the gatehouse at mile 4.6 where Wasque Road intersects with a dirt road to Norton Point Beach.

Take the option to turn right on that dirt road, where over-sand vehicles can access the southern barrier beach, Norton Point Beach. This beach used to connect to South Beach on the other side of Katama Bay, but in 2007 a storm caused a breach, making Chappaquiddick a separate island. The break in the barrier beach has been moving slowly eastward since 2007, and is expected to connect Norton Point Beach to South Beach in the next few years. As with the Outer Beach on the Cape Cod mainland from Eastham to Monomoy, the breaches and reforming of beaches are a constant cycle that has repeated over centuries. Interestingly, a 1775 map of Chappaquiddick, on the Trustees of Reservations website for Wasque, shows a break in the barrier beach that looks very much like it does today.

From the air, Chappaquiddick itself looks sort of like a mini-map of Massachusetts with its eastern barrier beach hooking around a large bay. Wasque

Chappaquiddick

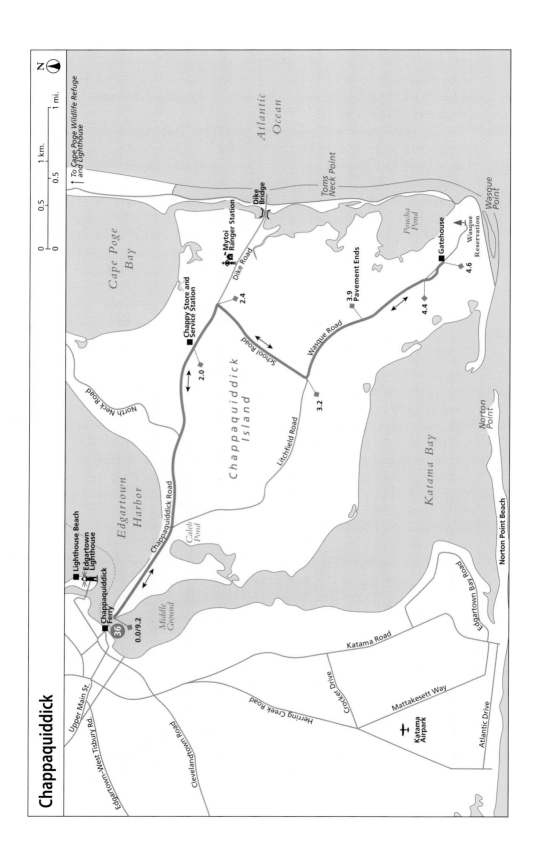

N

To Cape Poge Wildlife Refuge and Lighthouse

0   0.5   1 km.
0   0.5   1 mi.

Cape Poge Bay

Atlantic Ocean

Toms Neck Point

Dike Bridge

Mytoi Ranger Station

Dike Road

Chappy Store and Service Station

2.4

Poucha Pond

Wasque Point

Gatehouse

4.6

Wasque Reservation

3.9
Pavement Ends

Wasque Road

4.4

School Road

2.0

Chappaquiddick Island

North Neck Road

Edgartown Harbor

Chappaquiddick Road

Litchfield Road

3.2

Caleb Pond

Lighthouse Beach

Edgartown Lighthouse

Chappaquiddick Ferry

0.0/9.2

36

Middle Ground

Katama Bay

Norton Point

Norton Point Beach

Upper Main St.

Edgartown–West Tisbury Rd.

Clevelandtown Road

Herring Creek Road

Katama Road

Crocker Drive

Mattakesett Way

Atlantic Drive

Edgartown Bay Road

Katama Airpark

Point would be analogous to Chatham, and Poge Lighthouse would be something like Truro on the Cape Cod map. Wasque Reservation has hiking trails, porta-potties, picnic tables, shade, and a beautiful barrier beach. Turn around at the gatehouse when you have finished exploring Wasque. Although, you might not ever want to leave this peaceful place.

MILES AND DIRECTIONS

0.0 Start this ride at the Chappaquiddick Ferry on Chappaquiddick Road.

2.0 Pass the Chappy Store and Service Station on the left.

2.4 Turn right on School Road at Dike Road intersection. Or take an optional out-and-back side trip to Mytoi on Dike Road, the Dike Road Bridge, and Cape Poge (the barrier beach).

3.2 Turn left onto Wasque Road.

3.9 Come to the end of the paved road (now a sandy dirt road).

4.4 Continue straight on Wasque Road.

4.6 Opt to explore the vast and beautiful beach. Then turn around on Wasque Road by the Wasque Reservation gatehouse and return the way you came.

9.2 Finish the ride at the Chappy Ferry docks.

RIDE INFORMATION

Chappaquiddick has a fire station with trucks but no emergency medical services (there are many EMTs who reside on the island). There are no hospitals, restaurants, or high-speed Internet service. Bring your own food and water, as the only store on Chappaquiddick is the Chappy Store, open in season (but not always when you need it). EMS gets first priority on the Chappy Ferry, so an ambulance will get you to a hospital about as fast as anywhere else, if you need one. In case of emergency, call 911 if on a landline telephone or call (508) 693-1212 if on a cell phone.

Local Events and Attractions

Mytoi: Dike Road, Chappaquiddick, Edgartown; (508) 627-7689. Beautiful Japanese gardens with hiking trails. Public restrooms (year-round portable toilets). Picnic tables. Bike rack. Fresh water by hand pump located at entrance (seasonal).

Cape Poge Wildlife Refuge and Lighthouse Tours: Call (508) 627-3599 for a reservation. Family-friendly lighthouse, kayak, and seaside exploration tours on a daily basis (Memorial Day through Columbus Day). Complimentary van pickup for guided tour participants on the Chappaquiddick side of the Chappy Ferry.

Restaurants
There are no restaurants on Chappaquiddick. Stuff a backpack or jersey pockets with food and drink.

Restrooms
There are porta-potties at Wasque Reservation.

Edgartown to South Beach Loop

This is an easy and flat loop from bustling Edgartown along paved bike paths and roads to South Beach, also known as Katama Beach.

Start: Dock Street parking lot, Dock Street, Edgartown

Distance: 7.5-mile loop

Approximate riding time: 1 hour

Best bike: Road, hybrid

Terrain and surface type: Paved roads, paved bike paths

Traffic and hazards: Heavy traffic in Edgartown, with vehicles, pedestrians, other cyclists, multi-use traffic on bike path, vehicles entering and exiting South Beach parking lot, distracted drivers (vehicles, bicycles) watching planes taking off or landing at airport

Things to see: Edgartown, Edgartown Lighthouse, Lighthouse Beach, South Beach State Park, grass-runway Katama Airpark, Katama Bay, Chappaquiddick

Map: *Arrow Street Atlas: Cape Cod including Martha's Vineyard & Nantucket*, p. 104

Getting there: Follow the directions to the Chappy Ferry if riding from Oak Bluffs to Edgartown, then turn right at the ferry docks on Dock Street. The parking lot is on the left.

GPS coordinates: N41 23.35' / W70 30.71'

THE RIDE

Edgartown's busy streets and sidewalks are as crowded in summer as anywhere on Cape Cod or the Islands, lined with shops, art galleries, restaurants, and 19th-century sea captains' houses built when whaling was

Martha's Vineyard's main economy. Tourism took over in the late 1800s and then boomed again in the 1970s, and the Vineyard's summer population is roughly ten times its year-round population of 15,000. So with 150,000 people on-island, cyclists must keep their wits about them. Yet, despite all the hustle and bustle of Edgartown Center and all it has to offer, the number one attraction in Edgartown isn't downtown. It's the beach. And the number one beach is South Beach (also called Katama Beach by locals), the south-facing beach that currently extends east as a barrier beach, almost all the way to Chappaquiddick.

Start this ride at the Dock Street parking lot and turn left onto Dock Street. If you need coffee, breakfast, or lunch, a great place to start is at the Dock Street Coffee Shop, which you could easily miss, but is easy on the budget. Climb up Dock Street to South Water Street and turn left. The view to the left is of Edgartown inner harbor, filled with yachts, pleasure craft, and fishing boats that travel the waterway around the Middle Ground shoals, then south to the large but shallow Katama Bay. Ride down South Water Street and look left at the long, descending grassy strips of lawn between the two-story colonial homes to the water, where everyone's backyard seems to extend to a dock with attached yacht. The sea captain's houses line both sides of the road and remind you of the Martha's Vineyard seafaring and whaling past. The road bends away from the water a little to the right, past that house on the left with the white picket fence and beautiful tree (you'll know what I'm talking about), and at the end of South Water Street turn left onto the paved bike path on Katama Road.

Bike Shops

Edgartown Bicycles, 212 Main St., Edgartown, (508) 627-9008, edgartownbicycles.com
Martha's Vineyard Bike Rentals (R.W. Cutler), 1 Main St., Edgartown, (800) 627-2763, marthasvineyardbike.com
Wheel Happy Bicycle Shop, 18 North Summer St., Edgartown, (508) 627-7210, www.wheelhappybicycles.com

The bike path along Katama Road is a 2.5-mile stretch that takes riders past the red-and-white Katama General Store (seasonal) on the other side of the road. Continue on the path past Katama Farm and the Farm Institute on the right, where adults and children can take classes year-round on farming and nutrition and partake in the everyday activities of a working farm. The farm offers hayrides and tours, including self-guided walking tours and Chore Tours, where visitors can help with farm chores and work with the farm animals. The path rounds a big curve to the right around the farm and then ends at mile 3.0 as it approaches Atlantic Drive. Riders have to cross to the right of

South Water Street, Edgartown

Katama Road to turn right on Atlantic Drive, which parallels South Beach for almost a mile. And planes taking off and landing from nearby Katama Airpark might distract you or vehicle traffic on this road, so use caution here.

There are a few entrances to the beach on the left along Atlantic Drive, but this ride takes the last entrance at mile 4, into a parking lot with bike racks. Kick off your shoes and enjoy the white sand and warmer-water South Beach, or have a picnic and bask in the sun. South Beach also has a steep slope and strong undertow and is great for surfing. There is also a protected salt pond on the mainland side. You can't see the water from the parking lot here because the dunes block the view. Walk over them for a panoramic view of this beach that seems to go on forever, extending eastward 3 more miles to a break separating it from Chappaquiddick. The breach, which broke through in 2007, is expected to disappear in the next few years, reforming the sand bridge that existed for decades between South Beach and Norton Point Beach on Chappaquiddick, today still officially an island.

Turn around in the parking lot and proceed on Herring Creek Road. Cross over to the bike path on the left side of the road when it's safe to do so, keeping in mind the Katama Airpark is just ahead to the right, and the loud sounds or sight of low-flying planes may startle cyclists, pedestrians, and drivers. You won't hear gliders, but glider and biplane rides are available at the Airpark, which has three grass turf runways and is a favorite stop for pilots. The airport also has a great little restaurant called the Right Fork Diner (formerly Mel's), where you can sit out on the deck and watch the planes. Continue past the airport on the flat bike path and turn left on Katama Road. Turn right on South Water Street and head back into town.

Start a brief tour of downtown Edgartown by turning left on High Street, right on School Street, and then down Main Street. South Water Street is one-way beyond High Street, so the left turn at High Street is a requirement unless you want to walk back to the start of this ride on the sidewalk. You'll get a little flavor of the heavy traffic here, but it's worth it to check out all the shops. It's a short walk up Main Street from the corner of School and Main Streets to the 18th-century Greek Revival Old Whaling Church, used for performances by locals like Livingston Taylor (brother of James) and weddings. The organ takes up almost all of one wall. Turn left on North Water Street and have an ice cream sandwich made with homemade cookies at Mad Martha's (on the corner of Main and North Water). Turn right on Kelly Street and then right on Dock Street to return to the parking lot to finish this ride. If you're hungry or thirsty (try the fresh-squeezed orange juice), don't miss Among the Flowers Cafe on Mayhew Lane, opposite the Dock Street parking lot. You'll see a crowded set of bike racks lining the side of Mayhew Lane and other cyclists dining outdoors under the shade of the cafe, sharing stories about the adventures of the day.

MILES AND DIRECTIONS

0.0   Start this ride at the Dock Street parking lot and turn left on Dock Street.

0.1   Turn left on South Water Street.

0.5   Turn left on Katama Road onto the paved bike path.

3.0   The bike path ends. Cross Katama Road carefully and proceed along the right side of the road.

3.1   Turn right on Atlantic Drive.

4.0   Turn left onto South Beach (Katama Beach) parking lot.

4.1   Turn around and proceed straight on the bike path on Herring Creek Road.

6.3   Cross the crosswalk and turn left on Katama Road on the bike path.

6.6   Turn right on South Water Street off the bike path onto the right side of the street.

6.8   Turn left on High Street.

7.0   Turn right on School Street.

7.2   Turn right on Main Street.

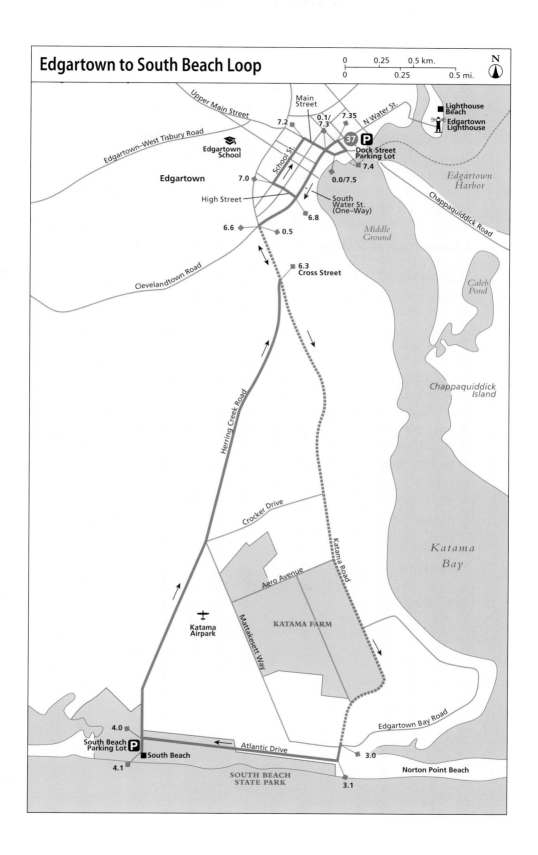

Edgartown to South Beach Loop

0   0.25   0.5 km.

0   0.25   0.5 mi.

N

Upper Main Street

Main
Street

Lighthouse
Beach

Edgartown
Lighthouse

N Water St.

7.2

0.1/
7.3

7.35

Edgartown–West Tisbury Road

Edgartown
School

37

Dock Street
Parking Lot

Edgartown
Harbor

School St.

7.4

Edgartown

7.0

High Street

0.0/7.5

Chappaquiddick Road

South
Water St.
(One–Way)

6.8

Middle
Ground

Caleb
Pond

6.6

0.5

Clevelandtown Road

6.3
Cross Street

Chappaquiddick
Island

Katama
Bay

Crocker Drive

Herring Creek Road

Katama Road

Aero Avenue

Katama
Airpark

Mattakesett Way

KATAMA FARM

4.0

South Beach
Parking Lot

South Beach

Atlantic Drive

Edgartown Bay Road

3.0

4.1

SOUTH BEACH
STATE PARK

Norton Point Beach

3.1

7.3 Turn left on North Water Street.

7.35 Turn right on Kelly Street.

7.4 Turn right on Dock Street.

7.5 Finish this ride at the Dock Street parking lot.

RIDE INFORMATION

Local Events and Attractions

Edgartown Lighthouse: Off N. Water St., Edgartown Harbor; (508) 627-4411. Lighthouse tours available and great views atop the spiral staircase in the lantern room overlooking the harbor. It's a tight squeeze and sturdy shoes are helpful, and you'll be glad you're a skinny cyclist near the top.

Katama General Store: 170 Katama Rd., Edgartown; (508) 627-5071. Stock up on beach supplies, food, and drink for the beach. Try the scones.

Restaurants

Right Fork Diner: 12 Mattakesett Way, Edgartown; (508) 627-5522. Watch the planes while having a great breakfast or lunch (dinners in July or August, open until sunset). It's a perfect spot for the beginning or end of a day-at-the-beach bike ride, at the fork in the road on Mattakesett Way.

Among the Flowers Cafe: 17 Mayhew Ln., Edgartown; (508) 627-3233. See the listing under Ride 35.

l'Étoile: 22 N. Water St., Edgartown; (508) 627-5187. See the listing under Ride 35.

Dock Street Coffee Shop: 2 Dock St., Edgartown; (508) 627-5232. It's a hole-in-the-wall but the locals eat here and the service is a throwback to earlier times. Try the grilled donuts.

Restrooms

There are restrooms at South (Katama) Beach (seasonal) and at the many restaurants in Edgartown.

Vineyard Up Island Tour

Tour every town on Martha's Vineyard and get a taste of what the rest of island is like, away from the touristy, bustling downtown areas. See the Gay Head Cliffs and Lighthouse in Aquinnah, ride through rural farmland in Tisbury, take the Menemsha Bike Ferry and ride through Chilmark and West Tisbury to Oak Bluffs. Complete the loop by adding Ride 39 around East Chop back to Vineyard Haven.

Start: The parking lot at the corner of Water Street and Union Street, across from the Steamship Authority ferry, Vineyard Haven (Tisbury)

Distance: 46.4 miles one-way

Approximate riding time: 3 to 4 hours

Best bike: Road

Terrain and surface type: Smooth pavement with some rough spots, rolling hills with some steeper climbs

Traffic and hazards: Heavy traffic in Vineyard Haven and Oak Bluffs during summer, dangerous travel on State Road, pedestrian traffic at ferry docks, narrow shoulders on other main roads

Things to see: Vineyard Haven, Tisbury farmland, Arrowhead Farm, Menemsha, fishing village and bike ferry across the Menemsha Pond inlet to Aquinnah, Gay Head Lighthouse, Gay Head Cliffs National Landmark, Gay Head Public Beach (Moshup Beach), Chilmark, West Tisbury, Alley's General Store, West Tisbury Library, State Forest, Oak Bluffs, Nantucket Sound

Map: *Arrow Street Atlas: Cape Cod including Martha's Vineyard & Nantucket*, p. 98

Getting there: The Steamship Authority Ferry from Falmouth arrives across the street from the start of this ride in Vineyard Haven. Or arrive in Oak Bluffs and ride to the start using Ride 39.

GPS coordinates: N41 27.33' / W70 36.08'

THE RIDE

This is the second-longest ride in this guidebook after Ride 29 (Grand Tour of the Outer Cape), and will take you through every one of Martha's Vineyard's six towns: Tisbury (Vineyard Haven is not a town, although most everybody traveling here seems to think so), West Tisbury, Chilmark (including Menemsha), Aquinnah (formerly called Gay Head but changed to its original Wampanoag name by a popular vote of 79 to 21 in 1997), Edgartown, and Oak Bluffs. This ride focuses on mostly the western half of the Vineyard, with a lot of time spent passing sheep, cows, and horses, but also with fabulous views of the ocean and other waterways connecting various parts of the island. And it's a leg-burner with its numerous hilly sections. This ride is titled "Up Island" because that's what Martha's Vineyard residents call this western, more rural and quiet part of the Vineyard. The terms "up island" and "down island" refer to its nautical past, when sea captains would navigate along longitudinal lines, with higher numbers (up) farther west.

Start this ride on the corner of Water Street and Union Street opposite the Steamship Authority ferry parking lot. If you arrived in Oak Bluffs, use Ride 39 to connect to Vineyard Haven, which will extend this ride by a distance of 5 miles, making it a little longer than 50 miles. If you start in Vineyard Haven, you'll have to use Ride 39 at the end of this ride to connect if you want to finish where you started. Ride through busy Vineyard Haven on Water Street past the Steamship Authority on the left, and turn right on Beach Road. Bear left onto State Road and ascend for a little more than 0.5 mile where the highway levels off. This is a busy and fairly dangerous two-lane road for experienced road riders only. Wear brightly colored clothes with a flashing rear light on your bike to maximize safety. Riders cannot be too cautious on this stretch of road leading uphill out of town, where vehicle traffic is fast or congested.

The road crests at the 1-mile mark, bends to the right, and then descends again for a nice long and fast stretch of road. At the bottom of the descent (mile 1.8), you finally feel like you're getting out of town, but the road climbs

Bike Shops

Martha's Bike Rentals: Vineyard Haven, (508) 693-6593, www.marthasbike rentals.com
Vineyard Bicycles: 344 State Rd., Vineyard Haven, (508) 693-8693, www.vine yardbicycles.com
Cycle-Works Martha's Vineyard: 351 State Rd., Vineyard Haven, (508) 693-6966
Anderson's Bike Rentals: 23 Circuit Avenue Extension, Oak Bluffs, (508) 693-9346, andersonsbikerentals.com
Oak Bluffs Bike Rentals: 7 Circuit Avenue Extension, Oak Bluffs, (508) 696-6255, oakbluffsbikerentals.com

back up for the next mile, and is still very congested with traffic. Vehicles are entering and exiting side roads and entrances to the many businesses lining State Road here, but less so than the first mile out of Vineyard Haven. State Road is fairly flat for the next 3 miles, descending gradually. Pass Arrowhead Farm on the right at mile 5.1, a great place to take kids for horseback riding lessons. State Road then turns right onto North Road and heads uphill. North Road climbs over gently rolling hills past forest and farmland for the next 5 miles, until it reaches a summit on North Road at mile 10.8 and then plummets downhill toward Menemsha for the next mile. This is a very fast and fun descent into the fishing village of Menemsha (in Chilmark), but there is no fog line and it's a dangerous shoulder in many places, and if you crash you might come face to face with one of the many stone walls lining the roads here. The traffic is typically light on North Road, but near the intersection with the Menemsha Crossroad it gets busier, nearing the end of the road in Menemsha by the water.

This ride is mapped for the Menemsha Bike Ferry's off-season. If it is running when you visit, catch the ferry and subtract 8.4 miles from all waypoints in this ride after the 12-mile mark in Menemsha. If not, check out Menemsha before turning around. It's a quaint little fishing village where part of Steven Spielberg's *Jaws* was filmed. The place to grab a bite here is Larsen's Fish Market on Basin Road (a side street off North Road that hugs Menemsha Basin), where you can sit outside and eat fresh lobster, clams, oysters, or mussels that they'll steam or shuck to-go. Head back up the hill on North Road and take a right on the Menemsha Crossroad, and continue through Chilmark by turning right on State Road.

State Road through Chilmark is a very different experience than its other end in Vineyard Haven. There are no sidewalks here, and the fog line is very close to the soft shoulder. But there aren't as many cars, and drivers here seem to be very used to road cyclists, often giving a wide berth or simply slowing down to near your speed before passing (the way it should be done). The road climbs and descends past beautiful views of Nashaquitsa Pond and Menemsha Pond farther in the distance on the right, and enters the Wampanoag town of Aquinnah over rolling hills. After 4 miles on this end of State Road, the ride turns right and descends on Lobsterville Road to the water, and then bends right along Menemsha Bight into Wampanoag-Aquinnah Trust Lands. Turning left onto West Basin Road, you are privy to a little-known stretch of road that most tourists to the Vineyard will never see because they don't ride a bike or take the bike ferry from Menemsha. It's barren but beautiful here, with dunes on both sides of the road, lined with bearberry and other dune plants that hold back the sands from the occasional high winds crossing from the bight's open bay. Head to the end of West Basin Road. It's a gorgeous view of

Menemsha on the other side of Menemsha Basin, with boats traveling in and out into the Bight and Vineyard Sound. Turn around at the Bike Ferry dock and turn right on Lobsterville Road and then right on Lighthouse Road at mile 22.1 (or mile 13.7 if you caught the ferry).

Now the road rises to the heights of Aquinnah toward the Gay Head cliffs, and ends at Aquinnah Circle, a beautiful spot for just about anything, with magnificent views of the Atlantic to the south and the rest of Martha's Vineyard to the east. Turn right on the circle and then right again up the path to the Gay Head Lighthouse. I rode up the path on my road bike, although it's a nice walk down. The top of the lighthouse towers above the trees as you ascend the path, and then at the top, the brush clears to give full view of the redbrick lighthouse with its black iron-encased lantern room. The current lighthouse was built in 1856 to replace the old wooden lighthouse, built in 1799 per order of President John Adams. Secretary of the Treasury Alexander Hamilton was granted funding from Congress for the lighthouse, and Paul Revere provided the metal used in the original roof. Today, Gay Head Light is in danger of falling over the cliffs, sitting on a shrinking one-acre plateau, 130 feet above sea level. The breathtaking multicolored clay Gay Head Cliffs are visible from the plateau here, with benches and a grassy area perfect for

Gay Head cliffs, Aquinnah

a picnic or rest break for tired legs. When Bartholomew Gosnold first saw the cliffs, he was reminded of the cliffs at Dover, but the usage of Gay Head was common by the late 17th century. Ride around Aquinnah Circle and enjoy the spectacular views.

Continue the ride by turning right onto State Road from the circle and riding over the rolling hills for 6 miles to the Chilmark General Store, which has a front porch with rocking chairs where you can chat or relax and watch the passersby. It's also a great place to refuel, with a deli and grocery store for anything you need to charge up the body for the last push across the island back to Oak Bluffs. Ride a short way up the road to a four-way intersection known as Beetlebung Corner, where State Road intersects with the Menemsha Cross-road, South Road, and Middle Road. The word "beetlebung" apparently exists only here on Martha's Vineyard, another word for the tupelo tree, whose wood was so hard that it was used for making both *beetle*, a wooden mallet, and *bung*, a plug for wooden barrels used in the whaling industry. Continue straight on Middle Road, which rides the rolling hills through farmland and forest to West Tisbury Center, where you have to stop at Alley's General Store, located here since 1858. A huge amount of stuff is packed into this old store, with creaky old wooden floors and dimly lit interior, with less and less room to walk every year. There is a good little farm stand and sandwich shop out back with ice cream, too.

Ride down the hill from Alley's on State Road and turn right on the Edgar-town–West Tisbury Road, where there is access to the bike path through the woods if you know where to turn. Otherwise, stay on the right side of this busy road, running parallel to the bike path, and ride straight for almost 4 miles past the Martha's Vineyard Airport. Turn left on Barnes Road, where there is also the option to ride the bike path through the state forest along the airport's edge. Ride through the rotary that connects the Edgartown–Vineyard Haven Road at mile 42.2, and continue on Barnes Road (the bike path ends at the rotary). There is the option to turn left at the rotary and return to Vineyard Haven on the Edgartown–Vineyard Haven Road or its bike path to loop back to the start of this ride. But this ride continues on to Oak Bluffs. Follow Barnes Road as it descends and crosses County Road at mile 44.8 and becomes Wing Road. At mile 45.4, continue straight onto Circuit Avenue, then turn right on Kennebec Avenue, right on Lake Avenue, and left on Seaview Avenue to get to the Oak Bluffs ferries at mile 46.4. To connect to Vineyard Haven from Oak Bluffs, connect with Ride 39 and add 5 miles to this ride past the East Chop Lighthouse and over Lagoon Pond to the corner of Beach Road and Water Street. If you're looking to do a killer century, ride the Up Island Tour again. Maybe this time you'll catch the Menemsha Bike Ferry.

MILES AND DIRECTIONS

0.0   Start this ride on Water Street at the corner of Union Street in Vineyard Haven across from the Steamship Authority ferry parking lot. Proceed down Water Street with the Steamship parking lot on your left.

0.1   Turn right on Beach Road.

0.2   Bear left on State Road.

2.4   Enter West Tisbury.

3.1   Bear right at the fork to remain on State Road.

4.2   Bear left at the fork with Indian Hill Road to remain on State Road.

5.1   Pass Arrowhead Farm on the right.

5.6   Turn right on North Road.

12.0   Turn around or take bike ferry to Aquinnah (in season).

12.6   Turn right on the Menemsha Crossroad.

13.6   Turn right on State Road (Beetlebung Corner).

17.8   Turn right on Lobsterville Road.

19.4   Turn left on West Basin Road.

20.4   Turn around at the inlet to Menemsha Pond (unless you took the bike ferry).

21.4   Turn right on Lobsterville Road.

22.1   Turn right on Lighthouse Road.

24.2   Turn right on Aquinnah Circle.

24.3   Ride the path up to Gay Head Lighthouse.

24.4   View the Gay Head cliffs next to the lighthouse, head back down the path, and turn right on Aquinnah Circle.

24.7   Turn right on State Road.

30.6   Pass by or visit the Chilmark General Store on the left.

30.7   Continue straight on Middle Road (Beetlebung Corner).

35.2   Turn right on Panhandle Road.

35.4   Turn left on Music Street.

35.8   Turn left on State Road.

35.9   Turn right on Edgartown–West Tisbury Road.

39.3   Pass Airport Road on the left.

39.8   Turn left on Barnes Road (opt to take the bike path).

Vineyard Up Island Tour

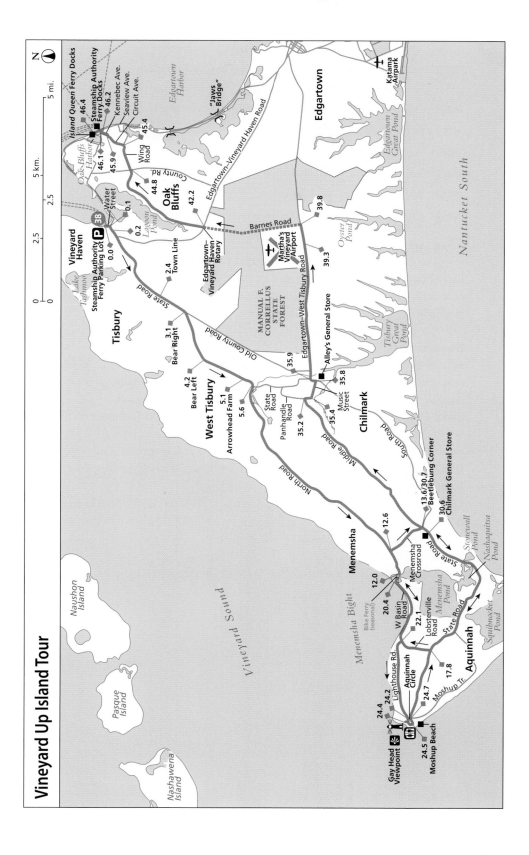

42.2 Arrive at Edgartown–Vineyard Haven Rotary (end bike path) and continue on Barnes Road.

44.8 Cross County Road and continue straight on Wing Road.

45.4 Continue straight on Circuit Avenue.

45.9 Turn right on Kennebec Avenue.

46.1 Turn right on Lake Avenue.

46.2 Turn left on Seaview Avenue.

46.4 Finish the ride at Oak Bluffs Harbor (*Island Queen* ferry docks).

RIDE INFORMATION

Local Events and Attractions
Martha's Vineyard Film Center: 79 Beach Rd., Vineyard Haven (Tisbury); (508) 696-9369. Cool movie theater for when it's raining or snowing.

Restaurants
Artcliff Diner: 39 Beach Rd., Vineyard Haven (Tisbury); (508) 693-1224. Cool, retro diner for breakfast and lunch, and a food truck close by during the dinner hours. Say hello to Gina, who makes the best breakfast in town.

Black Dog Tavern: 21 Beach St. Extension, Vineyard Haven (Tisbury); (508) 693-9223. Have breakfast here before the ride.

Larsen's Fish Market: 56 Basin Rd., Dutcher's Dock, Menemsha (Chilmark); (508) 645-2680. "The" place for lunch, with fresh, locally caught seafood and great water views.

Chilmark General Store: 7 State Rd., Chilmark; (508) 645-3739. Snacks and drinks or lunch.

Restrooms
There are restrooms at the Steamship Authority in Vineyard Haven and at the Oak Bluffs ferry docks.

Oak Bluffs–East Chop–Vineyard Haven

Do it as an out-and-back or combine with Ride 38 to see the rest of the island. Beautiful views of Vineyard Sound and Falmouth, riding the East Chop to the lighthouse. Explore Oak Bluffs and the gingerbread houses, then explore Vineyard Haven, a completely different feel. This one's an easy way to get a good taste of two very different Martha's Vineyard towns.

Start: Oak Bluffs Harbor parking lot (*Island Queen* ferry)

Distance: 10.0 miles out-and-back

Approximate riding time: 1 hour

Best bike: Road or hybrid

Terrain and surface type: Paved main roads, fairly flat route with a little climbing through East Chop

Traffic and hazards: Busy docks at the start in Oak Bluffs and the finish in Vineyard Haven, with vehicle traffic and ferry passengers coming and going, heavy traffic through Oak Bluffs and Vineyard Haven

Things to see: Oak Bluffs, Wesleyan Grove and Trinity Park Tabernacle, gingerbread houses, East Chop Lighthouse, Vineyard Haven

Map: *Arrow Street Atlas: Cape Cod including Martha's Vineyard & Nantucket*, p. 108

Getting there: The *Island Queen* Ferry in Falmouth takes passengers and bikes to the start of this ride in Oak Bluffs. The Steamship Authority docks are 0.1 mile away.

GPS coordinates: N41 27.60' / W70 33.45'

THE RIDE

This ride is an out-and-back from the busy Oak Bluffs to the busy Vineyard Haven, where you can see all the sights in both towns. Since getting to Martha's Vineyard usually means taking a ferry with a bicycle from Falmouth and arriving at either Oak Bluffs or Vineyard Haven, there is the option to take the *Island Queen* ferry from Falmouth Heights to Oak Bluffs or the Steamship Authority ferry to either town. This ride can also be used to connect to Ride 38 and make a 50-mile loop, or with Ride 35 to connect to Edgartown from Vineyard Haven or vice versa. It is not the shortest route from Oak Bluffs to Vineyard Haven, but it avoids heavy traffic on New York Avenue and most of Eastville Avenue, and rides around Oak Bluffs Harbor to East Chop, with water views for several miles. This ride could be named the Vineyard Sound Ride, since it essentially follows the north shoreline of Martha's Vineyard other than a quick side trip to Trinity Park. In Vineyard Haven, there is the option to head north and do a loop past the West Chop Lighthouse on Main Street and return via Franklin Street.

Start this ride in the Oak Bluffs *Island Queen* ferry parking lot and bear left out of the parking lot onto Seaview Avenue. Go over the crest of the hill and turn right on Oak Bluffs Avenue. There is a very short bike lane that ends as Seaview Avenue merges with Lake Avenue at a crosswalk, perhaps one of the shortest bike lanes in the world. Head up Lake Avenue just a very short way and turn left onto Central Avenue, make a quick left, and then a quick right onto Montgomery Avenue past some bike racks on the right. You are entering Wesleyan Grove, also known as Trinity Park, facing a huge wooden structure called the Tabernacle, home to the Trinity United Methodist Church. The Methodists have been coming to Oak Bluffs to camp since 1835, and after the Civil War, tents were replaced with the gingerbread houses that circle the

---

Bike Shops

Anderson's Bike Rentals, 23 Circuit Avenue Extension, Oak Bluffs, (508) 693-9346, andersonsbikerentals.com

Oak Bluffs Bike Rentals, 7 Circuit Avenue Extension, Oak Bluffs, (508) 696-6255, oakbluffsbikerentals.com

Martha's Bike Rentals, Vineyard Haven, (508) 693-6593, www.marthas bikerentals.com

Vineyard Bicycles, 344 State Rd., Vineyard Haven, (508) 693-8693, www .vineyardbicycles.com

Cycle-Works Martha's Vineyard, 351 State Rd., Vineyard Haven, (508) 693-6966

The author at East Chop Lighthouse, Oak Bluffs

church Tabernacle today. Ride around Trinity Park by turning right onto the circle and going counter-clockwise. The colorful gingerbread houses with intricate carvings are an architectural style known as "carpenter gothic," and between the colorful paint and beautiful gardens, there is really nothing quite like this circle anywhere else. Circle around just past Montgomery Avenue where you entered, then exit the circle by turning right on Jordan Crossing. Turn right onto Siloam Avenue, which takes you back to Lake Avenue.

At mile 1.1, turn right on East Chop Drive and head up the flat part of this road past Oak Bluffs Harbor on the right. East Chop Drive starts climbing where it bends just past the harbor, but not very much. It then levels off and passes the East Chop Lighthouse on the right. East Chop Lighthouse was the last of six lighthouses to be built on the Vineyard. It is maintained by the Martha's Vineyard Museum, which opens the lighthouse on Sundays in summer for sunsets. East Chop Drive descends rapidly past the lighthouse and bends left, where it stays flat at sea level past Crystal Lake on the left and alongside Vineyard Haven Harbor. The ride follows the harbor by turning right onto Temahigan Avenue and then right onto Beach Road (Eastville Avenue is at this corner, with Martha's Vineyard Hospital in front of you), which then bends left 90 degrees and continues as Beach Road (hospital on your left now) into Vineyard Haven. Beach Road passes the small Eastville Beach on the right and then goes over the bridge across Lagoon Pond into Vineyard Haven Center. Stop by the Black Dog Tavern, whose T-shirts and clothing line may be more popular than the actual restaurant. I've been eating at the Black Dog since I first started racing bikes, and if you need to fuel up, the pancakes here (try raspberry and chocolate chip) are amazing. You'll need them if you're continuing up-island on Ride 38. Or steel yourself for the ride back to the ferry docks with the Blackout cake for dessert.

MILES AND DIRECTIONS

0.0 Begin this ride at the Oak Bluffs Harbor parking lot and ride up the hill on Seaview Avenue.

0.1 Turn right on Oak Bluffs Avenue into the bike lane, and continue on Lake Avenue where the short bike lane ends.

0.2 Turn left on Central Avenue and continue on Montgomery Avenue, past the bike racks on the right, into Trinity Park.

0.4 Turn right on Trinity Park and ride the loop 1.5 times.

0.8 Exit Trinity Park and turn right onto Jordan Crossing.

0.9 Continue on Siloam Avenue.

Oak Bluffs–East Chop–Vineyard Haven

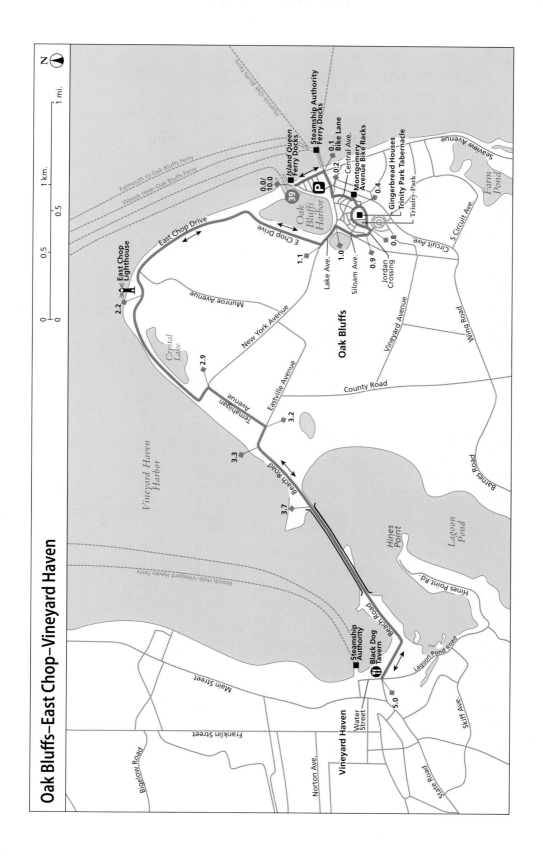

N

0   0.5   1 km.
0   0.5   1 mi.

Falmouth to Oak Bluffs Ferry

Woods Hole–Oak Bluffs Ferry

Hyannis–Oak Bluffs Ferry

Steamship Authority
Ferry Docks

Island Queen
Ferry Docks

0.1
Bike Lane

0.2
Central Ave.

Montgomery
Avenue Bike Racks

0.4

Gingerbread Houses
Trinity Park Tabernacle

Trinity Park

0.0/
10.0

39

P

Oak
Bluffs
Harbor

East Chop Drive

E Chop Drive

1.1

Lake Ave.

1.0

Siloam Ave.

0.9

Jordan
Crossing

0.8

Vineyard Avenue

S Circuit Ave.

Circuit Ave.

Wing Road

Seaview Avenue

Farm
Pond

East Chop
Lighthouse

2.2

Crystal
Lake

Munroe Avenue

New York Avenue

Eastville Avenue

Oak Bluffs

County Road

Barnes Road

2.9

Temahigan
Avenue

3.2

3.3

Beach Road

3.7

Vineyard Haven
Harbor

Woods Hole–Vineyard Haven Ferry

Hines
Point

Lagoon
Pond

Hines Point Rd.

Lagoon Pond Road

Skiff Ave.

State Road

Main Street

Franklin Street

Bigelow Road

Norton Ave.

Steamship
Authority

Black Dog
Tavern

Water
Street

Beach Road

5.0

Vineyard Haven

1.0 Turn left on Lake Avenue.

1.1 Turn right on East Chop Drive.

2.2 Visit East Chop Lighthouse, then continue on East Chop Drive.

2.9 Turn right on Temahigan Avenue.

3.2 Turn right on Beach Road.

3.3 Continue on Beach Road, which bends 90 degrees left.

3.7 Cross the bridge over Lagoon Pond.

5.0 Turn around at the intersection of Beach Road and Water Street to return the way you came.

10.0 Finish the ride at the Oak Bluffs Harbor parking lot.

RIDE INFORMATION

Local Events and Attractions
Martha's Vineyard Film Center: 79 Beach Rd., Vineyard Haven (Tisbury); (508) 696-9369. See the listing under Ride 38.
West Chop Lighthouse: Ride a loop from Vineyard Haven up Main Street and return on Franklin Street. Ask the local bike shop people or wing it.

Restaurants
See the listings under Ride 35 for restaurants in Oak Bluffs, or Ride 38 for restaurants in Vineyard Haven.

Restrooms
There are restrooms at the ferry docks in both Oak Bluffs and Vineyard Haven.

Nantucket-Siasconset-Wauwinet Tour

This is a nice tour of the island, with the option to see more. Get out of town quickly to Siasconset (pronounced and often spelled "Sconset"), loop around to Sankaty Light, head north to Wauwinet, and return for a tour of historical downtown. Lots to see and do, or just ride and ride. Head to Madaket to add another 12 miles to this ride.

Start: Straight Wharf, Nantucket Harbor (Hy-Line ferry)

Distance: 26.8 miles, two loops with one long out-and-back and one short out-and-back

Approximate riding time: 2 to 3 hours or more depending on stops

Best bike: Road

Terrain and surface type: Mainly flat paved roads and bike paths through downtown, with short stretches of dangerous cobblestones on Main Street and South Water Street; a rideable stretch of smoother brick road on Main Street and Upper Main Street; a stretch of dirt road at the end of Wauwinet Road; gently rolling hills on Milestone Road, Wauwinet Road, and Polpis Road

Traffic and hazards: Very congested traffic at the start/finish at Straight Wharf, with pedestrians, bicycles, pets on leashes, vehicles all navigating to and from Main Street, with busy shops, restaurants, and people everywhere in summer; some narrow roads without much shoulder, sand in the roads, other users of multi-use bike paths; dangerous cobblestones on Main Street and South Water Street

Things to see: Main Street in Nantucket Center, with many fine shops, restaurants, art galleries, and historic whaling-era mansions; the Moors Conservation land with optional off-road trips; Siasconset, Sconset Bluff Walk, Sankaty Lighthouse, Wauwinet Inn and Spa, Coskata-Coatue Wildlife Refuge, African Meeting House, the "Three Bricks" and "Two Greeks" historic whaling-era mansions, Madaket Bike Path option,

Nantucket's "Oldest House," Nantucket Whaling Museum, Nantucket Atheneum

Map: *Arrow Street Atlas: Cape Cod including Martha's Vineyard & Nantucket*, p. 114

Getting there: Ferry services with bicycle transport leave Hyannis and Harwich Port daily. GPS coordinates for the Ocean Street Docks: N41 65.15' / W70 28.09'

GPS coordinates: N41 17.08' / W70 05.67'

THE RIDE

Nantucket is Wampanoag for "faraway land," and getting to Nantucket is a bit more involved than getting to Martha's Vineyard, as the island is 30 miles out to sea from mainland Cape Cod. Ferries take cyclists and their bicycles to Nantucket from Harwich Port and Hyannis, with most bicyclists boarding the ferries from the Ocean Street Docks in Hyannis. Be sure to check ferry fares, as they can change without notice. The other way to Nantucket is to fly, and the trip over Nantucket Sound is worth the view all by itself. Getting there in 15 minutes is a real bonus if vacation time is limited. There are bicycle rentals at the airport and at least one bike shop offers free delivery. A new bike path connects the airport to downtown Nantucket.

Start this ride at Straight Wharf (Hy-Line Ferry) and walk your bike down the wharf to Main Street, which is a cobblestone street heading one-way into town from the wharf. (If you arrived on the Steamship Authority ferry at Steamboat Wharf, simply follow the directions for this ride from mile 26.4 at the corner of South Water Street and Broad Street to the ride start at Straight Wharf.) Use caution and walk through town on Main Street to Washington Street, where the cobblestones end and you can begin riding toward the Mile-stone Rotary and bike path.

There are more than 30 miles of bicycle paths on Nantucket, with plans to build more. Several new paths have been constructed in the last ten years, and the town is currently working on a project to provide a safer bike route from downtown to the Milestone Rotary and bike path. The plan is to build a shared-use path along an old railroad berm from Washington Street Extension to Orange Street, and then bike lanes along Washington Street and Orange Street. Currently, getting from the start of this ride to Orange Street requires riding Francis and Union Streets with vehicular traffic. It's a bit sketchy here, with very little room on narrow roads, as you ride up Washington Street,

Francis Street, and then Union Street. The left turn from Union Street onto Orange Street at mile 0.8 is a dangerous intersection, with vehicles merging from the right where Orange Street becomes a two-way street. It's easy to understand why the town wants to divert bicycles away from these side streets and build a bike lane on Orange Street. Orange Street ends at the James Coffin Memorial Rotary (traffic circle), known more commonly to locals as the "Milestone Rotary" at mile 1.3. Ride around the rotary, remembering that vehicles and bicycles in the rotary have the right of way, and exit onto the Milestone Road bike path.

The Milestone Road bike path travels 6 miles east, and is fairly flat, with a gradual uphill and then gradual downhill into Siasconset, passing connections to other bike paths that branch off to the left and right. At mile 1.8, a path on the right connects to the Old South Road bike path, which takes riders to Nantucket Memorial Airport and connects to the South Shore and Surfside Beach bike paths. On the left, there is a crosswalk connecting to the Polpis bike path, on which this ride returns. The Milestone bike path quickly takes cyclists away from the bustling downtown area along Milestone Road into a part of this island's natural beauty. On the left is the Middle Moors, 3,200 acres of Nantucket Conservation land, the largest area of undeveloped land on the island with miles of intersecting hiking trails and dirt roads. The Moors is home to bearberry, blueberry, huckleberry, heather, moss, and sedge. In summer and fall, the hills of the Moors are covered in aster, goldenrod, and many other wild flowers. The intensive grazing by sheep here in 19th century removed many of the original shrubs and trees, and the southern section of the Moors that borders the Milestone bike path is referred to as Nantucket's Serengeti. The habitat is now a sand plain grassland and coastal heathlands environment, with scrub oak and other shrub trees battered by the salt air and winds blowing across the Moors.

Bike Shops

Young's Bicycle Shop, 6 Broad St., Nantucket, (508) 228-1151, www.youngsbicycleshop.com

Nantucket Bike Shop, 4 Broad St., Nantucket, (508) 228-1999, www.nantucketbikeshop.com

Island Bike Company, 25 Old South Rd., Nantucket, (508) 228-4070, www.islandbike.com

Easy Rider Bicycle Rentals, 65 Surfside Rd., Nantucket, (508) 325-2722, www.easyridersbikerentals.com

Cook's Cycle Shop, 6 South Beach St., Nantucket, (508) 228-0800, www.cookscycleshop.com

On the right of the Milestone bike path are Madaquecham and Tom Nevers, also maintained by the Nantucket Conservation Foundation, and at mile 3.9, Madaquecham can be accessed via Russell's Way. Madaquecham was an early settlement of Native Americans, with scrub oak and no real hiking trails, making it ideal for deer (and hunters). Tom Nevers is an isolated beach with great surf, and Tom Nevers Road branches off the Milestone bike path at mile 5.2 and travels a straight path until a fork in the road, with Tom Nevers Road branching right and Old Tom Nevers Road to the left. The right fork takes you to a field with a playground, basketball courts, outdoor hockey rink, and baseball fields, and there is a restroom there. The left fork takes you to the beach, with its coarse sand and powerful currents, not recommended for younger children but a lesser known beach with not as many people in summer.

At mile 7.3, the paved bike path ends, and bicyclists must continue on the right of Milestone Road into Siasconset. The road gradually rises through the shade of some taller trees, approaches this old fishing village, and comes to the Siasconset Rotary at mile 7.7. Bear right up the hill onto Ocean Avenue and continue up over the crest for wonderful views of the Atlantic, with nothing but water between here and Africa. At mile 7.9, stop by the Summer House Beachside Bistro, with bike racks against a wooden fence and a long stairway down to the outdoor bar and restaurant under tents on a patio. Have lunch by the outdoor pool on hot summer days, or dine under the stars, with blankets and heaters provided by the staff for chilly nights on the Atlantic. Continue riding, past the stairway down to the bistro on the left, for more magnificent panoramic views of the Atlantic Ocean. This is a beautiful, long stretch of paved road that turns around at mile 8.6 so you can see it again.

Turn left at mile 9.0 on Morey Lane and head through a neighborhood of beautiful homes, then turn right on Milestone Road and head back to the rotary, this time taking note of the Siasconset Cafe on the far end of the rotary. If your schedule doesn't allow for a stop at the bistro, the cafe has outdoor seating and is a favorite stop for other cyclists looking to caffeinate or just hang out and take a break for lunch. Pass the cafe on the right around the rotary and now continue past the Sconset Market on the right, a hangout for teenagers and rows of bike racks. Turn left on Broadway and ride through the main part of the village, with historic homes, some dating to the late 17th century, with flowers and gardens planted everywhere. There is the option to turn right off Broadway onto Front Street and hike the Sconset Bluff Walk. Look for an opening at the far right end of Front Street (before it merges with the far end of Broadway) to this beautiful public walkway, then walk along the grass walkway on the edge of the bluffs and get a peek at the back yards of the elegant homes on Baxter Road. Like so much of Cape Cod, the bluffs keep falling into the ocean. And if you ask a Sconset fisherman, he'll tell you how much longer the houses to the left have before they fall in.

Continue north on Sankaty Road or opt to take the Polpis bike path at mile 10.2 at Annes Lane. (If you turn right on Annes Lane, you can ride on Baxter Road, which is paved all the way to Sankaty Head Lighthouse.) From this ride, the Sankaty Lighthouse is easily seen to the right at mile 10.9. From here, ride the Polpis Road to mile 13.9 and turn right on Wauwinet Road. This out-and-back takes you to the edge of the Coskata-Coatue Wildlife Refuge, just past the Wauwinet Inn and Spa. You can opt to stay at the Wauwinet for a while, and if you are independently wealthy you might decide never to leave, although a room will set you back several hundred dollars a night. A better choice for this ride is to continue past the Wauwinet, where the pavement ends and you reach mile 16.4, the turnaround point of this branch of the ride. A road bike isn't the best bike for riding this dirt road, so this ride only heads out far enough for a view. A fat tire bike or mountain bike would be ideal from here, or even a cyclocross bike. The ranger at the gatehouse can offer help with the best place to park if you come back with a different bike to explore the Coskata-Coatue Wildlife Refuge and Great Point Lighthouse at the northern tip on Nantucket. The Trustees of Reservations offer the best tour if you don't want to bike it.

In any case, enjoy the view, plan the next trip in the back of your mind, and head back to Polpis Road along Wauwinet Road. Turn right on Polpis Road at mile 18.8 and continue the loop around the Moors for the next 4.5 miles, then turn right on Milestone Road. At the rotary, exit onto Sparks Avenue, come to a second rotary, and stay on Sparks Avenue. Turn right on Sanford Road past the Stop & Shop (restrooms and groceries), then left on Lower Pleasant Street, which turns into Pleasant Street at mile 24.6 at the corner of York Street. The five-way intersection here is known locally as Five Corners, and was once the center of a segregated neighborhood called New Guinea, a thriving community of African Americans in the 19th century. At the far right corner of Pleasant and York Street is the African Meeting House, a National Historic Landmark, and the only public building constructed and occupied by African Americans in the 19th century still standing on Nantucket. Pleasant Street goes slightly uphill here, and the historic houses seem to get more impressive as you ride ahead, with beautiful mansions from Nantucket's whaling days on both sides of the street.

At mile 25.0, you are at the corner of Pleasant Street and cobblestoned Main Street, in the heart of the Nantucket Historic District. In front of you are the Three Bricks, three identical, Georgian-style brick houses built in 1839 by Nantucket master mason Christopher Capen for Joseph Starbuck, one of the richest whaling merchants of the day. Starbuck had these three homes

Sankaty Head Lighthouse, Siasconset

built for his sons, William, Matthew, and George, and while they are privately owned today, the middle one still remains in the Starbuck family. Starbuck's own home was around the corner at 4 New Dollar Ln., which had a candle factory behind it. Starbuck's daughter Eunice married her neighbor William Hadwen, who owned his own mansion at 100 Main St. Hadwen built the Two Greeks at 94 and 96 Main St. The Hadwen-Wright House at 94 Main St., built for Hadwen's niece on her marriage to George Wright in 1845, is also very impressive. It is likely the most detailed Greek Revival house on Nantucket with its portico, second floor ballroom and domed ceiling, and cylindrical stair hall and dome. Starbuck's daughter Eliza and her son Joseph built the Victorian house at 73 Main St. after Eliza's husband Nathaniel Barney passed away. The Eliza Starbuck Barney House is a blue and white H-style Victorian beauty, with two huge front doors hand-carved by James Walter Folger.

Opt to walk down the cobbles with your bike and check out the other mansions on Main Street, built when Nantucket was literally the world center of whaling. There are more than eight hundred pre–Civil War homes preserved on Nantucket, with the more elegant ones on Main Street and Orange Street. The list of family members of the whaling captains, ship owners, and wealthy merchants who built these homes reads like a Who's Who of America, like Tristram Coffin, ancestor of the famous whaling family and who purchased Nantucket Island for thirty pounds sterling and two beaver hats; J.A. Folger, who founded Folger's Coffee; Abiah Folger, Benjamin Franklin's mother; and R.H. Macy, who founded Macy's Department Store in New York City.

Turn left on Main Street and walk or ride the flat brick sidewalk to avoid the cobbles. Two houses ahead, the cobblestone street changes to a flat gray brick surface, and can be ridden much more easily than the round stone cobbles. Just past here, the Soldiers and Sailors Monument marks the intersection of Main, Upper Main, Gardner, and Milk Streets. Bear right past this Civil War monument and continue on Upper Main Street to mile 25.2, where the Madaket Road branches off to the left. Visible down that road and running parallel to it is the Madaket Bike Path, which travels 5.5 miles from here to Madaket Beach. You can opt to make the trip and add another 11 miles to this ride, or continue on Upper Main Street, bearing right and continuing this ride on New Lane. I'm taking you on a short loop around town so you can opt to see some of the more important sites, including Nantucket's oldest house, the Jethro Coffin House on Sunset Hill Lane. To see it, turn right on West Chester Street (mile 25.7), make your first left on North Liberty Street, and a quick right on Sunset Hill Lane. The "Oldest House," which was rebuilt and renovated after fire and other disasters, is set back from Sunset Hill Lane on the left. Sunset Hill Lane turns right, back onto West Chester Street, to continue on this ride.

At mile 26.0, West Chester Street merges with Center Street and turns immediately left onto Chester Street and continues on Easton Street. At mile 26.1, you can opt to turn left to connect to the Cliff Road Bike Path via North Water Street and Cliff Road. The Cliff Road Bike Path connects to the Madaket Bike Path, the Eel Point Bike Path, and Dionis Beach. Continue on Easton Street to mile 26.2 onto South Beach Street, then turn right on Broad Street at mile 26.4 (left if you're headed to the Steamship Authority ferry). The Nantucket Whaling Museum is on the right at the corner of South Beach and Broad Streets, and is well worth a visit. Make a quick left and continue on South Water Street, which also turns to cobblestones just past India Street, where the Nantucket Atheneum is located (around the corner to the right). The Atheneum is Nantucket's public library, built by Charles Coffin and David Joy in the Greek Revival style, and a place where abolitionist meetings took place. Frederick Douglass gave a speech here in 1841 on his experiences as a slave just four years after he escaped slavery in Maryland. The card catalogue system for libraries was invented here. Continue on foot along the South Water Street sidewalk at the intersection with Cambridge Street, then cross Main Street and turn left on Salem Street. Ride past the Stop & Shop (with restrooms) on the right. To finish the ride, turn left on New Whale Street back to Straight Wharf for the Hy-Line ferry. Don't forget to go home with some Nantucket rose hip or beach plum jelly available in September (when they ripen) and on sale in the shops on Straight Wharf.

MILES AND DIRECTIONS

0.0 Begin this ride on Straight Wharf, Nantucket Harbor.

0.1 Continue on Main Street over the cobblestones. Use caution or walk bicycles.

0.2 Turn left on Washington Street.

0.5 Turn right on Francis Street.

0.6 Turn left on Union Street.

0.8 Turn left on Orange Street.

1.3 Ride the Milestone Rotary and continue on Milestone Road on Sconset Bike Path.

1.8 Pass the connector to the Old South Road Bike Path.

3.9 Pass Russell's Way and Madaquecham on the right.

5.2 Pass Tom Nevers Road on the right.

7.3 Come to the end of the Sconset Bike Path and ride on the right side of the road.

Nantucket–Siasconset–Wauwinet Tour

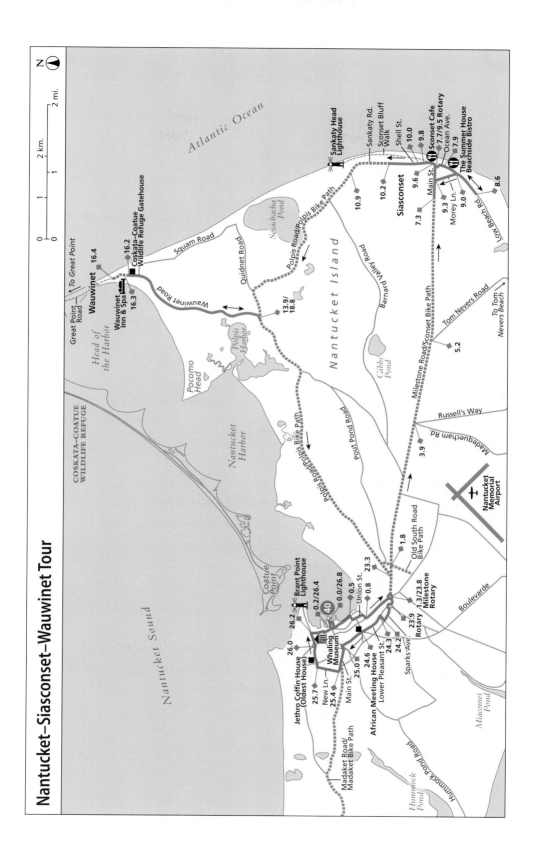

7.7 Ride the Main Street rotary and turn right onto Ocean Avenue uphill to the right.

7.9 Stop for lunch at the Summer House Beachside Bistro or continue on Ocean Avenue onto Low Beach Road.

8.6 Turn around on Low Beach Road.

9.0 Turn left on Morey Lane.

9.3 Turn right on Main Street.

9.5 Go around the Main Street rotary and pass the Sconset Cafe on the right. Continue on Main Street.

9.6 Turn left on Broadway.

9.8 Turn right onto Shell Street.

10.0 Continue straight on Sankaty Road at Coffin Sias Street.

10.2 Continue on Sankaty Road or cross the street left onto the Polpis Bike Path at Annes Lane.

10.9 View the Sankaty Lighthouse and continue straight on Polpis Road.

13.9 Turn right on Wauwinet Road.

16.2 Pass the Wildlife Refuge Gatehouse (pavement ends) and ride the dirt road.

16.3 Pass the Wauwinet Inn & Spa.

16.4 Turn around here.

18.8 Turn right on Polpis Road.

23.3 Turn right onto Milestone Road (Sconset Bike Path).

23.8 Go around the rotary and exit onto Sparks Avenue.

23.9 Go around another rotary and stay on Sparks Avenue.

24.2 Turn right on Sanford Road.

24.3 Turn left on Lower Pleasant Street.

24.6 Continue on Pleasant Street past York Street and the African Meeting House on the right.

25.0 Turn left on Main Street after exploring the whaling-era mansions.

25.2 Pass the Madaket Road on the left or opt to ride the Madaket bike path by turning left and crossing onto the bike path (11 miles out-and-back).

25.4 Turn right on New Lane.

25.7 Turn right on West Chester Street.

40

26.0 Merge right with Center Street and take an immediate left on Chester Street.

26.1 Continue straight on Easton Street.

26.2 Turn right on South Beach Street.

26.4 Turn right on Broad Street and make an immediate left on South Water Street.

26.6 Cross the cobblestones on Main Street and turn left on Salem Street.

26.7 Turn left on New Whale Street and then right on Straight Wharf.

26.8 Finish the ride on Straight Wharf (Hy-Line Ferry).

RIDE INFORMATION

Local Events and Attractions

Cisco Brewers: 5 Bartlett Farm Rd.; (508) 325-5929. Opt to check out this brewery/winery by turning left on Milk Street at the Soldiers and Sailors Civil War Monument at the intersection of Main, Upper Main, Gardner, and Milk Streets (just after mile 25.0 of this ride). From Milk Street and Milk Street Extension, take Hummock Pond Bike Path to Bartlett Farm Road on the left. Wine tasting, brew pub, live music.

Nantucket Wine Festival: 50 Easton Street; (617) 527-9473. One island, five days in May. Experience world-class wines and award-winning food.

Restaurants

Something Natural: 50 Cliff Rd., Nantucket; (508) 228-0504. Great sandwiches made with homemade bread. Take lunch outside on picnic tables in a lovely shaded setting.

Petticoat Row Bakery: 35 Center St., Nantucket; (508) 228-3700. The delicious breakfast pastries are not great for the waistline, so ride here and then ride more. Very good coffee.

Bean: 29 Center St., Nantucket; (508) 228-6215. Great coffee. Hang for a bit and you'll meet a lot of locals.

Sconset Cafe: Main Street, Post Office Square, Siasconset, Nantucket; (508) 257-4008. A great stop when you're out that way, and excellent food. Minutes from the beach. Open in summer.

Restrooms

There are restrooms at the ferry docks in Nantucket and in Siasconset at Post Office Square.

About the Author

Dr. Gregory T. Wright is a Cape Cod executive committee member of Mass-Bike and an original member of the Cape Cod Cycling Club. He is currently the team physician for Keough Professional Cycling Team and served as event physician for UCI and USA Cycling professional cycling races around New England. A twenty-year resident of the area, he loves to ride Cape Cod whether it's road, trail, or off-trail.